WITHDRAWN FROM
RCSJ LIBRARY

Becoming American

Becoming American

Why Immigration Is Good for Our Nation's Future

Fariborz Ghadar

ROWMAN & LITTLEFIELD
Lanham • Boulder • New York • Toronto • Plymouth, UK

Published by Rowman & Littlefield
4501 Forbes Boulevard, Suite 200, Lanham, Maryland 20706
www.rowman.com

10 Thornbury Road, Plymouth PL6 7PP, United Kingdom

Copyright © 2014 by Rowman & Littlefield

All rights reserved. No part of this book may be reproduced in any form or by any electronic or mechanical means, including information storage and retrieval systems, without written permission from the publisher, except by a reviewer who may quote passages in a review.

British Library Cataloguing in Publication Information Available

Library of Congress Cataloging-in-Publication Data

Ghadar, Fariborz.
  Becoming American : why immigration is good for our nation's future / Fariborz Ghadar.
    pages cm
  Includes bibliographical references and index.
  ISBN 978-1-4422-2894-8 (cloth : alk. paper) — ISBN 978-1-4422-2895-5 (electronic)
  1. United States—Emigration and immigration—Government policy. 2. Immigrants—Government policy—United States 3. United States—Emigration and immigration—Economic aspects. 4. United States—Emigration and immigration—Social aspects. I. Title.
  JV6465.G53 2014
  325.73—dc23
                                                                          2013042436

∞™ The paper used in this publication meets the minimum requirements of American National Standard for Information Sciences—Permanence of Paper for Printed Library Materials, ANSI/NISO Z39.48-1992.

Printed in the United States of America

Contents

Acknowledgments		ix
1	Beyond the Numbers	1
2	Debunking the Myths	5
	Myth #1: America Continues to Be a Nation of Immigrants	5
	Myth #2: All Immigrants Want to Come to the United States	6
	Myth #3: America Already Attracts the Best and Brightest Immigrants	6
	Myth #4: Immigrants Are a Drain on the Economy	6
	Myth #5: Immigrants Are a Threat to National Security (That Is, The War on Terrorism Can Be Won through Immigration Restrictions)	7
	Myth #6: Immigrants Do Not Want to Learn English	8
	Myth #7: Many Immigrants Are Criminals	8
3	How Did I Get Here?	11
4	What It Takes to Uproot Yourself	21
	Immigration as a Force of Change	21
	Immigration Laws	25

	Today's Pariahs	30
	Immigration Reform	32
5	How Did She Get Here: Margaret Ghadar	37
6	Why Do They Come?	43
	Immigration's Ebb and Flow	46
	Silicon Valley: A Microcosm	48
7	How Did He Get Here: Zbigniew Brzezinski	53
8	Hard Work Makes for a Successful Career	59
9	How Did He Get Here: Salomon Garay	69
10	Paying It Forward to the U.S. Economy	73
11	How Did He Get Here: Yoon-shik Park	81
12	The Bimodal Nature of Immigrants	87
13	The Lure of Clusters	95
	Case Study: Detroit's Automobile Industry	96
	Case Study: Silicon Valley	98
	Technological Revolutions	99
	Life Science Cluster	100
	Nanotechnology Cluster	102
	Other Revolutionary Fields	104
14	A Day in the Life	111
15	Prejudice Exits, But So What?	117
	The New Enemy	125
	Racial Profiling	128
16	Sticking to Your Own May Work, But It's Not Easy	133

17	Assimilation Is Critical	137
	When Assimilation Doesn't Occur	141
18	Next Generation, and the Next, and the Next	147
19	How Did She Get Here: Otessa Ghadar	151
20	Old Country Is Old	155
	Benefits	155
	Costs	157
21	How Did He Get Here: Michel Amsalem	161
22	Can You Go Home Again?	165
23	Lessons for the Next Generation	171
24	Blueprints for Policymakers	177
25	Would I Do It Again?	187
References		191
Index		203
About the Author		207

Acknowledgments

Because the significance of the immigration issue has recently been escalating, I have decided to publish *Becoming American: Why Immigration Is Good for Our Nation's Future*. As an immigrant myself, this topic is extremely close to my heart. While writing my book, I took a unique approach—one that weaves statistics, research, and theory with personal narratives and case studies. The book's publication has been encouraged by a number of scholars whom I would like to thank for their insight and support. In particular, I thank my Penn State advisory board members: Nabeel Al-Amudi, James Boland, Jim Clay, Gerald Kessler, and Laura Kohler. They, along with Andrew Schwartz from the Center for Strategic and International Studies (CSIS), convinced me that now is the appropriate time to publish my manuscript, and then they encouraged me to do so.

Becoming American would not have been possible without the help of a competent and enthusiastic core group of four people who served as researchers, writers, and editors throughout its process. I owe my gratitude to Hortense Fong, who was in charge of coordinating the project while also tirelessly researching and editing many of the chapters; and to Kathleen Loughran, who worked closely with Ms. Fong to ensure that the manuscript was well researched and properly edited. I would also like to thank Holly Graff, who was principally responsible for conducting many of the interviews featured in this book. Additionally, Nancy Dull, who (as always) helped to organize many of the documents and sought out permissions for many of the charts, also deserves my appreciation.

Of course, an immigration book largely told through the voices of successful immigrants could not have been completed without the gracious help and participation of those people willing to share their stories. Thus, I would like to thank Michel Amsalem, Zbigniew Brzezinski, Salomon Garay, Margaret Ghadar, Otessa Ghadar, and Yoon-shik Park—all of whom were willing to be interviewed and serve as case studies.

Additionally, I would like to thank my publisher, who saw the potential in the book's original concept and was willing to help make it a reality. Finally, I would like to thank my wife, Lis Ghadar, for her steadfast support throughout our lives together and for help in finessing *Becoming American*.

1

Beyond the Numbers

No one can rightly deny that what helped make America strong—economically, governmentally, politically, and militarily—have been immigrants. They came and continue to come to this country with grand ambitions to succeed in an open and free society—not to ride the dole, not to kick back, but to succeed and to do well.

These virtues were and unfortunately are still not always recognized, particularly in times of national tension or economic stress, when reactionary forces pursue obstacles to block the immigrants' paths toward assimilation and success.

Our nation's prosperity, however, is built on the renegade, risk-taking, entrepreneurial concoction of truly American innovation and invention. Wave upon wave of immigrants bought into the American Dream that anything was possible in the United States, and anyone who put in the effort could succeed here.

As an immigrant myself, I know the path an immigrant must take in order to succeed in this country. Additionally, as an academic, entrepreneur, and business consultant, I clearly see that "the continued failure to devise and implement a sound and sustainable immigration policy threatens to weaken America's economy, to jeopardize its diplomacy, and to imperil its national security."[1]

In an attempt to frame the current immigration debate in real terms, I have put faces on the statistics in order to avoid falling back into knee-jerk positions based on ignorance, fear, and racism. In addition to sharing my own personal experience as an immigrant, I have interviewed a number of immigrants who have not only achieved the success that they originally envisioned, but also who have helped shape our nation in significant and public ways. These immigrants have started companies in traditional as well as brand new fields of endeavor. They have created numerous jobs, have launched new industries, have educated thousands, and have helped grow our economy. Others have had a lasting and significant impact on our public policy roles both domestically and internationally. They have also promoted the privatization of global economies working within U.S. policy; have strengthened our relations with many developing and developed nations, most notably China; and have influenced the direction of the Cold War. Their stories help to flesh out the identity of the immigrant as inspirational innovator.

The results of my research and work are self-evident but nonetheless profound: no matter where you live or how you earn a living, immigrants will have made a significant impact on your life and on your career. They are not only the ones who have shaped the history of the United States but also they are the ones who are shaping our future, and how we treat them will lead to either our success or our downfall. This book is about these forces and their impact on our futures; in it, I have identified some of the key issues to be considered in this hot debate, their implications, and policy considerations for both the government and for the businessperson.

If you are a parent, a CEO, a manager, a student, an entrepreneur, a policymaker, an educator, or simply a concerned citizen (or a number of those things at once), you have important decisions to make and goals you want to achieve. Whether you realize it or not, immigrants will always play a role in each of these areas. My book is a new way of seeing one of the single most important, yet often overlooked, factors in the attempt to navigate the future.

Each of us is a decision maker. As parents, we need to decide whether to enroll our children in French, Spanish, or Chinese. As business leaders, we need to allocate resources, design new products and services, or develop marketing plans. As investors, we ponder whether health care, green technology, or emerging markets are the next growth areas. So as citizens or policymakers, immigration is one of the key issues we need to watch, as it relates to the developments taking place in our communities, our nations, and throughout the world. With proper knowledge, we can help steer all those choices in the best direction. What is more, we need to make those decisions not based on current reality but on the reality that will be in place five to twenty years from now. We cannot fail to address the impact that immigration will have on our future if we want to accurately plan for the reality of our tomorrow.

In this book you will come to know some immigrants and what the experience of being an immigrant has been like from their own perspectives—not just to understand the mind-set of the immigrant, but also to provide the perspective necessary to view the landscape of the future.

NOTE

1. Jeb Bush and Thomas McLarty, "Independent Task Force Report on U.S. Immigration Policy," Council on Foreign Relations, July 2009, www.cfr.org/immigration/us-immigration-policy/p20030 (accessed July 10, 2013).

2

Debunking the Myths

Before I begin telling my own story and those of other immigrants, I thought it would be helpful to expose some wildly accepted misconceptions about immigration. Here, I have identified seven myths, and through presenting the reality, I hope to aid readers in being able to approach this book with an informed, open mind.

MYTH #1: AMERICA CONTINUES TO BE A NATION OF IMMIGRANTS

While America at one point had a huge influx of immigrants, today the picture is quite different. Although the number of immigrants residing in the United States is almost four times what it was one hundred years ago, the percentage of the total U.S. population (about 13 percent) is not at an all-time high. Indeed, America's rate of foreign-born population is now on par with that of France and Germany.

When taken as a percentage of the population, illegal immigration is on the decline as well. The number of unauthorized immigrants living in the United States grew during the last decade, rising from 8.4 million in 2000 to 11.1 million in 2011. But this population peaked at 12 million in 2007 and then fell to 11.1 million in 2009.[1] It has remained at that level through 2011, the last year for which an estimate is available.

MYTH #2: ALL IMMIGRANTS WANT TO COME TO THE UNITED STATES

Only twenty years ago, many ambitious immigrants considered America to be the most promising destination. Today, this is no longer the case. At approximately 20 and 26 percent of their total populations, Canada and Australia, respectively, both have significantly higher rates of foreign-born residents than does the United States. Simpler immigration policies and more welcoming environments could explain why many foreign-born people are electing to move to those countries. In fact, Canada has actively solicited immigrants for years.

MYTH #3: AMERICA ALREADY ATTRACTS THE BEST AND BRIGHTEST IMMIGRANTS

America is no longer the forerunner for attracting the brightest people from around the world. In contrast to countries such as Canada, New Zealand, and Australia, the United States has a higher proportion of low-skilled rather than high-skilled immigrants. Nearly 30 percent of immigrants in the United States have a low level of education, and only 35 percent obtain a high level of education. In Canada, only 22 percent of immigrants possess a low level of education, while more than 46 percent of immigrants obtain a high level of education.[2]

One of the main reasons the United States does not attract high-skilled immigrants stems from the backbone of U.S. immigration policy. Countries such as Canada see a greater influx of immigrants with higher education levels and specialized skills through immigration policies that support visa applicants with advanced degrees or work experience. When granting permanent residence, U.S. policies favor family relationships.

Although the United States educates some of the best and brightest—the United States granted about five hundred thousand F-1 student visas in 2012—its employment visa, H-1B, is capped at a much smaller number. That same year, only 150,000 H-1B employment visas were granted.[3]

MYTH #4: IMMIGRANTS ARE A DRAIN ON THE ECONOMY

Possibly the largest and most insistent immigration myth is that immigrants are a drain on the U.S. economy. Immigrants generate revenue through buying power and through paying taxes, as well as by creating jobs in America.

Immigration on a whole has increased the U.S. gross domestic product (GDP). According to a 2007 report from the White House Council of Economic Advisers, immigrants are responsible for increasing the U.S. GDP by approximately $37 billion each year.[4] A cost estimate by the Congressional Budget Office in 2007 found a path to legalization for unauthorized immigrants would cost public services about $23 billion but, in turn, would increase federal revenues by $48 billion. This produces a surplus of $25 billion for the U.S. government.[5] Additionally, according to a Social Security Administration trustees report, increases in immigration have improved Social Security's finances.[6]

Although many undocumented immigrants currently pay lower taxes because they work off the books, their purchasing power allots for the sustainment of hundreds of thousand of U.S. jobs. One study estimates that Latino buying power totaled $951 billion in 2008 and would increase to $1.4 trillion by 2013, while Asian buying power totaled $509.1 billion in 2008 and is expected to increase to $752.3 billion by 2013.[7]

Immigrants have also played a key role in job creation. In 2012, immigrants founded 42 percent of America's Fortune 500 companies.[8] These companies have created over ten million jobs and have generated $4.5 trillion of annual revenue, which is about 30 percent of the U.S. GDP.[9] Additionally, according to the Fiscal Policy Institute, immigrant-owned small businesses generated a total of $776 billion in receipts and employed an estimated 4.7 million people in 2007.[10]

MYTH #5: IMMIGRANTS ARE A THREAT TO NATIONAL SECURITY (THAT IS, THE WAR ON TERRORISM CAN BE WON THROUGH IMMIGRATION RESTRICTIONS)

Since September 11, 2001, we have dramatically strengthened our borders through the use of biometrics at ports of entry, of secure cargo-shipment systems, of intelligence gathering, of integrated databases, and of increased international cooperation. Nonetheless, since 9/11, no security authority has said the terrorist attacks could have been thwarted with more suppressive immigration measures. Rather, the key is good use of good intelligence. Most of the 9/11 hijackers were here on legal visas. Since 9/11, the multiple measures targeting immigrants under the cloak of national security has resulted in zero terrorism prosecutions. In fact, several of these measures could have the opposite effect and actually make us less safe, as targeted communities of immigrants are scared to bring information forward.[11]

MYTH #6: IMMIGRANTS DO NOT WANT TO LEARN ENGLISH

Learning English is perhaps the most important factor in successful immigrant integration. Opponents of immigration often argue that immigrants do not want to learn English. This is certainly not the case, as nearly all immigrants recognize that English leads to upward mobility. When the Pew Hispanic Center report asked Latino immigrants whether they "need to learn English to succeed in the United States, or they can succeed even if they speak Spanish," 89 percent of Hispanics in the poll said they need to learn English.[12]

Non-English-speaking immigrants today learn the language at a similar rate of those who immigrated from Italy, Germany, and Eastern Europe during the nineteenth and early twentieth centuries. Though first-generation immigrants who do not speak English have lower rates of language proficiency than native speakers, 91 percent of second-generation immigrants are almost fluent. This percentage increases six points when considering the third generation.[13]

MYTH #7: MANY IMMIGRANTS ARE CRIMINALS

Immigrants in the United States have nearly always been associated with crime. Case in point: a Google search for "immigration + crime" immediately returns 57.2 million hits.[14] Yet immigrants have the lowest crime rates of any other demographic group in the United States.

In fact, "the incarceration rate of the U.S. born (3.51 percent) was four times the rate of the foreign born (0.86 percent)."[15] "The foreign-born rate was half the 1.71 percent rate for non-Hispanic white natives, and 13 times less than the 11.6 percent incarceration rate for native black men."[16]

According to a 2008 report from the conservative Americas Majority Foundation,[17] crime rates are lowest in states with the highest immigration growth rates. "From 1999 to 2006, the total crime rate declined 13.6 percent in the 19 highest-immigration states, compared to a 7.1 percent decline in the other 32 states."[18]

Many of these myths will be addressed in more depth later in this book. But I hope by presenting them up front, I have helped to establish a foundation through which you can consider the rest of my narrative and the stories of other immigrants.

NOTES

1. "A Nation of Immigrants," Pew Research Hispanic Trends Project, January 29, 2013, http://www.pewhispanic.org/2013/01/29/a-nation-of-immigrants/ (accessed July 14, 2013).

2. Fariborz Ghadar, "Dispel the Immigration Myths," *CNN.com*, December 11, 2012, http://www.cnn.com/2012/12/11/opinion/ghadar-immigration-policy (accessed July 14, 2013).

3. Randall Monger and James Yankay, "U.S. Legal Permanent Residents: 2012," *Department of Homeland Security: Annual Flow Report*, March 2013, http://www.dhs.gov/sites/default/files/publications/ois_lpr_fr_2012_2.pdf (accessed July 10, 2013).

4. "Immigration's Economic Impact," The White House Council of Economic Advisors, June 20, 2007, http://georgewbush-whitehouse.archives.gov/cea/cea_immigration_062007.html (accessed July 15, 2013).

5. Michael Greenstone and Adam Looney, "Ten Economic Facts about Immigration," The Hamilton Project, September 2010, www.brookings.edu/~/media/research/files/reports/2010/9/immigration%20greenstone%20looney/09_immigration (accessed July 10, 2013).

6. Ghadar, "Dispel the Immigration Myths."

7. Jeffrey M. Humphreys, "The Multicultural Economy 2008," *Georgia Business and Economic Conditions* 68, no. 3 (2008): 1, 2, 3, 4.

8. "The 'New American' Fortune 500," Partnership for a New American Economy, June 2011, www.renewoureconomy.org/2011_06_15_1 (accessed July 10, 2013).

9. "FactSet Data—FactSet Research Systems," Financial Research, Investment Analytics Tools—FactSet Research Systems, http://www.factset.com/data/factset_data (accessed July 10, 2013).

10. Cecilia Muñoz, Gene Sperling, Alan Krueger, and Sylvia Mathews Burwell, "The Economic Benefits of Fixing Our Broken Immigration System," *White House Blog*, July 10, 2013, http://www.whitehouse.gov/blog/2013/07/10/economic-benefits-fixing-our-broken-immigration-system (accessed July 10, 2013).

11. "10 Immigration Myths Busted," Christian Reformed Church Office of Social Justice, http://www2.crcna.org/pages/osj_immigrationmyths.cfm (accessed August 18, 2013).

12. Havovi Cooper, "Immigrants Should Learn English," *Businessweek.com*, http://www.businessweek.com/debateroom/archives/2008/08/immigrants_should_learn_english.html (accessed July 15, 2013).

13. "Countering the Myths," *Justice for Immigrants.org*, www.justiceforimmigrants.org/myths.shtml (accessed July 15, 2013).

14. Mathieu Deflem, *Sociology of Crime Law and Deviance* series, *EmeraldInsight.com*, www.emeraldinsight.com/books.htm?chapterid=1791225&show=html (accessed July 14, 2013).

15. "Beyond Myths and Stereotypes: Facts about Immigration and Crime," Coalition for Humane Immigrant Rights of Los Angeles (CHIRLA), http://chirla.org/files/FactsheetImmigrationanCrime.pdf (accessed July 14, 2013).

16. Rubén G. Rumbaut and Walter A. Ewing, "The Myth of Immigrant Criminality and the Paradox of Assimilation: Incarceration Rates among Native and Foreign-Born Men," Immigration Policy Center, Spring 2007, www.derechoshumanosaz.net/images/pdfs/the%20myth%20of%20immigrant%20criminality%20and%20the%20paradox%20of%20assimilation.pdf (accessed July 13, 2013).

17. Salvatore Colleluori, "Fox News Amplifies Fabricated Link between Immigrants and Crime," Media Matters for America.com, June 18, 2013, mediamatters.org/research/2013/06/18/fox-news-amplifies-fabricated-link-between-immi/194504 (accessed July 14, 2013).

18. "'They Take Our Jobs'—Debunking Immigration Myths," *SEIU.org*, Service Employees International Union, http://www.seiu.org/a/immigration/they-take-our-jobs-debunking-immigration-myths.php (accessed July 14, 2013).

3

How Did I Get Here?

Just like everyone else, my life has been a series of events, many outside of my control, which have carried me along like a feather meandering on a draft of air.

I don't actually remember coming to the United States, as I was only a year old at the time, but I know from family stories that in 1948 my mother and I left Tehran to join my father, who was attending school at Michigan State University. However, my own immigrant journey did not end there; it turned out to be a long and winding one, and it was not until political upheaval in the country of my birth—and opportunity in America—that I became a U.S. citizen.

While my father studied chemical engineering and my mother statistics in the United States, back home in Iran, the country roiled in geopolitical intrigue. Prime Minister Mohammed Mossadegh nationalized the country's oil industry, sparking a harsh response from Britain and the United States. The two allies feared, in an era of cold war, losing access to the Iranian oil fields on which they relied. To secure their situation, in 1953 the British and the U.S. governments chose to overthrow the duly elected government of Mossadegh in a coup, allowing Mohammad Reza Pahlavi, the Shah, to become ruler.

Before my parents and I returned to Iran in the early 1950s, my mother gave birth to my sister, Margaret, and the family moved to Baton Rouge, where my father earned his degree from Louisiana State University. Due to a political crisis in Iran, currency restrictions were put in place, and thus both of my parents were forced to work in whatever jobs they could find in order to help support us.

My family had a tradition of producing men and women who were well educated and served in academia and public office. Early in the 1920s, my paternal grandfather was among the first teachers at the newly renamed American University of Beirut in Lebanon, and my maternal grandfather was a governor of one of Iran's states, Kermanshah, on the Iraq border. My mother, who had worked for IBM, had supervised Iran's first census and once ran for the Iranian congress.

Upon the family's return to Iran, my father went back to the military, then changed fields and entered the diplomatic corps, which kept the family moving around the world in places such as Jordan, Syria, Lebanon, and Israel. I did my best to survive the gusts of wind that buffeted me from one country and culture to the next.

While I ultimately ended up graduating from Massachusetts Institute of Technology (MIT) and Harvard Business School, my original postsecondary choice would have led me down a very different path. My parents had sent me to American Community Schools in high school due to my family's frequent moves, and they insisted that I attend classes twelve months a year: summers attending Persian classes and passing the Iranian exams so as not to fall behind in the Iranian system as well. However, when it came time to apply to a university, I had little guidance from either the American Community School system, since I was Iranian, or my parents. I ended up attending Ursinus College in Pennsylvania, with the intention of eventually becoming a physician. My first year there I did exceptionally well in math and the sciences and caught the attention of my English professor, Richard Richter, who sat down with me and helped me bring my English grade up to an A. He went on to advise me that I really should be going to a school with a more challenging math and science curriculum and set about helping me transfer to MIT. While I would eventually shelve the plans to go to medical school, this important mentoring helped set me on a path to achieve success. Richter subsequently became the president of Ursinus College, and when I contacted him years later to express my appreciation, he did not initially remember me or the wonderful mentoring he had done.

So, in the mid-1960s, when I turned seventeen years old, I went to MIT in Cambridge, where my supplemental year-round education in Iran had prepared me well. My first year was easily accomplished, but by my junior year, I had to roll up my sleeves. I ended up earning two undergraduate degrees in chemical engineering and biology, specializing in the biomedical area, and a master's degree in mechanical engineering. Then it was on to Harvard Business School, where I earned an MBA and a doctorate.

At MIT, I joined the Chi Phi fraternity, where an Iranian name like Fariborz was either too difficult or too intimidating to pronounce. My frat brothers in the house decided to call me "Bob." They didn't have a "Bob" in the house, so I became "Bob." To this day, I am still greeted by old fraternity brothers as "Bob."

This was not the first time I had encountered major differences between my culture and the dominant one. You see, in my high school days I enjoyed a unique opportunity studying in international American schools during the academic year and then during the summer retaking the same coursework in Farsi with the Iranian school system flunkies (Tajdeedeeha). While this helped to bolster my already substantial understanding of my subjects, it also made me more deeply aware of my ethnic and cultural roots in the long shadow cast by an economic powerhouse like the United States.

I still remember the essay I wrote about Alexander the Great for a history class while I was in the American Community School system. I am proud to say I received an A+ on the paper. I wrote about how Alexander of Macedon spread Hellenic culture, was undefeated in battle, and ruled one of the largest empires of the ancient world. Coming across a similar writing prompt in my summer class in Iran, I shamelessly translated and submitted the same essay after a few edits. Having received an excellent grade on it previously, I was shocked to receive an F from my Iranian teacher. He asked me how I could write such things, for "Alexander the Terrible" brought death and destruction to Persia's capital, Persepolis, which was located in what is now modern Iran. He burned its libraries and looted its treasury. I learned then that the collision of cultures could lead to major misunderstandings and cause both great and terrible outcomes.

Living as a young boy in the segregated 1950s of Louisiana, I had begun to notice the collision of cultures in small but not insignificant ways. There was an African American man named John, whose daily work break at the local gas station coincided with the end of my school day. Since my mother was working, he would accompany me home from school each day. In order for us to take the bus together, I had to ride in the last row of seats for whites, while John sat in the first row of seats for blacks. The message I took from this was that we are not all the same, even in America, the land of the free.

I would hear local whites refer to John as "boy," and when I referred to him once by that name in front of my mother, she quickly corrected me. My mom said, "He's not a boy; he's a man, and you call him Big John from now on." Big John responded to his new moniker by christening me "curly top."

By the time I was in college, the Jim Crow laws had been overturned, and I found the experience of studying alongside students from other cultures and countries positive and reaffirming. I think there is a sense of gratitude to be educated in this country; the sense your parents made this sacrifice; the sense you are representing your country. I threw myself into the experience and became the president of the foreign student association at MIT. In this role, I communicated the concerns and expectations of our multicultural student body to the administration and planned multicultural events that allowed students of all ethnicities to integrate more broadly in the MIT and Boston environment.

Additionally, during my time at MIT and then Harvard, while working on two research projects along with my full academic course load, I (along with another Iranian immigrant) bought a derelict apartment building as an investment. We rolled up our sleeves, and while until this point for us working hard had been relegated to the realm of academic pursuits, we cleaned up the building, redid the plumbing, painted, rewired the electrical system, and hauled out trash. We went on to rent the units and to manage the building while working on our academic studies.

During this time, I met a lovely, blond, blue-eyed American girl named Lis, who was studying studio art at Wellesley College. We fell in love, and while there were a number of cultural differences in our upbringings, we felt we were sufficiently educated and committed enough to conquer all odds, and eventually we married.

While both our families were happy we had each settled down with suitable partners, there were many small hurdles we had to navigate in order to meld our seemingly dissimilar families. Lis, on her part, immersed herself in learning Farsi, and while visiting us in Iran when the rest of the family was traveling, she helped take care of my ailing grandmother. I made sure that I was duly solicitous of her parents and was never without a gift on every occasion that I visited them in Penn Valley outside of Philadelphia.

Upon finishing academics, I followed the example my grandfather and father had made in service to their country, by working in Iran's Ministry of Finance as a deputy vice minister for international investments. I cautiously attempted to navigate the currents and forces blowing me along my path. But my career there soon became tenuous when I came across corruption in the ministry and reported it, not realizing how high up the practice went in the ministry. I did not know the minister himself was involved.

So I resigned and returned to the States to join the World Bank Group as an investment officer at the International Finance Corporation. Becoming bored with the bureaucracy I found, I started a computer company in Washington, D.C., on the side. I named the company The Computer Emporium, and I had partners from Egypt, Canada, and the United States. In the 1970s, this was a bold move, as computers were still viewed as the domain of governments and industry titans, filling entire air-conditioned rooms. Even my own mother, who had worked for IBM and was actively involved in the computerization of the first Iranian census, thought it was a crazy idea to open a microcomputer store. I still remember her saying to me, "Who would want a computer in their home?" After all, she was used to IBM-360 computers in large, air-conditioned rooms. Despite all of the doubt, we managed to obtain the distribution rights to Apple, Commodore PET, and other computers, and our company grew.

A couple of years later, however, in 1977, when Iranian politics turned in my favor and a number of my colleagues came into power, I left the World Bank Group, hired an MIT alumni to manage the computer store, and returned to Iran. There I was made president of the Export Promotion Center, a vice ministerial post, under the government of Mohammad Reza Shah Pahlavi. The Shah had previously brought about a program known as the White Revolution, which called for land reform, the extension of voting rights to women, and the elimination of illiteracy. He also brought many young, educated technocrats into government, me being one of them, and he modernized Iran. While the Shah brought social reform and economic growth to Iran, he also tried to hold on tightly to power and used the secret police to control the country. Thus, opposition grew, primarily within the mosques, and Ayatollah Khomeini, who advocated a populist ideology tied to Islamic principles, led the movement. Although Khomeini lived in exile in Iraq and later France, he was able to spread his message through music cassettes. Khomeini received the support of the conservatives in Iran, who believed that the Shah was leading Iran away from its traditional and religious roots.

I held the vice ministerial post for just over a year until late 1978, when I realized the Shah's government was about to be toppled in revolution. Everything rapidly fell apart. This time the prototypical winds of change felt more like a jet stream propelling me forward. I still remember when the National Iranian Gas Company's headquarters' building burned to the ground. I believed, as we were told by the regime, that it was due to an accidental fire in the basement because of a machine malfunction. It was not until I talked to one of my colleagues that I found out it was set on fire by a group of radicals. The amazing thing about revolutions is how rapidly the societal system falls apart. One day there were demonstrations with thousands of women in dark head coverings (chadoors), and the next week the system collapses. My father had given his resignation and asked to retire. He was staying in London, where Lis and my sister had joined him. Dad, due to having had senior positions in the foreign service, military, and intelligence organizations, was concerned about possible problems if I stayed in Iran. My family repeatedly urged me to leave as soon as possible.

But it was difficult for government officials to leave the country. Assuming we could even book a flight to leave Tehran, we needed special permission from ministers. Finally, after a number of requests, a colleague of mine, who had become Minister of Finance (Minister Hassanali Mehran), approved my trip for a conference. With Dad's connections with his majesty King Hussein of Jordan, I was able to leave Iran on a Jordanian flight.

I once again came back to the United States after much struggle. Upon returning, I took charge of The Computer Emporium and accepted a tenured position as a professor at George Washington University (GWU) in Washington, D.C. I held little hope that I would ever be able to rejoin the Iranian government ranks, as my being awarded a "Royal Decree" by the Shah had forever tainted me in the eyes of the ruling opposition. Those who supported the Shah back in Iran were executed or jailed by the hundreds. The Shah left Iran on January 16, 1979, and Ayatollah Khomeini returned to Iran on February 1, 1979. Events truly no longer moved linearly but rather exponentially.

My arrival back in the United States coincided with the Iranian hostage crisis, when fifty-two Americans working in the embassy in Tehran were held hostage for 444 days by a group of militants in Iran's revolutionary movement. The hostages were only released under the condition that the United States transfer money and export military equipment to Iran.

Network television competition had a notable effect on the coverage of the crisis. *ABC* added a half-hour segment, hosted by Ted Koppel, to its national nightly news programming. Originally titled "America Held Hostage," it went on to be renamed *Nightline*. In response, Walter Cronkite added to his famous sign-off, "and that's the way it is," a count of the days the hostages endured captivity.

During this time, it was a little disturbing being an Iranian, as the media whipped the public into a never-before-seen media frenzy. When dealing on a personal level, I was relieved to find my students at GWU being very respectful. This is the way it is in America. While prejudice may exist against a whole group of people, it disappears after people come to know you.

It was also during this time that I made the decision to become a naturalized U.S. citizen.

At GWU, I became a tenured faculty member and the director of the international business department. Continuing to teach, I decided to sell The Computer Emporium because of increasing market competition from IBM, which had opened retail outlets close to our store. My computer pioneering days were over, yet I was about to embark on another groundbreaking endeavor.

While remaining a professor, in 1982 I began another company, Intrados International Management Group, which provided executive education programs for officials from developing countries. While the Harvards and

MITs of the world were also conducting executive education programs, they were ignoring the vast need and desire of the developing world for these same services. We started to provide executive education to managers and government officials of developing countries, building on the network I had developed while working at the World Bank and teaching in executive programs. The business grew and became quite successful. One of the programs we developed was running and managing state-owned enterprises. Thus, we found our niche in the Reagan-inspired privatization boom of the 1980s and soon became consultants and contractors for many USAID projects around the world, as privatization became an active policy initiative of many nations. What started out as running two-week courses in Washington, D.C., with officials from places such as Cameroon, Nepal, and the Philippines, soon grew into a global endeavor needing additional staff and global support. Here, I tapped my sister, who was a vice president at JPMorgan, to help run the company, as there was no one else I felt I could trust as much with seeing my vision to fruition than family.

The same year I started Intrados, my first child, Otessa Marie, was born. She, being my parents' only grandchild, was loved, as any cherished child would be. Initially going by the name of Otessa, she insisted on being called Marie once reaching middle school. We reluctantly obliged her teenage attempts at assimilation.

Meanwhile, in the boom of the late 1980s and early 1990s, Intrados ended up winning many government contracts, including providing technical assistance services to support the privatization and economic restructuring program for Eastern Europe and the New Independent States of the former Soviet Union. We went on to develop the software, to train the people, and to set up the stock exchanges in Russia, Romania, Kazakhstan, and Moldova for one-fortieth the price of what NASDAQ or the French Bourse would charge. And we did it all on desktop computers, not the typical mainframes.

Unfortunately, government contracts and contractors are of a different breed. Intrados ended up in a multiyear legal battle with the U.S. government, which resulted in exorbitant lawyers' fees. The battle was a result of the U.S. government not willing to pay us for the work we had done. The designated contract administrator did not have the authority or the budget to ask for the task we were instructed to carry out. When we submitted the invoices, the government retaliated by repeatedly auditing and harassing our operations. I realized that in order to achieve any kind of resolution, I would have to spend even more of my employees' and my time, with the only guarantee being that the lawyers would be able to buy another luxury vacation home. By 1998, we decided it was time to cut our losses, so we settled with the government and shut the doors. The disappointing part of the experience was that major accounting and consulting firms were asked to step in, to hire a number of our staff, and simply to continue the work we were doing without providing us any compensation. The lesson I learned from the whole debacle is that you need to be an insider when it comes to working with the government. It seemed as if the upward trajectory I had taken in this endeavor was now slowly spiraling to the ground.

While Intrados was underway with my sister at the helm, I continued to teach at the university level and grew my own consulting and executive education business for Fortune 100 companies. I became sought after as an authority on future business trends, global economic assessment, and global corporate strategy and implementation. I found myself consulting with major corporations, governments, and government agencies, and regularly conducting executive programs for multinational corporations. Luckily, the breeze that my life had come to represent had drifted in an entirely new and unexpected direction.

While at George Washington University, I had been promoted to chair of the International Business Department, with the expectation that by increasing the standing of this department, it would in turn lead to the university increasing staff. George Washington was selected as one of the top five international business programs in the nation. Thus, I was stunned when I finally approached the school administration asking for more professors to carry the increasing workload of students enrolling and was told by the dean that they had no plans for doing so—partially because they never really expected me to stay indefinitely in the United States! "We thought you would be returning to Iran," stated the dean.

Armed with the knowledge I had reached the limits of opportunity at GWU, I kept my ears open for other prospects in academia. One of my colleagues at the executive education program I taught at Penn State University approached me about a potential appointment to a soon-to-be-created chair in 1992.

I interviewed with Penn State benefactor William A. Schreyer, chairman emeritus of Merrill Lynch, along with Dean J. Hammond, and I accepted the newly endowed position as professor of Global Management, Policies, and Planning, with the understanding that I would additionally be the founding director of the new Center for Global Business Studies. Schreyer became my friend and mentor and later encouraged me to join the Center for Strategic and International Studies (CSIS), one of the world's preeminent foreign policy think tanks.

Moving from Washington, D.C., to State College, Pennsylvania, was another culture shock. Instead of being in a multiethnic city with world stature,

I was now in the bucolic seat of college football mania, also fondly known as Happy Valley.

After a couple of years settling into the Penn State community, my twins, John Cyrus and Anna Shahrzad, were born. Having learned the lesson with our daughter Otessa, we decided to give them American first names and Persian middle names.

My consulting had me traveling globally, so regardless of where I was, I never stopped working. One of the opportunities my new position afforded me was to create my own board of directors for my center, and I chose a number of leaders from industry powerhouses whom I had worked with as a consultant. Eventually, I began to wonder when I would be asked to serve on any boards. While these Fortune 100 companies readily asked (and paid handsomely) for my insight and guidance, over the course of fifteen years I saw many board positions come and go with no offers proffered in my direction. I eventually figured out I would have to swallow my pride and actually ask to be considered. In 2006, I was granted a seat on the board of directors at Westfield Insurance Group. Headquartered in the Cleveland region, Westfield is an insurance and banking group of businesses. In addition to having a strong presence in Ohio, Westfield provides commercial and personal insurance in twenty-one states and surety services in thirty-one states. It has $3.7 billion in consolidated assets. Needless to say, I was honored to be selected to serve on the board.

The following year, the former vice president of Kodak North America and prior head of Kodak's Healthcare Business Unit, Bob Hamilton, approached me to sit on the board of the newly formed Nason Medical Center, an innovative company that provides emergency and urgent care at one-sixth the cost of hospital emergency rooms. Nason is headquartered in Charleston, South Carolina, and it has served over five hundred thousand people in the region since the company started in 2005. The wait times at the emergency and urgent care centers are significantly shorter than the wait times at hospitals. As a board member, I helped to raise money for the firm as well as expand Nason from one facility to five.

Here I was, feeling as if I had finally been accepted into the bastion of white America. But now, looking back on all of my choices and the impetus upon which they were based, I cannot help but wonder if my story is unique.

Like many other immigrants before and after me, I had become aerodynamic, shaped by the stronger-than-normal forces I had encountered in my lifetime as an immigrant. I worked hard not to be knocked over by these forces, which often led to sacrifices. Having worked over seventy hours a week for most of my life, my family life was at times set aside. I relied on my wife, Lis, and my children to fend for themselves when I worked abroad for weeks and months at a time. Sometimes I wonder how it must feel to marry an immigrant like myself, and then I wonder how I was so lucky to find such a supportive wife. She has helped me withstand life's storms and has kept me moving forward. She has tolerated moves from one place to another, from urban D.C. to bucolic State College to Tehran, Iran, and she has traveled all around the globe to grow our companies.

This is only one story of an immigrant. My success is built on hard work, a supportive family, and the American culture, which is based more on meritocracy and the tolerance of immigrants than on one's heritage. But it would not have been possible without a number of mentors over the years—such as former Ursinus president Richter, who recommended I transfer to MIT; Professor Stobaugh of Harvard Business School, who always encouraged me; and William Schreyer, who not only supported me and my center at Penn State but also encouraged me to join CSIS.

4

What It Takes to Uproot Yourself

IMMIGRATION AS A FORCE OF CHANGE

As a nation of immigrants, the United States has wrestled with immigration since its founding. Who should be allowed to pass through the Golden Door? How many? The issue is always approached with an array of sentiments—from ambivalence to ignorance, xenophobia to embracement, nationalism to fear.

Yet no one can rightly deny that what helped make America strong economically, governmentally, politically, and militarily has been immigrants. They came and continue to come to this country with grand ambitions to succeed in an open and free society.

Our nation's prosperity is built on the renegade, risk-taking, entrepreneurial concoction of truly American innovation and invention. Wave upon wave of immigrants bought into the American Dream that anything was possible in the United States, and anyone who put in the effort could succeed here. Immigrants, having taken the risk to come to the United States, are often entrepreneurial in nature. It is the entrepreneur who comes up with new ideas, takes risks, and tries new things. It is the entrepreneur who works long and hard, who finds the money for risky ventures, who breaks the rules, who is the pioneer and the inventor. Truly, entrepreneurs are the heroes of a growing economy.

However, "the continued failure to devise and implement a sound and sustainable immigration policy threatens to weaken America's economy, to jeopardize its diplomacy, and to imperil its national security," concludes a Council on Foreign Relations Independent Task Force cochaired by former Florida governor Jeb Bush and former White House chief of staff Thomas "Mack" McLarty.[1]

For most immigrants in the twenty-first century, coming to America is about the chance to start anew, to begin again, said author Joseph O'Neill, who is half Irish and half Turkish. He was raised in Holland, but he now lives in New York with his family. "One of the great pluses of being an immigrant is you get to start again in terms of your identity," O'Neill said. "You get to shed the narratives which cling to you."[2]

Our immigrants are truly the Mothers of Invention. As Google vice president Omid Kordestani told the graduating class at San Jose University in 2007, "To keep an edge, I must think and act like an immigrant. There is a special optimism and drive that I benefited from and continue to rely on that I want all of you to find. *Immigrants are inherently dreamers and fighters*."[3]

Within today's political and media discourse, immigration is generally framed as a social problem in need of solving. Newspaper headlines, editorials and blogs, as well as talk radio and television reveal a number of widely held negative perceptions about immigrants, including that they are reluctant to learn English, take jobs from native-born Americans, add to the crime problem, and contribute less to the tax revenue system than they use.

Yet a careful reading of the research debunks each of these myths. Additionally, while reviewing the research literature, I found that immigrants demonstrate a remarkable pattern of strengths. They have high levels of engagement in the labor market, and the children of immigrants go on to outperform their parents.

Children of immigrants learn from watching their parents work hard at making something of their lives in a country offering a chance to succeed. Many of them carry on to achieve great things. They do so in part to give something back to the country that allowed them and their parents the chance for a better life.

Immigrants have contributed to their new country in so many significant, positive ways. They have made American society and culture richer. As the sixty-nine-year-old, Indian-born novelist Bharati Mukherjee, who came to the United States in her twenties, said, "America has transformed me. It does not end until I show that I (along with the hundreds of thousands of immigrants like me) am minute by minute transforming America. The transformation is a two-way process: It affects both the individual and the national-cultural identity."[4]

Many of today's immigrants arrive already prepared to contribute to a global economy. They are frequently the best and brightest (if not also the most motivated) from their countries, and they come possessing the risk-taking personality of the entrepreneur.

Still, these virtues were and unfortunately are not always recognized, particularly in times of national tension or economic stress, when reaction-

> Peter Linder, second-generation Austrian immigrant, whose parents fled Vienna near the beginning of Hitler's rise to power, is a successful entrepreneur and investor. In Philadelphia, he started three companies, two of them successful.
>
> He says, "The mold of Jews coming here was that parents believed education was the most important thing. For a lot of cultures, education is very, very important, but it's not so important for people in this country."

ary forces place obstacles to block the immigrants' path toward assimilation and success.

Yet as Charles Darwin said, "It is not the strongest of the species that survive, nor the most intelligent, but the ones most responsive to change." Particularly in times of political tension or economic stress, immigrants have been the most responsive to change. Despite the obstacles, immigrants adapt and keep moving forward.

If we look at some of the statistics on immigrants in our society, we begin to recognize patterns. While the number of immigrants according to the 2010 Census is almost four times what it was in 1910, the percentage of immigrants with respect to the total U.S. population is not at an all-time high.

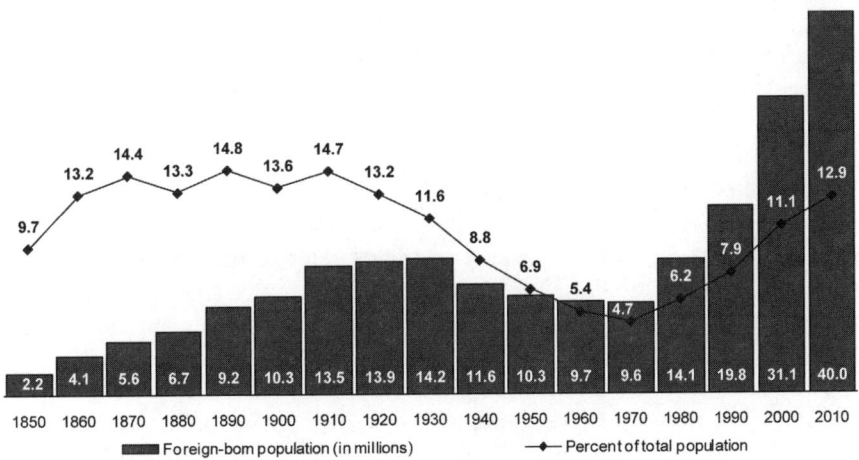

Foreign-Born Population and Foreign-Born as Percentage of the Total U.S. Population, 1850 to 2010

Elizabeth M. Grieco, Edward Trevelyan, Luke Larsen, Yesenia D. Acosta, Christine Gambino, Patricia de la Cruz, Tom Gryn, and Nathan Walters, U.S. Census Bureau, Population Division, *The Size, Place of Birth, and Geographic Distribution of the Foreign-Born Population in the United States: 1960 to 2010*. Annual Meetings of the Population Association of America, San Francisco, CA, May 3–5, 2012.

Some of the misconceptions about immigration have to do with its effects on the economy, and immigrants are easily singled out as exacerbating our economic woes. In particular, mass immigration and illegal immigration are the focus of much concern and anxiety, while much less attention is given to immigrants who enter legally.

> ### "The Founding Immigrants"—
> ### a *New York Times* op-ed by Kenneth C. Davis
>
> Often, the disdain for the foreign was influenced by religion. Boston's Puritans hanged several Friends after a Bay Colony ban on Quakerism. In Virginia, the Anglicans arrested Baptists.
>
> But the greatest scorn was generally reserved for Catholics—usually meaning Irish, Spanish, and Italians. Generations of white American Protestants resented newly arriving "Papists," and even in colonial Maryland, a supposed haven for them. Roman Catholics were nonetheless forbidden to vote and hold public office.
>
> Once independent, the new nation began to carve its views on immigrants into law. In considering New York's constitution, for instance, John Jay—later to become the first chief justice of the Supreme Court, suggested erecting a wall of brass around the country for the exclusion of Catholics."[5]

During the boom economic years in the last quarter of the last century and the coinciding period of deregulation, the undocumented immigrant population grew from less than one million in 1980 to a peak of nearly twelve million in 1996. Between 2007 and 2009, however, the undocumented population declined by one million, coinciding with the economic downturn. The current estimate of the undocumented population is 10.8 million: approximately 19 percent entered the United States prior to the 1990s; 44 percent entered during the 1990s; and another 37 percent entered since 2000. All told, undocumented immigrants (adults and children) only make up approximately 4 percent of the total U.S. population.

A host of opinions about immigration today is based on a set of beliefs about this country's past. Yet these opinions are most likely distorted because they are based upon a sanitized version of our nation's history. We believe our country was founded on the principle of equal rights, and while we acknowledge that these rights were gradually expanded to include new groups of people (Native Americans, African Americans, and women, for example), we believe that we have finally achieved this high ideal.

As we can see by the incremental inclusion of these new groups, however, each generation had rationales for maintaining legal inequality; so, too, we have our own rationale for excluding non-native residents from equal rights. Our individual lenses color the way we see things that are really black-and-white.

A Chinese student studying at Penn State University remarked, "I did not know what discrimination based on race was until I came to the United States."

IMMIGRATION LAWS

Ignorance and racism guided the nation's first law regulating immigration. The Naturalization Act of 1790 limited citizenship to "any alien, being a free white person" and to people of "good moral character."

Africans and Asians, as well as free blacks and indentured servants, were left out. Despite several appeals of the law, racial barriers remained in place and were not removed until 1870 for Africans and 1952 for East and South Asians.

Perhaps the most egregious of statutes regulating immigration came about after an economic boom in the western United States, when fortunes and jobs dried up at the end of the Gold Rush and work on the transcontinental railroad in the mid-1800s ceased.

The tens of thousands of Chinese immigrants mining gold and laying rails across the great expanse were tolerated during those flush years, but when the rare metal's vein was tapped, the Chinese were forced from the mines. They resettled in cities, working in laundries and restaurants.

As the post–Civil War economy declined, public sentiment in West Coast states turned against the Chinese. In 1882, Congress passed and President Chester A. Arthur signed the Chinese Exclusion Act, which kept out "skilled and unskilled laborers and Chinese mining employees." It was the nation's first law to restrict free immigration.

Ironically, according to historian David Hackett Fischer, Congress passed the law "while Chinese laborers were actually at work on Bedloe's Island, helping build the pedestal for America's great icon of liberty. Saum Song Bo wrote angrily in 1885, 'The word liberty makes me think of the fact that this country is the land of liberty for men of all nations except the Chinese. I consider it as an insult to us Chinese to call on us to contribute toward building in this land a pedestal for the Statue of Liberty.'" Fischer further wrote, "Saum Song Bo wondered whether this *statute* against the Chinese or the Statue to Liberty will be the more lasting monument."[6]

The Exclusion Act went even further by restricting any Chinese from becoming citizens, making their status as immigrants permanent and intending to prevent their assimilation into society and culture. The law essentially created a nation within a nation, attempting to exclude any Chinese from the opportunity to share in American prosperity.

That same year, Congress also banned "any convict, lunatic, idiot, criminals, or any person unable to take care of him or herself without becoming a public charge" under the 1882 Immigration Act.

From this point onward, for more than forty years, the United States continued to impose restrictions. Eventually, even white Europeans, who since the nation's founding immigrated freely, felt restrictions, but not like what Asians and Africans felt.

In 1917, the U.S. Congress passed the Immigration Act of 1917 (also known as the Asiatic Barred Zone Act) with an overwhelming majority. This act added to the number of undesirables banned from entering the country, including but not limited to "homosexuals," "idiots," "feeble-minded persons," "criminals," "epileptics," "insane persons," "alcoholics," "professional beggars," all persons "mentally or physically defective," polygamists, and anarchists. Furthermore, it barred all immigrants over the age of sixteen who were illiterate. The most controversial part of the law was the section that designated an "Asiatic Barred Zone," a region that included much of Asia and the Pacific Islands from which people could not immigrate. Previously, only the Chinese had been excluded from admission to the country.

Then, the Immigration Act of 1924 excluded all classes of Chinese immigrants as well as Asians in general. It limited the number of immigrants allowed entry into the United States through a national origins quota. The law was aimed at further restricting the southern and eastern Europeans, mainly Jews fleeing persecution in Poland and Russia, who were immigrating in large numbers starting in the 1890s, as well as prohibiting the immigration of Middle Easterners, East Asians, and Indians. Congressional opposition was minimal.

It was not until 1943 that Congress repealed the Chinese Exclusion Act. Certainly the specter of what had started in 1941 with Hitler's "Final Solution" played into the change in U.S. immigration policy. However, by this time tens of thousands of Japanese Americans, many U.S. citizens by birth, had been confined to internment camps because the United States was at war with Japan.

Japanese Americans were treated more harshly because of their appearance. The country was at war with Germany and Italy, too, but the Americanized citizens and immigrants from those countries had only to pledge a loyalty oath. As a group, the government may have monitored them, but they were not imprisoned.

The U.S. Immigration and Nationality Act of 1952, also known as the McCarran-Walter Act, only revised the quota formula assigned to each

They sought to have their citizenship restored but were denied and almost sent back to Japan. A Justice Department official, reading their case and their reason for wanting their citizenship, allowed them to remain in the United States. However, they did not have their citizenship restored until 1968.

Itaru and Shizuko Ina were both born in the United States, yet in 1941 they were among the many Japanese Americans who lost their homes and businesses. They were rounded up and shipped to what the government termed *internment* camps but what Japanese Americans, and even President Roosevelt, called *concentration* camps.

Shizuko was four months pregnant when she and Itaru boarded a Greyhound bus that took them to Topaz. They were first taken to a horse race track for processing, where they were forced to live in a stall. By the time they reached Topaz, where the arid and dusty climate made noses bleed, Itaru had become indignant at their treatment.

He began to fight for his and his family's civil rights and made a speech, arguing the military took the internees' constitutional rights based on discrimination. "We should be treated equal to the free people," he said. That branded Itaru a troublemaker.

Feeling that their country had betrayed them and not wanting to cut ties to their ancestral country, the Inas' refused to swear undivided loyalty to the United States in a survey all internees were given. They then renounced their citizenship.

When camp authorities demanded to know why he refused, Itaru told them he bought war bonds, registered for civil defense, and always voted, yet his country decided he was a threat based solely on his ethnic appearance. He now no longer believed he and his family had a future in the United States because of their ethnicity.

For speaking out in protest and refusing to swear loyalty, Itaru was charged with sedition, and in 1944, he was separated from his family and sent to a U.S. Justice Department camp. The camp, actually a military fort, had been converted to detain German prisoners of war, and Americans of Japanese decent were deemed enemies.

At war's end in 1945, Japan was in ruin, firebombing raids had devastated its cities and industry, and two atomic bombs had leveled two major cities. Reports back to the camps convinced the Inas there was nothing for them or their children to return to in Japan.

country of origin. Countries could send one-sixth of 1 percent of each nationality's population in the United States in 1920. Because the law was based on U.S. population percentages, immigrants during this period were primarily from Western Europe. McCarran and Walter were afraid the United States could face communist infiltration through immigration and were concerned about national security. Thus, their solution was selective immigration, which did not take economics and, to a certain extent, foreign policy into account. Although the law technically ended Asian exclusion by allotting each Asian nation a minimum quota of one hundred visas each year and allowing Asians to become naturalized American citizens, the law ensured low immigration numbers from Asian countries. President Truman vetoed the law because he believed it to be discriminatory, but it was passed with the support of Congress.

By the early 1960s, calls to reform U.S. immigration policy had mounted, thanks in no small part to the growing strength of the civil rights movement. The movement's focus on equal treatment regardless of race or nationality led many to view the quota system as backward and discriminatory. With the passing of the historic Civil Rights Act of 1964 to end overt discrimination within the nation, the next logical step was to purge it of its external discriminatory policies toward the rest of the world as embodied in its prevailing immigration policies.

In particular, Greeks, Poles, Portuguese, and Italians—of whom increasing numbers were seeking to enter the United States—claimed the quota system discriminated against them in favor of Northern Europeans. At that time, 70 percent of all immigrant slots were allotted to natives of just three countries: the United Kingdom, Ireland, and Germany. These slots went mostly unused, while there were long waiting lists for the small number of visas available to those born elsewhere in eastern and southern Europe.

The resulting Immigration and Naturalization Act of 1965 was as much a manifestation of civil rights policy as it was an instrument of immigration reform. It marked a dramatic break with past immigration policy and had an immediate and lasting impact. In place of the national-origins quota system, the act provided for preferences to be made according to categories, such as relatives of U.S. citizens or permanent residents, those with skills deemed useful to the United States, or refugees of violence or unrest. Though it abolished quotas per se, the system did place caps on per-country and total immigration, as well as caps on each category. As in the past, family reunification was a major goal, and the new immigration policy increasingly allowed entire families to uproot themselves from other countries and to reestablish their lives in the United States.

In 1965, nearly twenty-five years after the repeal of the Chinese Exclusion Act, Congress finally completely abolished immigration restrictions on

Asians and also eliminated the federal policy of discrimination based on race, place of birth, sex, and residence. In 1976, it went on to eliminate preferential treatment for people from the Western Hemisphere.

A similar story of the United States using and then limiting the immigration of a group of foreigners can also be found in Mexican immigration to America. When the United States entered World War I, the country had a great need for Mexican labor so that American workers could fight overseas. Consequently, the Mexican government exported Mexican workers to America as contract laborers. However, after the war ended, a nativistic United States wanted to cut back the flow of Mexicans and created the U.S. Border Patrol in 1924. Economic demand for unskilled laborers did not end with the creation of the Border Patrol, so Mexicans continued to immigrate to America both legally and illegally.

In the 1930s, as a result of the Great Depression, Mexican workers were deported en masse. In *Beyond Smoke and Mirrors*, Douglas Massey, Jorge Durand, and Nolan J. Malone point out, "Mexicans were accused, paradoxically, of both 'taking away jobs from Americans' and 'living off public relief.'"[7]

World War II brought back another surge in demand for Mexican immigrants. While Americans were away at war, braceros, Mexican farm laborers, helped to run the American economy. The Bracero Program continued even after the war ended, but the number of legal braceros allowed could not fulfill the demand for workers. As a result, growers recruited undocumented workers. The cycle continued with the government needing workers and then shutting them out.

In 1986, the next significant change in policy came about with the Immigration Reform and Control Act (IRCA). This required employers to attest to their employees' immigration status, made it illegal to knowingly hire or recruit unauthorized immigrants, granted amnesty to certain seasonal agricultural illegal immigrants, and granted amnesty to illegal immigrants who entered the United States before 1982 and had since resided in the United States. In all, 2.3 million Mexican illegal immigrants were granted amnesty. However, IRCA also began a process of border fortification and militarization. Besides the military, the U.S. Border Patrol is the largest arms-bearing branch of the U.S. government. Intended to keep illegal immigrants out, the border fortification instead kept illegal immigrants in. According to Princeton sociologist Douglas Massey, "From 1965 to 1985, 85 percent of undocumented entries from Mexico were offset by departures and the net increase in the undocumented population was small. The build-up of enforcement resources at the border has not decreased the entry of migrants so much as discouraged their return home."[8]

Current immigration policy then shifted after the enactment of the Homeland Security Act of 2002. The U.S. Immigration and Naturalization Service

(INS) became part of the Department of Homeland Security (DHS). The department's new U.S. Citizenship and U.S. Immigration Services (USCIS) handles U.S. immigration services and benefits, including citizenship, applications for permanent residence, nonimmigrant applications, asylum, and refugee services.

Unlike most other federal agencies, USCIS is funded almost entirely by user fees. Under President George W. Bush's fiscal year 2008 budget request, direct congressional appropriations made up about 1 percent of the USCIS budget, and about 99 percent of the budget was funded through fees. The total USCIS fiscal year 2008 budget was projected to be $2.6 billion.

In President Obama's fiscal year 2013 budget proposal, the total USCIS budget of $3.8 billion for immigration enforcement remained a priority. USCIS remains a mostly fee-dependent agency, as there was no request for additional appropriations from Congress to cover the costs of processing refugees and asylees. As usual, the Immigration and Customs Enforcement (ICE) and the Customs and Border Protection (CBP) budget dwarfed the USCIS's budget. Even within USCIS's budget, there were proposed increases for enforcement in the form of an expanded E-Verify program.

All in all, education and human capital do not figure prominently in the eligibility criteria for most immigrants in the United States. Since 1965, U.S. immigration policy has been built around family unification, and two-thirds of permanent immigrants to the United States are now admitted on the basis of family ties (two-fifths as the spouses of U.S. citizens, and the rest as the children, siblings, or parents of U.S. citizens or as the spouses of permanent residents). My own mother and father (and subsequently his second wife and their child) and I became U.S. citizens thanks to my sister being born here.

TODAY'S PARIAHS

We would like to believe that 1965 marked the year that discriminatory immigration laws were abolished; however, this is not truly the case. Both Arab Americans and Iranian Americans have excelled in the United States, and in an array of fields, from academics and politics to entertainment and science. Although they have been welcomed to this country for decades, Middle Eastern people—like Japanese Americans sixty years earlier—have found after the terrorist attacks on September 11, 2001, how harsh America can be toward someone who is nonwhite and professes a faith other than one based upon Judeo-Christian beliefs.

The history of Middle Eastern immigration to the United States dates back to the end of the nineteenth century. For decades, Middle Easterners came into the country at various rates, but after the United States defeated its foes in the Pacific and Europe, assumed superpower status, and locked horns with communist Russia, immigrants began to flood in.

The first wave from the Middle East occurred between the late 1800s and 1910, when approximately sixty thousand Arabs arrived on American shores, mostly from what was then Greater Syria (present-day Lebanon), and they were overwhelmingly Christian. They were by and large unskilled men intent on making money and then returning home to live in prosperity.

The second wave occurred in the 1950s. The bulk of this group was comprised of professionals and university students who sought citizenship and permanent residency in the United States, which was transforming itself into the world's largest economy with an expanding middle class.

Whereas the early Arab immigrants were mainly uneducated and relatively poor, the new arrivals included large numbers of relatively well off, highly educated professionals: lawyers, professors, teachers, engineers, and doctors. Many of the new immigrants began as students at American universities and then decided to stay, often as a result of lack of employment opportunities back home or because of the unstable political conditions in their homelands—conditions that often threatened imprisonment or death for returnees.

The third wave began in the mid-1960s and continues today, with an estimated 3.7 million Arab Americans living in the United States.[9] Most reside in and around the larger cities, such as Detroit and Los Angeles, according to the Arab American Institute.

The reasons for the third wave of Middle Eastern immigration differ from the reasons for the second wave. In addition to economic need and the attraction of a major industrial society, immigrants from the third wave often are driven out of their homes as a result of regional conflicts or as a consequence of major social and political changes in the homeland that make life difficult, especially for the wealthy or the middle classes. The search for a democratic haven, where it is possible to live in freedom without political or economic harassment and suppression by the government, was a strong motivation, even more so than during the earlier period.

These later immigrants come from all parts of the Arab world, but especially from Palestine, Lebanon, Syria, Egypt, Iraq, and Yemen. Arab Americans represent twenty-two different Arab countries. To many people's surprise, only 25 percent of Arab Americans are Muslim, even though most Arabs are Muslim. And although most Muslim Arab immigrants have been Sunni (reflecting the population in the region), there is a substantial Shi'a minority, as well. Some 65 percent of the remaining Arab Americans are Christian, and 10 percent profess other faiths. Arab Americans are generally more educated than the average U.S. citizen, with 45 percent having a bachelor's degree compared to 28 percent of Americans. Further, 18 percent of Arab Americans hold a postgraduate degree, while 10 percent of Americans can say the same.

Excluded from this group are the Iranian Americans, whose numbers are believed to be between one and two million. It is not clear how many Iranian Americans there really are because Census data has historically underrepresented the number of Iranian Americans in the country. After the Iranian hostage crisis, Iranian Americans took a low profile due to political tensions and hesitated in participating in civic activities. Extrapolated Census data and independent surveys performed by Iranian Americans estimated there to be one million Iranian Americans in the United States in 2009.[10] They tend to concentrate in certain areas, such as Los Angeles, New York, New Jersey, and Washington, D.C. A Zogby International survey found that around 40 percent of Iranian Americans identify as Muslims, around 40 percent are not religious, and the remainder is split among Christians, Jews, Bahais, and Zoroastrians.[11] Thus, an Iranian American is more likely to be Muslim, but less likely to be Christian, than an Arab American. Over 25 percent of Iranian Americans hold a postgraduate degree, according to research conducted by the Iranian Studies Group, an independent academic organization at MIT. Iranian Americans are truly some of the most educated people in the country.

Today, Iranians are often denied visas without an ounce of evidence under the claim they may engage in espionage, sabotage, or the prohibited export of sensitive information. In 2012, Bloomberg News found that some Iranian engineering graduate students, who were planning on attending American universities, could not come because they were denied their visas under the accusation of potential espionage.[12] Iranians have immigrated to the United States for decades and have greatly contributed to its economy through profitable businesses and well-educated students, but current political tensions between Iran and the United States are spilling out of the political arena into academics and ultimately into economics.

Nonetheless, in July 2012, President Obama signed a piece of legislation that ordered the secretary of state to deny visas to any Iranians who wanted to take coursework that could help Iran's energy industry.

IMMIGRATION REFORM

It is estimated that there are around eleven million undocumented immigrants currently residing in the United States. These undocumented immigrants are largely from Mexico and Central America. In 2011, the Department of Homeland Security estimated that Mexico, El Salvador, and Guatemala were the three greatest contributors of illegal immigrants to America. Mexico represented the most with 6.8 million, while El Salvador and Guatemala each have over half a million.[13] According to the Center on Foreign Relations, "A January 2013 Gallup poll found that only 36 percent of Americans are satisfied with the current level of immigration to the United States."[14] Because of this dissatisfaction, the general public widely favors immigration reform.

In early 2013, four Republicans and four Democrats were able to come together to draft an immigration reform bill, which advocates for a thirteen-year pathway for undocumented persons to gain legal status, among other stipulations. In late June, with a vote of 68–32, the Senate passed the bill.[15] This bill also provides stricter guidelines to control future immigration—an aspect the general American public would support. As shown through a Rasmussen poll, "66 percent of likely voters say that gaining control of the border is more important than amnesty for illegal aliens."[16]

Historically, conservative Americans compose the population segment that is vehemently opposed to amnesty, as they believe it adds incentive to immigrate illegally. Additionally, conservatives view it as rewarding undocumented people for doing something unlawful. Conservatives also have been at the forefront of arguing for tighter border patrol policies in order to solve the illegal immigration issue. They believe that a lack of enforcement has fostered problems such as gang violence and human and drug trafficking. Liberals, on the other hand, have advocated for establishing a system through which undocumented persons could eventually obtain citizenship. In regard to border control, they generally believe the current state of border enforcement is at its strictest.[17]

In addition to the topics of amnesty and border control, discussions on workplace enforcement have been widespread. Liberals believe the United States should strive to hold employers responsible for whom they hire, while conservatives typically favor a more proactive approach. More explicitly, many conservatives advocate for the mandatory nationwide use of E-Verify, a system that crosses an employee's Form I-9 with records from the U.S. Department of Homeland Security and Social Security Administration to ensure eligible employment. Conservatives also generally support stricter deportation and detention regulations than their liberal counterparts. While conservatives believe in using the help of state and local governments for enforcement, liberals think immigration regulations should largely be the responsibility of the federal government.[18]

Though the issue of illegal immigration has been a major point of contention, conservatives and liberals seem to hold fairly similar beliefs when it comes to legal immigration. Both support a system that emphasizes family through giving priority to spouses and children of persons already residing in the United States. Recognizing the value immigrants offer to the U.S. economy, conservatives and liberals have also both stated that they wish to attract and to retain immigrants who are highly skilled.[19] In order to do so, there have been recent discussions about altering the U.S. allocation of visas to establish both an entrepreneur's visa and one for foreign professionals specializing in science, technology, engineering, and math (STEM) fields, in addition to eliminating visa quotas for individual countries.[20]

The idea that immigrants are self-selective for persistence and resilience is one that is seen throughout the stories and data. Although many recently arrived immigrants face a wide range of risks, including poverty, discrimination, taxing occupations, sometimes fewer years of schooling, and social isolation, they do better than expected on a wide range of outcomes especially when compared with their counterparts who remain in their country of origin.

Just like the pioneers of the American Old West, immigrants are the ones who have the courage and drive to leave their home countries and who are the world's most likely to succeed.

Aiding the immigrant's success is the immigrant's family. Isolated abroad, immigrants rely heavily on their family and often recruit their family members to join them and work with them. Current U.S. immigration policy works in the favor of the family members of American citizens and permanent residents. Indeed, I trusted no one more than my sister, Margaret, to help me run Intrados.

NOTES

1. Jeb Bush and Thomas McLarty, "Independent Task Force Report on U.S. Immigration Policy," Council on Foreign Relations, July 2009, http://www.cfr.org/immigration/us-immigration-policy/p20030 (accessed July 10, 2013).

2. Joseph O'Neill, "The New Immigrant Experience," *NPR.org*, November 26, 2008, http://m.npr.org/story/97468340 (accessed July 2013).

3. Cokie Roberts and Steven Roberts, "Think Like an Immigrant," *Evening Sun*, April 16, 2010, http://www.evesun.com/news/stories/2010-04-16/9417/Think-like-an-immigrant-/ (accessed July 2013).

4. Luminita Frentiu, Romanian Journal of English Studies, no. 6, 2009; www.litere.uvt.ro/vechi/RJES/no6.htm.

5. Kenneth C. Davis, "The Founding Immigrants," *New York Times*, July 3, 2007, http://www.nytimes.com/2007/07/03/opinion/03davis.html?_r=0 (accessed August 28, 2013).

6. David Hackett Fischer, *Liberty and Freedom: A Visual History of America's Founding Ideas* (New York: Oxford University Press, 2005).

7. *Harvard Magazine*, "Uneasy Neighbors: A Brief History of Mexican-U.S. Migration," May–June 2007, http://harvardmagazine.com/2007/05/uneasy-neighbors-a-brief-html (accessed August 14, 2013).

8. Harvard Magazine, "Uneasy Neighbors."
9. Heather Brown, Emily Guskin, and Amy Mitchell, "Arab-American Media," Pew Research Journalism Project, November 28, 2012, http://www.journalism.org/analysis_report/arabamerican_population_growth (accessed July 24, 2013).
10. Azadeh Ansari, "Iranian-Americans Cast Ballots on Iran's Future," *CNN.com*, June 16, 2009, http://www.cnn.com/2009/US/06/12/iran.elections.voting/ (accessed July 24, 2013).
11. "Survey of Iranian Americans: 84% Support Establishing U.S. Interest Section in Iran," *Payvand.com*, December 11, 2008, http://www.payvand.com/news/08/dec/1117.html (accessed July 24, 2013).
12. Daniel Golden, "Iranians Denied U.S. Visas Hit by Political Crossfire," *Bloomberg.com*, September 19, 2012, http://www.bloomberg.com/news/2012-09-20/iranians-denied-u-s-visas-hit-by-political-crossfire.html (accessed August 13, 2013).
13. Michael Hoefer, Nancy Rytina, and Bryan Baker, "Estimates of the Unauthorized Immigrant Population Residing in the United States: January 2011," Department of Homeland Security, *Population Estimates*, March 2012, http://www.dhs.gov/estimates-unauthorized-immigrant-population-residing-united-states-january-2011 (accessed August 4, 2013).
14. Brianna Lee, "The U.S. Immigration Debate," Council on Foreign Relations, April 19, 2013, www.cfr.org/immigration/us-immigration-debate/p11149 (accessed August 14, 2013).
15. Ashley Parker and Jonathan Martin, "Senate, 68 to 32, Passes Overhaul for Immigration," *New York Times*, June 27, 2013, www.nytimes.com/2013/06/28/us/politics/immigration-bill-clears-final-hurdle-to-senate-approval.html?_r=0 (accessed August 14, 2013).
16. "Public Opinion Polls on Immigration," Federation for American Immigration Reform, www.fairus.org/facts/public-opinion (accessed August 14, 2013).
17. "Democratic Party on Immigration," OnTheIssues, www.ontheissues.org/celeb/Democratic_Party_Immigration.htm (accessed August 14, 2013).
18. "Republican Party of Immigration," OnTheIssues, www.ontheissues.org/celeb/Republican_Party_Immigration.htm (accessed August 14, 2013).
19. "Democratic Party on Immigration," OnTheIssues, www.ontheissues.org/celeb/Democratic_Party_Immigration.htm (accessed August 14, 2013). "Republican Party of Immigration," OnTheIssues, www.ontheissues.org/celeb/Republican_Party_Immigration.htm (accessed August 14, 2013).
20. Doug Hardy, "Entrepreneurship-friendly Immigration Reform," Entrepreneurship of All Kinds, May 2, 2013, http://entrepreneurshipofallkinds.org/2013/05/02/entrepreneur-friendly-immigration-reform/ (accessed August 14, 2013).

5

How Did She Get Here: Margaret Ghadar

Margaret Ghadar, my younger sister, was born in 1951 in Mount Pleasant, Michigan. Soon after, our family moved to Baton Rouge, Louisiana. She was too young to have any childhood memories of the United States, as we all returned to Iran when she was four years old.

Her youth was spent moving around the Middle East, where our father, Mansour, was an ambassador in places such as Lebanon and Jordan. At the time, her impression of why we were not located in more prestigious locales was that our father was being punished for some undisclosed action. She later came to understand that he was in fact in charge of the Iranian Intelligence Agency and that this stationing was quite strategic and important.

She graduated high school in 1969 from the American Community School in Tehran, where the few Iranian students were unfortunately largely treated as second-class citizens. She was not advised or guided by the school to prepare for postsecondary education. So, since I was already in school at MIT, she asked for my help. Ever the protective older brother, I helped her enroll in Regis College in Wellesley, Massachusetts, an all-girl Catholic institution, not too far from where I was living so that I could keep an eye out for her.

Even though Margaret was used to adapting to different countries, cultures, and climates, the atmosphere perpetuated by the nuns who taught there was restrictive and particularly discriminatory to non-Catholics. Her first month in, she was summoned to Father McMullen's office to be chastised for not having gone to confession since her arrival, even though it was understood that she was raised Muslim. Her best friend from New York had a similarly unpleasant experience, and so after their first year, they both transferred to Boston University for a bit more independence and freedom.

While in Boston, she met Mourad, a Harvard Business School student in the same program I was in but a year lower. He was the ultimate international student—Egyptian father, British mother, born in Hawaii, grew up in Switzerland, spoke five languages, and now working toward his master's in the United States. At the age of twenty-one, Margaret and Mourad married and moved to Paris, where he worked for Continental Grain, a commodities trading company. A yearlong move to Rome led to Mourad's father asking him to join the family commodities trading company back in Switzerland.

It was in Geneva that Margaret found a niche where she was able to put to use her background and talents. She went to work for the Iranian ambassador and was tasked with identifying and recruiting Iranian medical doctors who were working outside of Iran to go back home to practice their profession.

Unfortunately, it soon became clear that her marriage had been mostly a headstrong whim, destined to fail. After five years, she returned to the United States, where our mother was living in Washington, D.C., and she obtained a divorce.

With nothing tying her to one geographic location, she decided to return to Iran, where Lis and I were living. She went to work at an international company that worked with the Iranian stock exchange, a prescient move for her future.

Yet it was not long before the revolution was upon us in Iran. Margaret and Lis stayed indoors together, watching burnings of posters and garbage cans in the streets and people being dragged from stores with displayed images of the Shah.

I was still working for the government and not free to leave the country, but for their safety, Margaret and Lis decided to leave as soon as possible. Because of our father's deep friendship with King Hussein of Jordan, my wife and sister were put on the next (previously full) Air Jordan daily flight out of Tehran. Meanwhile, our father, seeing the handwriting on the wall, wrote a letter to the Shah saying that he was regrettably handing in his resignation due to pressing health concerns. It was three long months before I was able to leave the country.

The entire family was now uprooted back to Washington, D.C. Fortunately, because Margaret was born in the United States, she was able to pave the way for the immigration of the rest of the family. This was typical and still is of U.S. immigration to America. While I taught at George Washington University, Margaret and Lis helped run The Computer Emporium, the computer store we had opened in the area. Margaret recalls feeling as if this was only a temporary move, and that while it might take a year, or maybe two, eventually things would settle down and we would all go back to Iran. To pass the time, she thought it might be a good idea to get her master's degree in international finance in order to be prepared for an upward career move once back in Iran.

She finished her degree early by going to summer school, and she began interviewing for jobs in the Washington, D.C., area. However, it was also during this time that the Iranian hostage crisis was going on, making it difficult for her to find a job in the politically charged city. She decided to set her sights on an industry and a city that would be less discriminatory based upon her ethnicity. Thus, she obtained a job with Morgan Guaranty Trust, the company name JPMorgan went by until the 1980s, in New York City, where she was a financial analyst responsible for banks around the world. She eventually worked her way up to become a vice president at JPMorgan.

Meanwhile, I had started Intrados, and in 1988, I called upon Margaret to help out this rapidly growing, fledgling company. She came on as president and was immediately immersed in training all the highest-level government officials from developing countries. We had named the company *Intrados*, "the underlying support of an arch." Just as an intrados is the underlying support of an arch, our company became the underlying support of many government projects of developing countries.

At this time, no other company would pay attention to this previously untapped (and soon to be immensely important) market segment. The caliber of individuals who came through our programs soon would read as the who's who of the future. When these individuals went on to privatize a company, they approached the major U.S. funding source, USAID, and specifically requested that Intrados be included in the project.

It became clear to Margaret that there was another potentially untapped market where privatization was occurring, which was in setting up capital markets for these countries. The initial projected trading volume for the capital markets of developing countries was so low that Wall Street and the World Bank were barely aware of the possibilities.

Intrados, under Margaret's leadership, went on to forge a path in not only privatization but also in setting up stock exchanges, in equipping Central Banks to handle the trades, and in establishing depositories for funds in a number of countries around the world. With a home office of fourteen people, Intrados bid on and won its first U.S. government contract for the privatization and setting up of capital markets in the former states of the Soviet Union. The contract was worth $12 million and grew the company to two hundred employees.

Margaret was amazed by how immense the opportunities were and was proud the company was pioneering into a new frontier. Taking advantage of the opportunities, Intrados went on to develop the stock exchange and trading system for Romania, Moldova, Kazakhstan, Ukraine, and the eight member countries of the Eastern Caribbean.

All of this was no small feat, as in some places it was even necessary to set new telephone lines in order to handle the clearance and settlement transactions. Now it was time for NASDAQ to be a subcontractor to Intrados in this Wild West scenario. In Romania, during a meeting with Ion Iliescu, the head of state, he declared he wanted a trade to occur before the end of his term, which was in six months! The day the first trade was to occur, Margaret recalls having her staff on standby in sneakers, ready to run like old-time traders on Wall Street, if the electronic system should fail. Thankfully, all went according to plan, and the first registered trade occurred between the ambassador and the head of state.

> According to a 2012 report from The Partnership for a New American Economy, immigrant-owned business owners in America make less than native-born business owners on average ($49,779 vs. $62,695). However, there were a few exceptions to this finding. For example, Iranian immigrants who start businesses make $83,555 a year on average.[1]

The rewards for all this hard work were much more than monetary. While having been successful at JPMorgan, Margaret had been disheartened by having to sell the riskiest of derivatives, but at Intrados she was helping birth new capital markets around the world. The feeling of being part of something so big was heady.

Margaret says she owes a lot of success to the fact that when these officials from developing countries were looking for assistance and partners from the United States, they looked favorably on her being an immigrant to America. These officials viewed her as one of them, for she could understand from where they came. She was someone who did not ignore or dismiss them, someone who understood them, and someone who believed enough in their potential to invest time and resources.

Margaret typifies the immigrant as a person of the world, a global citizen. And being a global citizen can be advantageous personally but also on a broader level. As Madeleine F. Green, a Senior Fellow at the National Association of Foreign Student Advisors (NAFSA) and the International Association of Universities, explained, global citizenship requires that one be self-aware, and "self-awareness enables students to identify with the universalities of the human experience, thus increasing their identification with fellow human beings and their sense of responsibility toward them."[2] This, in turn, often translates into global citizens seeking out participation in their various communities in order to fulfill that sense of responsibility. Because of these traits, which many immigrants already possess, global citizens are inherently valuable to their country at large. Governments and businesses can make use of their communication skills, thereby strengthening relations with foreigners and increasing productivity.

NOTES

1. Robert W. Fairlie, *Open for Business: How Immigrants Are Driving Small Business Creation in the United States* (Princeton, NJ: The Partnership for a New American Economy, 2012), 1–40.

2. Kris Olds, "Global Citizenship—What Are We Talking About and Why Does It Matter?" *Inside Higher Ed.com*, March 11, 2012, http://www.insidehighered.com/blogs/globalhighered/global-citizenship-%E2%80%93-what-are-we-talking-about-and-why-does-it-matter (accessed August 14, 2013).

6

Why Do They Come?

The inscription on the interior pedestal of the Statue of Liberty reads:

> Not like the brazen giant of Greek fame,
> With conquering limbs astride from land to land;
> Here at our sea-washed, sunset gates shall stand
> A mighty woman with a torch, whose flame
> Is the imprisoned lightning, and her name
> Mother of Exiles. From her beacon-hand
> Glows world-wide welcome; her mild eyes command
> The air-bridged harbor that twin cities frame.
> "Keep, ancient lands, your storied pomp!" cries she
> With silent lips. "Give me your tired, your poor,
> Your huddled masses yearning to breathe free,
> The wretched refuse of your teeming shore.
> Send these, the homeless, tempest-tossed to me,
> I lift my lamp beside the golden door!"
>
> —"The New Colossus" by Emma Lazarus[1]

Mass migrations are seldom random. Shocks to the cultural and natural ecology create the potential for mass migration as a way to adapt to a crisis. Great economic transformations, wars, violence, and environmental cataclysms create crises in countries of origin, which then set off mass migrations. Three factors in particular drive migration trends: family reunification, search for work, and humanitarian refuge. These factors also parallel this country's national immigration policy.

> Between 1881 and 1924, 2,800,000 Jews emigrated from Europe to the United States, 94 percent of them from Eastern Europe, and some 97 percent of these remained on the eastern seaboard. By 1925, one of every three New Yorkers was a Jew.[2]

A century ago, the Industrial Revolution served as a catalyst for immigration. Today, an increasingly global economy serves much the same role. The global production, distribution, and consumption of goods and services stimulates migration because where capital flows, immigrants tend to follow. Labor markets in globally coordinated economies are reliant on foreign workers in both the knowledge-intensive sector and in the more labor-intensive sector.

Just as most of today's American forebearers came to the United States at the turn of the last century in search of economic opportunity and a better life for their children, immigrants continue to do the same today.

Despite what advertisement men on Madison Avenue have tried to peddle, there is no single American Dream, but many. In post–World War II, the dream for many who struggled through the Great Depression and fought the bloodiest war in history was a home with a plot of land; for others, it was higher education. Both these dreams were realized thanks to a prosperous economy and the GI Bill, which paid for former soldiers to go to college.

In the 1950s and 1960s, the dream was grander than property ownership and a sheepskin. It was equal rights for African Americans and other minorities in a nation still trying to break with its slave-trading past and pre-enlightened thinking.

The winds of ignorance and intolerance still buffet America today, but within the last thirty years, more Americans, particularly the younger generations, have come to embrace diversity, viewing it as America's strength, not its weakness.

Nowadays, the best friend of my own twin children is a combination of black and Japanese. When I was their age, we were required in Louisiana schools to memorize the taxonomy of race. I am chagrined to remember that 100 percent black was known as "Negro," one-half as "Mulatto," one-fourth as "Quadroon," one-eighth as "Octoroon," and those that could pass as black but presented themselves as white were "Passe Blanc." These were the days when 1/32 of black blood classified you as black. Remembering about this calls to mind Martin Luther King's "I Have a Dream" speech, in which he hopes his children will not be judged by the color of their skin but by the content of their character.

Perhaps in a similar way, another grand dream is the one sought for more than two centuries by immigrants. No matter what country they leave behind, which continent they sail from or fly out of, the immigrant sees America as a beacon of tolerance and promise, of hope and opportunity—as a nation governed by ideals and values far greater than those of their homeland.

This beacon only grew brighter as the United States succeeded in World War II, showed an unprecedented generosity toward former enemies as well as allies through aid and rebuilding programs such as the Marshall Plan, and produced a dynamic economy that remains unparalleled in history.

The United States remains one of the world's premier magnets for immigrants today. There are currently forty-two million immigrants in the United States—representing one in seven American residents and one in six workers.[3] Due to changing economies and laws, the makeup of today's immigrants looks significantly different from the makeup of immigrants fifty years ago. In 1960, three-quarters of immigrants in the United States came from Europe. Today, half come from Latin America and a quarter come from Asia. In 2010, the United States accounted for roughly 27 percent of the world's permanent immigration flows and 23 percent of temporary labor migration (with Russia and Germany, numbers two and three, respectively, trailing far behind).[4] The demand for U.S. visas dramatically exceeds the supply.[5]

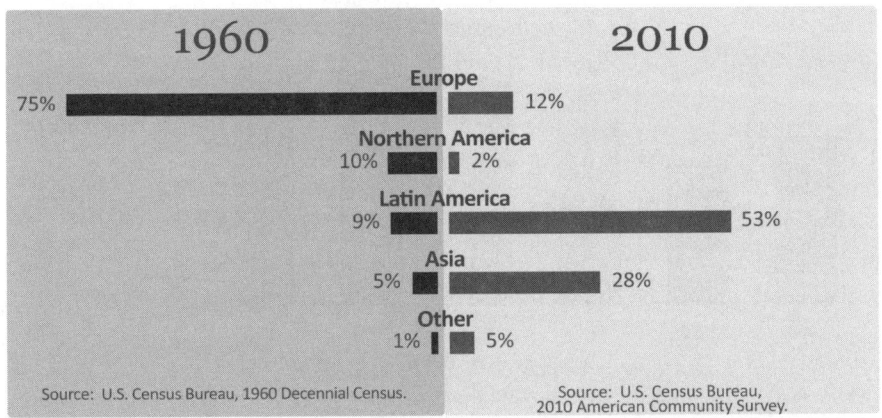

Immigrant Composition in the United States
U.S. Census Bureau Economics and Statistics Administration, *America's Foreign Born in the Last 50 Years*, http://www.census.gov/how/infographics/foreign_born.html (accessed October 22, 2013).

In the twenty-first century, millions of people around the world are affected by the experience of migration. While the United States attracts the largest number of immigrants, when looking at the percentage of immigrants out of the national population, Singapore, Israel, Saudi Arabia, and Canada all surpass the United States in percentage. Immigration is transforming nations the world over.

IMMIGRATION'S EBB AND FLOW

While the absolute number of immigrants in the United States is at an all-time high, the rate of immigration today is actually lower than it was during the last era of mass migration, when Europeans began a massive exodus from the Old World. Further, while there was a peak in unauthorized migration in 2000, the rate has dropped dramatically (over 60 percent) a decade later.[6]

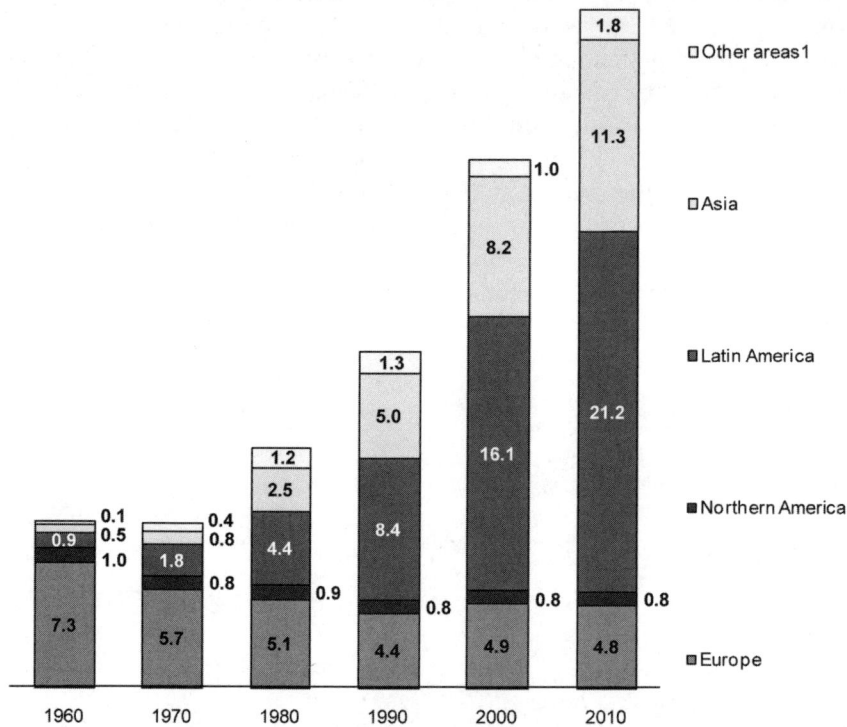

Foreign-Born Population by Region of Birth, 1960 to 2010

Elizabeth M. Grieco, Edward Trevelyan, Luke Larsen, Yesenia D. Acosta, Christine Gambino, Patricia de la Cruz, Tom Gryn, and Nathan Walters, U.S. Census Bureau, Population Division, *The Size, Place of Birth, and Geographic Distribution of the Foreign-Born Population in the United States: 1960 to 2010*. Annual Meetings of the Population Association of America, San Francisco, CA, May 3–5, 2012.

Since 2007, when 11.8 million unauthorized immigrants—most of them from Mexico—entered the country, illegal immigration has been declining. According to a February 2010 report complied by the U.S. Department of Homeland Security,

> The unauthorized immigrant population living in the United States decreased to 10.8 million in January 2009 from 11.6 million in January 2008. Between 2000 and 2009, the unauthorized population grew by 27 percent. Of all unauthorized

immigrants living in the United States in 2009, 63 percent entered before 2000, and 62 percent were from Mexico.

According to "Nation Digest" in the *Washington Post*, the decline in 2008 and 2009 "coincides with the national economic downturn" and "marked the first back-to-back drops in the number of illegal immigrants since the federal government allowed many to obtain legal status after a 1986 amnesty."[7]

We have all heard the age-old adage that America is the land of hope and opportunity, but there may be a darker side: Is there enough hope and opportunity to go around? Are there hoards of immigrants from Mexico constantly trying to sneak over our border and steal our jobs? Many people in the United States believe that the Mexican economy is a mess and the country is run by drug cartels, so Mexicans come running to our homeland to take a slice of the American Dream.

While Mexico is certainly poorer than the United States, the connection between poverty and immigration may not be as clear-cut as we imagine. For most of the two countries' histories, the United States has been the richer country. Yet until 1970, immigration from Mexico was not nearly as significant as immigration from Europe. Between 1970 and 1980, immigration from Mexico almost tripled according to the Census Bureau. In the following decade, immigration from Mexico increased twofold.

In the state of Puebla, the source of hundreds of thousands of immigrants to the United States, the economy grew at a 6.6 percent rate in the fourth quarter of 2012, and the unemployment rate in Puebla was just above 4 percent in April 2013.[8] The U.S. unemployment rate during the same time period was 7.6 percent. Opportunities exist in Puebla, yet the citizens still decide to immigrate to America. They immigrate to America because they buy into the American Dream. They believe that they can make a better life for themselves. Yet the Mexican economy has consistently outperformed the U.S. economy for most of the past forty years. Specifically, in the decade of 1970 to 1980, Mexican GDP grew at an annual rate of 6.7 percent. Even in 2012, the Mexican economy grew at 4 percent, while the U.S. economy grew at 2.2 percent. Mexico's rapidly growing economy may reduce the incentive for Mexicans to immigrate to the United States. As the economy of Mexico continues to grow faster than the United States' and the birthrate of Mexico continues to decline, the attraction of the United States will continue to rely on the American Dream. The 2008 to 2009 decrease that coincided with the U.S. economic downturn could signal a turning point in Mexican immigration, or it could simply be a hiccup. On the other hand, the attractiveness of a growing Mexican economy may cause a fading of the American Dream and the reduction of the type of immigrants that come from Mexico that our aging demographic requires.

Just as America can open its Golden Door to those "yearning to breathe free," it can, particularly in times of great stress, turn on the "foreigner," blaming him for taking away jobs or harshly generalizing his behavior or motives based on race and religion.

Yet if foreign-born workers have always been drawn to the United States, our reliance on them to boost our economy is less understood.

Generations of policymakers around the world have successfully promoted the expansion of trade in goods, services, and capital across international borders, regulated by a wide array of multilateral institutions and agreements. Yet migration—particularly from developing countries to developed countries—continues to be defined primarily as a matter of national sovereignty, where governments impose arbitrary numerical limits unrelated to global economic forces or even domestic labor demand. As a result, immigration that exceeds those limits is viewed simply as a law-enforcement issue largely unconnected to economic policy.[9] Where U.S. immigration policy does address economic realities is in the H1-B visa classification for highly skilled workers. However, the caps, quotas, and numbers do not address the real demand of the economy.

This outdated view of immigration would seem to imply that migration is something that occurs in spite of globalization rather than because of it. In fact, much of modern-day migration, especially from developing to developed nations, is an intrinsic part of globalization. However, arbitrary numerical limits on immigration are much lower than the actual movement of workers across national borders. As a result, a large share of this labor migration has been driven underground.[10] Illegal immigrants still continue to uproot themselves and to risk their lives to come to the United States in the hope of a better life.

The immigrants' story, though, is far more than just the journey to the Golden Door and the struggle to succeed in the "New Colossus." It is about the achievements made by millions of immigrants; achievements that not only lead to their great success, but also to the great success of that idea that is called the United States of America. It is not a coincidence that immigrants thrive on and drive future-oriented industries.

SILICON VALLEY: A MICROCOSM

One geographical example of significant immigrant contribution is that of Silicon Valley. It was in 1971 that the phrase "Silicon Valley" was coined by Don Hoefler to describe the mass of electronics firms mushrooming in Santa Clara County. "He pioneered the coverage of Silicon Valley as a distinct community," said Michael Malone in his book *The Big Score*, chronicling the industry. He goes on to aptly describe how we now "think of Silicon Valley as a collection of characters and eccentrics."[11] This was the same year that Intel created the world's first microprocessor, the Intel 4004.

Silicon Valley flourished and continued to generate additional startups. But why was Silicon Valley so different from older industrial regions such as Detroit and Pittsburgh, where entrepreneurial ventures were swallowed up into a handful of big firms?

Professor AnnaLee Saxenian decided to investigate this phenomenon and researched the contrast between the relative decline of the minicomputer industry along Route 128 (Massachusetts' long-established engineering hotbed) with the success of the upstart ventures south of San Francisco.[12] Key to the difference in outcomes, Saxenian argued, was the disparate cultures of the regions. Route 128 technologists, working in abandoned textile mills, created large, bureaucratic firms that jealously preserved corporate autonomy and secrecy, seeing no reason to collaborate on projects or to share technologies. By contrast, the engineers in what came to be called Silicon Valley forged a spirit of joint enterprise along with their counterparts at Stanford, Berkeley, and other local institutions. As Saxenian explained,

> Far removed from the East Coast centers of political and economic power, everyone in Silicon Valley in the '70s felt like an outsider, so they banded together to work cooperatively. They shared information freely, moved frequently between companies and invested earnings in other people's ventures. Venture capital and other professional services emerged to support a continuing flow of new start-ups and a more open, networked model for growing them.

The resulting decentralization gave Silicon Valley an edge in the unstable business environment of the 1980s and 1990s. While Digital, Wang, and other giants that anchored 128 ran aground on the shores of rapid change, Silicon Valley's networks of specialized startups and team-based firms were able to adapt quickly to circumstances, sailing beyond defense work into semiconductors, computer hardware, software, Internet, e-commerce, web services, and applications.

In "Silicon Valley's New Immigrant Entrepreneurs" (1999), Saxenian showed how the original Silicon Valley demographic, "mostly white guys from the Mid-West," had expanded to accommodate a growing number of engineers, who had originally come overseas for graduate school.

"Most of what we previously knew about immigrant businesses focused on small firms with marginal jobs: the Korean grocer, the Chinese textile worker. But in Silicon Valley I found immigrants starting companies that stood at the leading edge of technology in the global economy," Saxenian said.[13] Immigrants perfectly fit into the adaptive model of Silicon Valley, for the characteristics needed to start a new life and to assimilate into a foreign culture are much like those needed to survive in an ever-changing and competitive technological world.

Though many immigrants have found success in Silicon Valley, it is not the only hub that has attracted promising immigrants. The immigrant's typically strong work ethic, persistence, and adaptability often make him suitable for multiple career paths, within one lifetime. Zbigniew Brzezinski—who has worked in academia, for the U.S. government, and as a leader—is a perfect example.

NOTES

1. Emma Lazarus, "The New Colossus," *Poets.org*, http://www.poets.org/viewmedia.php/prmMID/16111 (accessed July 2013).

2. Rhoda G. Lewin, "Stereotype and Reality in the Jewish Immigrant Experience in Minneapolis," *Minnesota History* 46, no. 7 (1979): 258–73, http://collections.mnhs.org/MNHistoryMagazine/articles/46/v46i07p258-273.pdf (accessed August 27, 2013).

3. Audrey Singer, "Immigrant Workers in the U.S. Labor Force," *Brookings.com*, March 15, 2012, http://www.brookings.edu/research/papers/2012/03/15-immigrant-workers-singer#4 (accessed July 9, 2013).

4. "International Migration Outlook," Organisation for Economic Co-operation and Development (OECD), http://www.oecd.org/els/mig/imo2013.htm (accessed October 22, 2013).

5. Peter Whoriskey, "U.S. Manufacturing Sees Shortage of Skilled Factory Workers," *Washington Post*, February 19, 2012, http://articles.washingtonpost.com/2012-02-19/business/35444240_1_factory-workers-laid-off-workers-jobs (accessed July 9, 2013).

6. "Crossroads: The Psychology of Immigration in the New Century," *American Psychological Association, APA.org*, http://www.apa.org/topics/immigration/report.aspx (accessed August 16, 2013).

7. "Nation Digest," *Washington Post*, February 10, 2010, http://articles.washingtonpost.com/2010-02-10/world/36891238_1_illegal-immigrants-gallbladder-immigration-advocates (accessed July 2013).

8. Sara Murray, "Fewer Mexicans Head to U.S. as Home Exerts More Pull," *Wall Street Journal*, June 21, 2013, http://online.wsj.com/article/SB10001424127887324069104578529522746064526.html (accessed July 24, 2013).

9. Douglas S. Massey, "International Migration at the Dawn of the Twenty-First Century: The Role of the State," *Population and Development Review* 25 (1999): 303, 307.

10. Jorge Durand, Douglas S. Massey, and René M. Zenteno, "Mexican Immigration to the United States: Continuities and Changes," *Latin American Research Review* 36, no. 1 (2001): 107, 109.

11. Michael S. Malone, *The Big Score: The Billion Dollar Story of Silicon Valley* (New York: Doubleday, 1985).

12. AnnaLee Saxenian, *Regional Advantage: Culture and Competition in Silicon Valley and Route 128* (Cambridge, MA: Harvard University Press, 1994).

13. MIT Political Science, "Alumni Spotlight: AnnaLee Saxenian, PhD, 1989—A View of the Valley," http://web.mit.edu/polisci/news/2012/alumni-saxenian-feature.html (accessed August 29, 2013).

7

How Did He Get Here: Zbigniew Brzezinski

A few decades before Dr. Zbigniew Brzezinski was born, at the turn of the twentieth century, thousands upon thousands of Poles left Poland. Many headed for America because of imperial repression, land shortages, and chronic unemployment. Many of the immigrants were known as *za chlebem* ("for-bread") immigrants because they did not intend to stay abroad and only hoped to make some money before returning to the land they knew and loved. Nonetheless, many ended up staying in America but remained faithful to their Polish language and culture. The Library of Congress estimates that by the 1920s, more than two million Poles had immigrated to the United States.[1]

A decade after the end of World War I, Zbigniew Brzezinski was born in 1928 in Warsaw, Poland. His father was a diplomat posted to Germany from 1931 to 1935 and then to the Soviet Union from 1936 to 1938. Brzezinski thus spent some of his earliest years witnessing the rise of the Nazis as well as Stalin's Great Purge.

The family moved to Canada in 1938, the result of a new diplomatic posting. In the meantime, Poland was invaded by Nazi Germany and the Soviet Union, with the eventual allocation of Poland to the Soviet Union by the Allies in 1945. With this decision, the family could not safely return to their home country, and so they decided to remain in Montreal, Canada.

The Second World War had a profound effect on Dr. Brzezinski. In fact, in an interview, he said, "The extraordinary violence that was perpetrated against Poland did affect my perception of the world and made me much more sensitive to the fact that a great deal of world politics is a fundamental struggle."[2]

Dr. Brzezinski obtained his master's degree from McGill University in 1950, with a thesis focusing on the various nationalities within the Soviet Union. His plan for doing further studies in Great Britain in preparation for a diplomatic career in Canada fell through on a technicality. Brzezinski then attended Harvard University to work on a doctorate, focusing on the Soviet Union and the relationship between the October Revolution, Vladimir Lenin's state, and the actions of Joseph Stalin. He later collaborated with Carl J. Friedrich to develop the concept of totalitarianism as a way to more accurately and powerfully characterize and criticize the Soviets in 1956.

Of his life spent in the Polish community in Canada, he says, "I admired the dedication and the determination of the first generation of Polish immigrants who struggled against adversity to shape for themselves a better life abroad and who in the process retained their links with Poland."

It is important to place his statement within a greater historical context. After Poland became part of the Soviet Bloc in 1945, Poland's migration policies became isolationist and remained so until the collapse of communism in 1989. Consequently, passport and exit-visa policies became tight, and it was difficult for Polish citizens to leave the country. Those who made it out were only granted permission to leave temporarily and had to return by a predetermined date. Some took advantage of this system and left Poland to try to build a better life for themselves abroad. However, those who did so knew that they would never be able to return to Poland again. It truly took great dedication and determination to leave.[3]

Inspired by what he saw, Dr. Brzezinski became a U.S. citizen in 1958. Despite years of residence in Canada and the presence of family members there, he decided to immigrate to the United States because he felt he could make a greater difference in America.

> I felt that America had the greater capacity for influencing world affairs for the good, and thus helping to fashion a more just international system that would therefore also help Poland.[4]

In 1960, Brzezinski moved to New York City to teach at Columbia University, where he went on to head the Institute on Communist Affairs. He remained at Columbia until 1989, but in the meantime he started a parallel political career.

He was an advisor to the John F. Kennedy 1960 U.S. presidential campaign, urging a nonantagonistic policy toward Eastern European governments. Seeing the Soviet Union as having entered a period of stagnation, both economic and political, Brzezinski correctly predicted the future breakup of the Soviet Union along lines of nationality (expanding on his master's thesis).

In regard to his personal life, he married Czech-American sculptor Emilie Benes, and in 1963, his first son, Ian, was born. His second son, Mark, was born in 1965. And his last child, a daughter, Mika, was born in 1967.

Meanwhile, in 1964, he supported Lyndon Johnson's presidential campaign, the Great Society, and civil rights policies, and he saw Soviet leadership as having been purged of any creativity following the ousting of Khrushchev.

Brzezinski continued to support engagement with Eastern European governments while warning against De Gaulle's vision of a "Europe from the Atlantic to the Urals." He also supported the Vietnam War. From 1966 to 1968, he served as a member of the Policy Planning Council of the U.S. Department of State (President Johnson's October 7, 1966, "Bridge Building" speech was a product of his influence).

Events in Czechoslovakia further reinforced his criticisms of the right's aggressive stance toward Eastern European governments. His service to the Johnson administration and his fact-finding trip to Vietnam made him an enemy of the New Left, despite his advocacy of deescalation of the United States' involvement in the war.

Brzezinski called for a pan-European conference, an idea that would eventually find fruition in 1973 as the Conference for Security and Co-operation in Europe.

In his 1970 book, *Between Two Ages: America's Role in the Technetronic Era*, he argued that a coordinated policy among developed nations was necessary to counter global instability erupting from increasing economic inequality. Out of this thesis, he cofounded with David Rockefeller the Trilateral Commission and served as its director from 1973 to 1976. The Trilateral Commission is a group of prominent political and business leaders and academics primarily from North America, the European Union, and Asia. Its purpose is to strengthen relations among the three most industrially advanced regions of the capitalist world. The Commission helps countries "fulfill their shared leadership responsibilities in the wider international system."[5] Brzezinski selected Georgia governor Jimmy Carter as a member.

Upon becoming president in 1977, Carter chose Dr. Brzezinski for the position of National Security Adviser. Brzezinski credits Henry Kissinger as having paved the way for an immigrant to attain a cabinet-level position within the U.S. government.

> Henry Kissinger was born in Germany under the name Heinz Alfred Kissinger. He served as National Security Advisor as well as Secretary of State for presidents Richard Nixon and Gerald Ford, and he received the Nobel Peace Prize in 1973.

As Carter's National Security Advisor, Brzezinski encouraged the president to engage the People's Republic of China beginning in 1978. He personally traveled to Beijing to lay the groundwork for the normalization of U.S.–

People's Republic of China relations and developed a strong relationship with Deng Xiaoping, who led China after Mao Zedong's death. The United States and China established official diplomatic relations on January 1, 1978. By this point, China was already a third pole of power besides the Soviet Union and the United States. The new relationship between the United States and China was instrumental in the Cold War, for it brought China to the side of the United States. Scientific, technological, and cultural interchange, as well as trade relations also resulted from the diplomatic relations.

For all of the world-changing ideas Brzezinski set in motion, he never forgot his roots. Brzezinski made a visit to Poland in 1977, and of his visit he says, "There was a shift in the definition of my identity. I realized that I was no longer a Pole, but an American of Polish descent. Subsequent visits deepened my sense of cultural and historical attachment to Poland, as well as a heightening of my awareness—the way I understood it—of my being an American of Polish descent."[6]

Some cultures are more resilient, while others assimilate more easily. The Polish culture is a resilient one. Since the beginning of Polish immigration to America, many immigrants moved into Polish communities that preserved Polish culture and heritage. Newspapers, social clubs, and radio and television stations were created to help keep the Polish language alive in a foreign country.[7] Thus, the concept of identity for an immigrant is an interesting one. In America, Brzezinski is Polish, but in Poland, Brzezinski is American.

> Polish-language newspapers in the United States have been present for as long as Poles have been immigrating to America. Polish weekly newspapers were especially popular in the early 1900s, when they created a feeling of unity among immigrants as well as reinforced the responsibilities of citizenship and kept immigrants up to date on world affairs. In the early part of the nineteenth century, popular newspapers such as Chicago's *Dziennik Zwiazkowy* (meaning "Alliance Daily" in Polish) kept Poles informed on workers' rights and other labor movements, while Philadelphia's *Gwiazda* (meaning "Star" in Polish) reached a large portion of the Polish American community.

Brzezinski, however, eventually came to understand the immigrant identity and remarked that "the element of conflicting duality that may have existed gradually receded."[8]

By the 1980s, Brzezinski argued that the general crisis of the Soviet Union foreshadowed communism's end. In 1981, he was awarded the Presidential Medal of Freedom for his role in the normalization of U.S.-China relations and for his contributions to the human rights and national security policies of the United States.

As a scholar, he has developed his thoughts over the years, fashioning fundamental theories on international relations and geostrategy. During the 1950s, he worked on the theory of totalitarianism. His thoughts in the 1960s focused on a wider Western understanding of disunity in the Soviet Bloc, and he developed the thesis of intensified degeneration of the Soviet Union. During the 1970s, he propounded the proposition that the Soviet system was incapable of evolving beyond the industrial phase into the "technetronic" age.

He is currently a professor of American Foreign Policy at the School of Advanced International Studies at Johns Hopkins University and a counselor and trustee of the Center for Strategic and International Studies, both located in Washington, D.C.

His younger brother, Lech Brzezinski, continues to live in Montreal, where he works as the head of a large engineering company. Lech's wife, Wanda (also from Poland), has a medical practice. Lech and Wanda's oldest child, Matthew, a newspaper reporter, spent two years in Poland and has been a reporter for the *Wall Street Journal*. He has written some controversial and interesting articles as well as a book on the Wild West of capitalism in post–Soviet Russia.

Like their father and grandfather before them, Brzezinski's children have gone on to achieve much in the realm of political influence and discourse. Their oldest son, Ian, having spent almost two years in Ukraine as a volunteer, helped the Ukrainians with their national security problems. He also served as Deputy Assistant Secretary of Defense for Europe and NATO and was a principal at Booz Allen Hamilton. He is a Senior Fellow in the International Security Program and is on the Atlantic Council's Strategic Advisors Group. Key highlights of his tenure as Deputy Assistant Secretary of Defense for Europe and NATO Policy (2001–2005) include the expansion of NATO membership in 2004, the consolidation and reconfiguration of the Alliance's command structure, the standing up of the NATO Response Force, and the coordination of European military contributions to U.S.- and NATO-led operations in Iraq, Afghanistan, and the Balkans.

Brzezinski's second son, Mark, spent two years in Poland as a Fulbright scholar, both studying and occasionally teaching at Warsaw University. He then went to Oxford, where he completed a doctorate, focusing on the introduction of constitutionalism into Polish democracy. He became a lawyer who served on President Clinton's National Security Council as an expert on Russia and Southeastern Europe and was a partner in McGuire Woods LLP. He now serves as the U.S. ambassador to Sweden.

His daughter, Mika, is a television news presenter and cohost of MSNBC's weekday morning program, *Morning Joe*, where she provides regular commentary and presents the news headlines for the program. She appears under her maiden name and is often invited by Polish American communities to speak on special occasions.

The effects of Brzezinski's immigration to the United States has provided this country with an immeasurable repository of knowledge, insight, and career dedication to the furtherance of our standing, interactions, and influence in the global community. His Polish heritage combined with his diverse upbringing helped to shape his goals, which truly contributed to a more just international system. Brzezinski's children continue his contribution to the country. They, too, have not forgotten their Polish background, as can be seen in their work. We cannot begin to quantify the legacy his family has made in modern politics.

The Brzezinski family is one of many Polish families who have helped shape America. Today, the Census Bureau estimates that there are less than half a million Polish foreign-born immigrants in America. These immigrants work in a diverse range of sectors, ranging from manufacturing to health care to construction.[9] They all have their own story. Their story may not be as grand as Brzezinski's, but all of their stories will share at least one common plot point. Each and every single Polish immigrant had the bravery to uproot himself or herself and move to an unfamiliar land in hope of a greater future.

NOTES

1. "Polish/Russian Immigration: The Nation of Polonia," *Library of Congress*, http://www.loc.gov/teachers/classroommaterials/presentationsandactivities/presentations/immigration/polish4.html (accessed July 8, 2013).
2. Al Jazeera English, "One on One: Zbigniew Brzezinski," *YouTube.com*, http://www.youtube.com/watch?v=03ApSE6mgHE (accessed July 8, 2013).
3. Krystyna Iglicka and Magdalena Ziolek-Skrzypczak, "EU Membership Highlights Poland's Migration Challenges," *Migration Information Source*, September 2010, http://www.migrationinformation.org/feature/display.cfm?ID=800 (accessed July 8, 2013).
4. Aleksandra Ziólkowska-Boehm, "Conversation with Zbigniew Brzezinski, from 'The Roots Are Polish' by Aleksandra Ziolkowska-Boehm," *RootsWeb: Freepages*, http://freepages.genealogy.rootsweb.ancestry.com/~atpc/heritage/articles/aleksandra/roots-brzezinski.html (accessed July 8, 2013).
5. The Trilateral Commission, "About the Trilateral Commission," http://www.trilateral.org/go.cfm?do=Page.View&pid=5 (accessed August 27, 2013).
6. Aleksandra Ziólkowska-Boehm, "Conversation with Zbigniew Brzezinski."
7. Ziólkowska-Boehm, "Conversation with Zbigniew Brzezinski."
8. Ziólkowska-Boehm, "Conversation with Zbigniew Brzezinski."
9. Iglicka and Ziolek-Skrzypczak, "EU Membership Highlights Poland's Migration Challenges."

8

Hard Work Makes for a Successful Career

The clichéd image of the immigrant includes the Chinese dry cleaner, the Greek restaurateur, the Korean greengrocer, and the Mexican construction owner. These examples are still occurring, but with an important addition to the twenty-first-century immigrant story. Today we see an astounding increase in immigrant influence in the high-tech fields. Both immigrant narratives share a common thread: perseverance and hard work.

> Nguyen and Phong Phan came to Lancaster County, Pennsylvania, in 1991 from Vietnam. As new U.S. citizens under an arrangement that allows the United States' old allies who were ranking officers to become citizens, they received government assistance. Within a few weeks, they both landed jobs at the local factory of New Hampshire–based Anvil International, which manufactures piping products.
>
> They worked hard for several years, saving their money until they had enough to purchase a restaurant. They opened the Vietnamese Garden in Harrisburg, Pennsylvania, in 2003. It is a family-run enterprise. After five years at the factory, Phong Phan quit to help run the restaurant with her son, Loc, and his wife. Nguyen still works at the factory, but the family has expanded their property holding, and their daughter opened a hair salon two doors down from the restaurant.

Today's immigrants arrive in the United States with varied levels of education. At one end of the spectrum are highly educated immigrant adults. These immigrants comprise a quarter of all U.S. physicians, 24 percent of the nation's science and engineering workers with bachelor's degrees, and 45 percent of scientists with doctorates. These highly educated immigrant adults are participating in and driving innovations, research, and development—and contributing substantively to technological progress. Today, more than 40 percent of America's Fortune 500 firms were started by an immigrant or the child of an immigrant.

Immigrants are also frequently the risk takers who launch restaurants, convenience stores, dry cleaners, lawn care operations, and other small businesses in the service industry. Just a couple decades ago, only 12 percent of small business owners were immigrants. Today the number is 18 percent—a disproportionate ratio given that immigrants make up just 13 percent of the U.S. population. The largest number of owners is found in the professional and business services sector, but many are found in retail, construction, educational and social services, and leisure and hospitality.

For those immigrants who do not have educational or financial resources, they find employment in the labor market in construction, house and child care positions, and agricultural work. When we note that approximately 75 percent of all hired farm workers in the United States are immigrants, and that U.S. farms produce more than 9 percent of U.S. exports and almost all the food consumed in the United States, we can see that immigrant labor contributions are staggering.

Immigrant education levels are bimodal, meaning that immigrants are both better and worse educated than U.S.-born citizens. At one end of the spectrum, more than 1.9 percent of foreign-born workers have PhDs, almost twice the share of U.S.-born citizens. Yet, at the other end of the spectrum, nearly 30 percent of immigrants lack a high school diploma, nearly four times the figure for U.S.-born citizens. It is both ends of this spectrum that provide the diverse set of skills needed to fuel the U.S. economy. Immigrants perfectly complement U.S. workers and fill the gaps in the workforce.

In further support, noncitizens make up one-quarter of all international patent applicants from the United States, and college-educated immigrants have been found to be twice as likely to register patents as their U.S.-born counterparts. Indian and Chinese immigrants and their descendants are also thought to be overrepresented among inventors, holding 14 percent of U.S. patents. When we keep in mind that the foreign born only represent 13 percent of the U.S. population, it is impressive to note that they make up 27 percent of the U.S. workforce with a doctoral degree.

Today's successful high-tech immigrants include an impressive accounting of the world's most influential companies. Google, eBay, Yahoo!, PayPal, Zappos, and Amazon were all started by immigrants. These companies are now household names around the world.

Google

What began as a simple research project for graduate school turned into a multibillion-dollar company called Google. While at Stanford University, Sergey Brin and Larry Page decided to create a search engine that filters web pages based on popularity. Realizing its potential, Brin and Page raised money and named their search engine *Google*, as a pun on the mathematical term *Googol*, which means one followed by one hundred zeros. Half of the duo is foreign born. Brin immigrated to the United States from Russia in 1979 to escape Jewish persecution.[1] Because his father was a mathematician and valued education, he would teach Brin after hours. Brin followed in his father's footsteps by majoring in mathematics and computer science while at the University of Maryland at College Park.

But Brin isn't the only immigrant who has had a major influence on Google. Omid Kordestani joined the team as the company's twelfth employee in 1999. He is credited "for developing the business model that capitalized on the powerful, new internet search engine," according to San Jose State University, from where he received his bachelors degree.[2] Kordestani is originally from Tehran, Iran, but he immigrated at the age of fourteen to San Jose with his family, a year before Khomeini seized power in Iran.[3] After graduating with a degree in electrical engineering, he was recruited by Hewlett-Packard. There, he realized how beneficial it would be to have skills in both engineering and business, so he also obtained an MBA from Stanford University. Both Brin and Kordestani were instrumental in growing Google from its inception to the $268 billion market capital it sees today.[4] With over fifty-thousand employees and more than $50 billion in sales, Google clearly has a huge impact on the U.S. economy.

But the company doesn't just stop there; it's also a leader in technological innovation. Headed by another immigrant from Tehran, Project Glass, a Google-led endeavor, has created glasses that allow wearers to take photos, shoot videos, translate their voice, and more. Babak Parviz from Iran is leading the project, along with Google X lead product manager Steve Lee and founder and head of Google X, Sebastian Thrun.

eBay

Born in Paris, France, to Iranian parents, Pierre Omidyar was originally named Parviz, after his Iranian roots. In the early 1960s, both sets of Omidyar's grandparents moved their children to Paris so that they could receive a proper education, unavailable to most students in Iran at the time.[5] Omidyar and his parents moved to the United States when he was six years old. Though they eventually separated, both of his parents played an instrumental role during his childhood. In an interview in 2000, Omidyar spoke about his "fond memories" of doing medical rounds with his father, a surgeon and doctor, on weekends.[6] While his father worked in a hospital, his mother established a nonprofit that helped fellow Iranians remain closely connected to their heritage. Additionally, she was an executive director at the Institute of Comparative Social and Cultural Studies, which advocated for a greater appreciation of cultures among people of varying backgrounds.[7]

In Washington, D.C., Pierre enrolled at St. Andrews Episcopal High School. While there, he began programming an Apple II computer and digitizing the school library's card catalogue at $6 per hour. He also helped with the school's computer program that created class schedules.[8]

In 1995, Omidyar, then twenty-eight years old, wrote the original computer code for what would become eBay. The first item Omidyar sold on the site was a broken laser pointer. He was amazed that anyone would pay for such a thing, but he learned the buyer wanted the device for his laser-pointer collection.[9] The site soon exploded in popularity. Though the site initially sold collectibles, it grew to include a wide spectrum of items, from furniture to airline tickets to cars. After eBay went public in 1998, Omidyar became a billionaire.

With the help of his wife, Pam, Omidyar created the Omidyar Network in 2004. Broadening the scope of the Omidyar Foundation, which had only financed nonprofit endeavors, the Network also provides money for profit ventures that advance its goals.[10] Omidyar said one of the results of eBay has been in its ability to show the trust strangers can share when exchanging money and goods online. Despite never having met in person or having mutual friends, these people still make these transactions, with the only physical proof being a photograph. Equal funds are set aside for nonprofit and profit concerns.

In addition to having served as a Tufts trustee, Omidyar was selected by President Barack Obama to serve as a commissioner on the President's Commission on White House Fellowships in 2009.[11] In 2010, Omidyar founded *Honolulu Civil Beat*, a local online news service devoted to civic engagement and public affairs journalism.[12]

Chegg

Aayush Phumbhra, a native of India, is cofounder of Chegg, Inc. and serves as senior vice president. Prior to moving to the United States in 2001, Aayush founded two additional companies, one of which popularized peanut butter and chocolate spreads in his native country.

Phumbhra's next business venture, Chegg.com, was his big break. Phumbhra conceived of the idea of Chegg through his personal experience and frustration with his own university's bookstore. Thus, the mission of Chegg is "to enable college students to save a significant amount of money by letting them rent textbooks rather than buy them."[13]

The name of the company itself is a bit humorous. While studying in Iowa in 2001, Aayush Phumbhra contemplated "the chicken and egg dilemma" for students searching for a job. Employers look for work experience, but students need to have a job to have work experience. By mashing the words *chicken* and *egg* together, Phumbhra came up with Chegg.[14]

Because of how it operates, Chegg is often referred to as "Netflix for textbooks." It allows students at more than six thousand colleges to rent from an online bookstore equipped with 4.2 million books.

Yet Chegg's success story varies from the common tale of other breakout startups, such as Groupon and Zynga. Instead of founding a completely new industry, Chegg introduced an established service idea and relied on traditional customer behavior (mail-order rentals) in an archaic, defective category, whose customers felt confined by high costs. Although Chegg did not initially find success in 2003, it established a steady business flow within four years.[15]

However, most countries often consider two persistent questions about lower-skilled immigrants: given concerns about competition with native workers, how many immigrants should be permitted, under which circumstances, and into which occupations? And should these flows be temporary, permanent, or circular?

The United States is no exception to this concern. Its employment-based visa regime is divided into two separate systems: temporary (known as nonimmigrant) and permanent (known as immigrant). Most long-term employment-based immigrants must apply through both systems, one to enter the country and again to gain permanent residence. In the vast majority of cases, both applications require an employer sponsor. Receiving a green card for permanent residence takes considerable time, in part because of the strict, permanent, numerical limits on visas. Virtually all (about 90 percent) of employment-based green-card recipients, therefore, arrive on temporary visas and later adjust to permanent residence from within the country.

The chart below shows the level of employment-based visas over the past two decades (1992–2010) issued to permanent immigrants (employment-based preference) and temporary nonimmigrants (B-1 temporary visitor for business purposes).

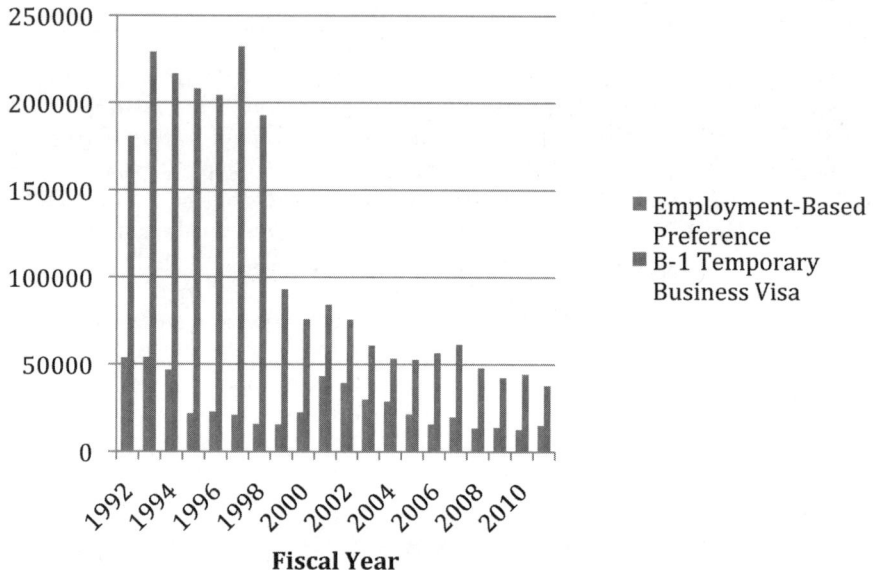

Fiscal Year

Employment-Based Visas (1992–2010)

U.S. Department of State, *Classes of Nonimmigrants Issued Visas (Including Crewlist Visas and Border Crossing Cards) Fiscal Years 1992–2010*, http://www.travel.state.gov/pdf/MultiYearTableI.pdf. *Immigrant and Nonimmigrant Visas Issued at Foreign Service Posts Fiscal Years 1992–2011*, http://www.travel.state.gov/pdf/MultiYearTableXVI.pdf.

Only about 15 percent of visas for legal permanent residence ("green cards") are issued to economic-stream immigrants in the United States. About half of the visas go to the family members of employer-sponsored immigrant workers (the "principal" applicants). The share of employment-based immigrants in the United States is low compared to other immigrant-receiving nations in the English-speaking world (even if the United States remains the largest recipient of skilled migrants). In Australia, for example, economic-stream immigration accounts for about two-thirds of the total, and in the United Kingdom, it accounts for just over two-fifths, excluding the substantial flows of primarily labor-motivated immigration from within the European Union.

The United States operates two strictly temporary, employment-based migration schemes for mostly perishable-crop agricultural and seasonal or temporary nonagricultural jobs. Agricultural visas, also known as H-2A visas, are uncapped but subject to a complex web of requirements that leave neither employers nor workers and their advocates satisfied; in recent years approximately sixty thousand have been issued per year. The number of nonagricultural visas, also known as H-2B visas, is capped at thirty-three thousand per six-month period. Even though the labor demand during the economic crisis was incredibly low, the thirty-three-thousand cap was typically exhausted after an average of 100 to 150 days. Note that, while these visas are not used exclusively for low-wage workers (H-2B recipients include small numbers of more highly skilled workers, including architects, engineers, managers, and creative artists, for example) and not all low-wage workers have low levels of formal education, the majority of immigration through this category is into low-paying, less-skilled occupations.

H-1B visas, on the other hand, are administered to immigrants who have a higher education degree. Only five days after the application-filing period opened for H-1B visas for the fiscal year 2014, the U.S. Citizenship and Immigration Services had reached the statutory cap of eighty-five thousand. The H-1B cap is comprised of the regular cap, for which sixty-five thousand visas are available, and the ADE cap, for which twenty thousand visas are available. Most people are familiar with the sixty-five-thousand regular cap, which is for those who are living abroad and are obtaining their first H-1B visa and for those who are in the United States and want to change their visa status to H-1B. The ADE cap, or Advanced Degree Exemption cap, is given to foreign students who graduate from a U.S. university with a graduate degree. H-1B visas are typically valid for between three to six years. They are typically applied for by companies, rather than by individuals, and most often by companies seeking engineers, computer programmers, and other high-tech workers.[16]

The H-1B visas submitted in 2012 for fiscal year 2013 ran out in just ten weeks. In 2012, the unemployment rate for computer and math occupations was 3.5 percent, according to the Bureau of Labor Statistics, which indicates a lack of U.S. workers with these skills. This visa limitation thus stifles economic growth for months and months until the next H-1B visa-application-filing period begins. As Karen Jones, vice president and general counsel at Microsoft indicates,

> Companies like Microsoft—who employ significant numbers of American workers and generate high-paying jobs in the U.S. both directly and indirectly—must be able to hire top talent in areas where we have a shortage of workers in order to succeed and grow in a highly competitive global market. This barrier to hiring puts our country at a competitive disadvantage. While U.S. employers are precluded from hiring high skilled workers from around the world, other countries—like Australia, Canada, Chile, Germany and Singapore—are actively attracting these same types of workers and thereby strengthening their competi-

tive capabilities in the global market. Some countries are also actively engaged in programs to repatriate top talent from the U.S. For example, China has offered significant economic incentives to encourage the repatriation of Chinese nationals who have established themselves in the U.S. as scientific elites, high-level managers and entrepreneurs.

As a result of the visa restrictions, smaller tech companies have begun to set up operations abroad to gain access to highly skilled labor. In the past, foreign workers were hired to cut costs, but today foreign workers are hired because companies want the cream of the crop, regardless of geographic location. According to the article "Tech Firms Go Abroad to Hire," written by John Shinal for *USA Today*, "A growing number of small, private U.S. technology companies—who . . . are late-stage start-ups with more than $100 million in annual sales—now have engineering offices overseas."[17]

Rather than restricting access to top global talent, our country's approach to highly skilled immigration should be enabling U.S. companies to attract and to retain the world's brightest minds so that our economy and our workforce can reap the economic benefits of their brainpower and contributions over the long term.

> Wernher Von Braun, a German rocket scientist who worked for the Nazis during World War II, developed the V-1 and V-2 rockets that terrorized London. He, along with many of his fellow engineers and scientists, was recruited by the Americans after the war to help in the development of missiles and rocketry. He became a naturalized citizen in 1955 and led the team of mostly German-immigrant scientists in the development of the Saturn rockets, which were used to send men to the moon.

A recent study by the Kauffman Foundation highlighted entrepreneurs as the job incubators, with data that indicates an entrepreneur has the potential to create, on average, 512 jobs in his or her lifetime. Research has also found that for every one hundred foreign students who receive an advanced STEM degree and stay in the United States, 262 additional jobs are created. Thus, the low visa numbers do not make economical sense for three reasons: first, we lose the foreign students we spent vast resources training; second, we lose all of the secondary jobs that would have been created had we kept the students; and third, other countries reap the benefits of our education system, and secondary jobs are made abroad instead of in America. In addition, we limit our own access to the top talent of other countries and thereby limit our access to hardworking, entrepreneurial immigrants who have historically contributed to America's wealth and knowledge.

Regardless of education level, method of entry into the United States, or country of origin, immigrants seem to have two traits in common: perseverance and hard work. Since they are the ones who have had the courage, desperation, or necessity to leave home and to pursue an uncertain future in a frequently foreign culture, for them, failure is not an option. They are determined to make a new life for themselves, and their hard work pays off. The single most important factor in successful companies is the people, and this is why we see immigrants make such a huge success of their efforts once they reach our shores.

We need not look much further than Zbigniew Brzezinski, Emilie Benes, and their family; Sergey Brin; Omid Kordestani; Pierre Omidyar; Aayush Phumbhra; and Nguyen and Phong Phan, and their son Loc to see how in each of these different stories of immigration, each immigrant was determined to see his or her hard work pay off, and it did.

I have met many hardworking immigrants in my lifetime from different industries and places. One man that has left an impression on me is Salomon Garay, my family's house painter, because he produces the highest quality work and then goes above and beyond.

NOTES

1. "Sergey Brin," *Biography.com*, http://www.biography.com/people/sergey-brin-12103333 (accessed October 22, 2013).

2. "Alumni Profiles: Omid Kordestani, Google Inc. Senior Vice President of Global Sales and Business Development," *Engineering @ San Jose State University*, http://www.engr.sjsu.edu/alumni/profiles/omid-kordestani (accessed October 22, 2013).

3. Arash Norouzi, "Omid Kordestani: Educate People about Iran," *The Mossadegh Project*, http://www.mohammadmossadegh.com/news/omid-kordestani/ (accessed October 22, 2013).

4. "World's Most Innovative Companies: Google," *Forbes.com*, http://www.forbes.com/companies/google/ (accessed October 22, 2013).

5. Jennifer Viegas, *Pierre Omidyar: The Founder of eBay* (New York: Rosen Publishing Group, 2007).

6. "Pierre Omidyar, Academy of Achievement," *Achievement.org*, http://www.achievement.org/autodoc/page/omi0int-4 (accessed July 17, 2013).

7. General Books, LLC, *eBay Employees: Meg Whitman, Pierre Omidyar, Randy Wigginton, John Donahoe, and Rajiv Dutta* (Memphis, TN: General Books LLC, 2010).

8. Marty Gitlin, *eBay: The Company and Its Founder* (Edina, MN: ABDO Publishing, 2011).

9. Viegas, *Pierre Omidyar*.

10. "Omidyar Group: Pierre and Pam Omidyar," *Omidyar Group.com*, http://omidyargroup.com/ (accessed July 17, 2013).

11. "Pierre Omidyar (Founder of eBay): 20 Fascinating Fun Facts," *People with Impact.com*, http://www.peoplewithimpact.com/pierre-omidyar/f67e77/ (accessed July 17, 2013).

12. "Pierre Omidyar," *Tufts Now, Tufts.com*, October 23, 2013, http://now.tufts.edu/commencement-2011/pierre-omidyar (accessed July 22, 2013).

13. "Management Team," *Chegg.com*, http://www.chegg.com/managementteam (accessed July 17, 2013).

14. Rituparna Chatterjee, "How Silicon Valley's New Indian Entrepreneurs Are Blooming in All Hues," *Economic Times*, July 31, 2011, http://articles.economictimes.indiatimes.com/2011-07-31/news/29835690_1_indian-entrepreneurs-sramana-mitra-serial-entrepreneur (accessed July 17, 2013).

15. Steven Carpenter, "TC Teardown: Chegg Is a Money Machine," *TechCrunch.com*, June 5, 2010, http://techcrunch.com/2010/06/05/teardown-chegg/ (accessed July 17, 2013).

16. "H1B Visa Cap and H1B Quota 2013 (FY2014) System Explained—Latest H1B 2013 Status for Quota, Cap, News Updates—H1B 2012 Cap Count and Tracker—USCIS H1B Quota Filing Updates and Cap Numbers Count—H1B cap 2011, h1b cap 2012, h1b quota 2012," *h1base.com*, http://www.h1base.com/visa/work/H1Bvi (accessed August 18, 2013).

17. John Shinal, "Tech Firms Go Abroad to Hire," *USA TODAY*, June 5, 2013, http://usatoday30.usatoday.com/MONEY/usaedition/2013-07-05-Silicon-Valley-not-waiting-for-US-immigration-reform_ST_U.htm (accessed August 18, 2013).

9

How Did He Get Here: Salomon Garay

In 1981, Hector Salomon Garay was twenty-five when he crossed the Rio Bravo from Mexico into an unknown small town in southern Texas. Although the United States and Mexico share water from the same river, the different perspectives on life in America is exemplified by the two names of this river. South of the border it is called the Rio Bravo, which means "furious" or "agitator," while in the United States it is called the Rio Grande or "big." Depending upon where you were born, your experience with the same river is entirely different.

Salomon was born in El Salvador, and with the idea that he could find steady work in the United States, he saved up the $1,200 needed to pay the "coyote" to take him in a group of thirty-four across the border in the middle of the night. His ultimate destination was the Washington, D.C., area, where his older sister already lived. From beginning to end, his journey took him nineteen days to complete.

He and his group had to walk and swim through the river and hide in bushes and behind trees until a prearranged Toyota pickup truck took all thirty-four of them piled up like sardines on an hour-long ride to Corpus Christi, where they were again unceremoniously dumped in the bushes in the middle of the night. Trash of empty gallons of water and bread bags littered the area, making it obvious that they were not the first to come this way.

By 9 a.m., another vehicle pulled up to take the ten women in the group to Houston, but it took another eight hours for someone to come check on the men. This person left only some yellow cheese and bread for the remaining men. After dividing the provisions up among themselves, they waited out the night in the pouring rain until 2 a.m., when they decided to try to find some kind of temporary shelter. By daylight, they had come across a building in an oil field, and the man inside greeted them with a "Cómo estás?" They asked if they could stay awhile, and he responded in the affirmative, under the condition that they not smoke.

The group was stranded here for three days, taking turns each day to walk the five miles to a small grocery store run by a local Chicano woman. They politely asked to use the phone, and it wasn't until the third day, when the woman told them they could no longer use her phone for free, that they told her of their plight. She told them not to worry, as she had seen this happen many times before. The next morning, she showed up with some food and clean clothes for them, and it wasn't long until the man taking them to Houston showed up and relocated the group to a nearby barn.

One morning, around 3 a.m., three men with guns woke the group members and took them through the countryside, ensuring through whistle commands that they hid in bushes from the roving helicopter lights above. They were passed off to two women driving a green Chevy van, where they sat huddled for an hour, hoping to eventually make it to Houston. They finally arrived safely to a small, basementless house, which provided living conditions that were only a little better than the original pickup truck. Salomon and his fellow group members, now totaling sixty-four residents, had to take turns sleeping sitting up against the walls. Now stuck in Houston, Salomon was forced to pay an additional $400 to arrange for transportation to D.C. and into the safety of his older sister's apartment.

Soon he was given a false Social Security number to use so that he could apply for jobs, and he quickly and easily found work in construction. As long as he worked hard and did a good job, nobody looked too closely at his documentation. Early the following year, his sister received her U.S. citizenship, and she took him to apply for his own Social Security number. Even though the office personnel noticed he did not have a visa to be in the country, they were lenient and allowed him to apply, and within four weeks, he was working legally and paying taxes.

Eight years after arriving in this country, Salomon started his own house painting business, while also doing a few related small jobs as needed. In the beginning, he employed solely family members and friends, but he soon found that consistently getting good work out of family members was tricky. Now, he only hires family members whom he trusts will be able to competently complete the job. A perfectionist, Salomon values strong customer service and thorough work. While serving clients, he not only paints their houses but also completes minor maintenance work that he feels needs to be done. As one of his clients, I can attest to the superb job Salomon does with every task. For example, one time, when he was painting a room in my house, the wood of a doorframe was loose and broke off. Even though it was not stipulated in his contract, he took it upon himself to fix the doorframe. This occurrence is just one example of the numerous times Salomon has gone above and beyond the call of duty. Through his hard work and ambitious nature, he truly exemplifies the common characteristics of many successful immigrants.

> Of the ten immigrant groups in the United States with the largest number of new business owners per month from 2007 to 2011, five of them were from Central America. With the highest number of new business owners per month first, the countries were Guatemala, Cuba, El Salvador, Dominican Republic, and Honduras. (Mexico had the highest number of new business owners who were immigrants, but the country is located in North America.)[1]

In 2005, he finally became a U.S. citizen, and while today he has to turn down work, he recognizes it is not so easy for new immigrants. In fact, a number of his friends back in El Salvador have asked for his advice and assistance in coming to the United States. They often relay stories of the daily lines, full by 7 a.m., for a visa at the U.S. Embassy. Even with the $125 application fee, there is no guarantee. Salomon truthfully tells them it is now very hard to find work in the United States, and that while he will do his best to help them, he cannot assure them of their fate. He wishes that the immigrants already in this country could be given their papers. He is also involved in raising funds through a church picnic for a family who has been detained and needs $10,000 for legal fees to attempt to stay and continue working.

Salomon also says that unfortunately the president and Congress cannot understand what it is like for poor people, and he thinks they are too old and don't really care. They have been raised in "good hands," whereas, for people from Central America, everything is different—probably as different as the two names of the same river that border Texas and Mexico.

NOTE

1. The Partnership for a New American Economy, "Open for Business: How Immigrants Are Driving Small Business Creation in the United States," August 2012, www.renewoureconomy.org/sites/all/themes/pnae/openforbusiness.pdf (accessed July 20, 2013).

10

Paying It Forward to the U.S. Economy

In our time of economic stagnation, attention on the part of many political figures is turning to the question of immigration.

The most recent academic research suggests that, on average, immigrants raise the overall standard of living of American workers by boosting wages and by lowering prices. One reason is because immigrants and U.S.-born workers generally do not compete for the same jobs; instead, many immigrants complement the work of U.S. employees and increase their productivity. Similar to education levels, the skill levels of immigrants are also bimodal, so they take the low- and high-skilled jobs; whereas U.S.-born citizens typically take the middle-skill jobs. Another reason is because businesses adjust to new immigrants by opening stores, restaurants, or production facilities to take advantage of the added supply of workers; more workers translate into more business.

Because of these factors, economists have found that immigrants raise average wages slightly for the United States as a whole. Estimates from opposite ends of the academic literature arrive at this same conclusion and point to small but positive wage gains of between 0.1 and 0.6 percent for American workers.[1]

By affecting the prices of the goods and services they purchase, immigrants also have an impact on the well-being of U.S. workers. Recent research suggests that immigrant workers enhance the purchasing power of Americans by lowering prices of "immigrant-intensive" services, such as child care, gardening, and cleaning services. By making these services more affordable and more widely available, immigrant workers benefit U.S. consumers.

Immigration laws can both benefit and damage the economy, and in the case of Arizona, its laws have drastically damaged its economy since mid-2007, according to an analysis by the Cato Institute. The Legal Arizona

Workers Act (LAWA or employer sanctions) was the first such law, and it tried to regulate unauthorized workers out of the market. Its chief tool is E-Verify, an electronic employment eligibility verification system used to weed out unauthorized immigrants when they apply for a job. The E-Verify program scared a lot of investors and businesses out of the state. It was largely responsible for a business formation rate *decline* of 14.3 percent in the third quarter of 2007 in Arizona, while rates of business formation in California and New Mexico *increased* over the same time. Proponents of Arizona's new immigration laws claim that E-Verify will force unauthorized immigrants out of jobs so Americans can fill them. In reality, however, some unauthorized immigrants are forced out of jobs that mostly remain unfilled.

In the immigrant-heavy farming industry, crop production employment dropped by 15.6 percent in the first four years after LAWA was passed. American workers did not fill the gaps. In neighboring New Mexico and California, crop production employment *increased* over the same time period. E-Verify can explain much of that difference.

Yet we often hear the real economic issue is immigrants create a drain on the federal government budget, but taxes paid by immigrants and their children—both legal and illegal—exceed the costs of the services they use. In fact, a 2007 cost estimate by the Congressional Budget Office found a path to legalization for unauthorized immigrants would increase federal revenues by $48 billion but would only incur $23 billion of increased costs from public services. This would produce a surplus of $25 billion for government coffers. According to the Social Security Administration Trustees' report, increases in immigration have also improved Social Security's finances.

Many government expenses related to immigrants are associated with their children. From a budgetary perspective, however, the children of immigrants are just like other American children in that they are expensive when they are young because of the costs of investing in children's education and health. Those expenses are paid back through taxes received over a lifetime of work. The consensus of the economic literature is that the taxes paid by immigrants and their descendants exceed the benefits they receive.

Even with undocumented immigrants, the Internal Revenue Service estimates they paid almost $50 billion in federal taxes from 1996 to 2003. These taxes include payroll and Social Security (about $8.5 billion per year), property (directly, or as part of rental payments), and sales taxes. Nonetheless, about 40 percent of undocumented immigrants currently work off the books and consequently pay lower taxes.[2] Yet the purchasing power alone of undocumented immigrants sustains hundreds of thousand of U.S. jobs.

Meanwhile, it is astonishing to also note that immigrants are 30 percent more likely to start new businesses than U.S.-born citizens.[3] About 10 percent of native-born Americans own a business. Koreans and Iranians living in the United States, in particular, are more than twice as likely to own a business than native-born Americans.[4] The traits needed to uproot yourself from your home—bravery, perseverance, diligence—are much like the traits you need to start a business.

> Greg Fairchild, associate professor of Business Administration at the University of Virginia's Darden School of Business, says, "Even if [immigrants] have a college degree from a home country, people don't know those schools in the U.S. They have credentials and knowledge and drive but they're not recognized by typical employers. They begin by hiring themselves."[5]

Such investments in new businesses and in research may provide spillover benefits to U.S.-born workers by enhancing job creation and by increasing innovation among their U.S.-born peers. Over the last three decades, startup companies less than five years old created forty-four million new jobs, and they account for all net new jobs created in the United States during that time.[6] Because there is such a large entrepreneurial gap between immigrants and U.S.-born workers, it makes sense to harness this untapped source of growth and to develop sound economic policy around it.

In some states, the immigrant contribution to the general economy is substantial. About 30 percent of all businesses in California are immigrant owned, as are 25 percent of businesses in New York and 20 percent of businesses in New Jersey and Florida. Across America, immigrants helped to start 25 percent of the new technology and engineering companies of the past decade. Where skilled immigrants congregated the impact was even more profound. During 1995 to 2005, immigrants helped to launch 39 percent of the new high-tech companies in California, 38 percent of the new companies in New Jersey, and 29 percent of the new companies in Massachusetts. Researchers estimated in 2005 that immigrant-founded companies were generating $52 billion in sales and employing 450,000 people.[7]

> According to a 2010 study by the Fiscal Policy Institute, Mexico has the most small business owners in the United States for any one country's immigrants, with over one hundred thousand immigrants, followed by India and Korea. Iran came in eighth and Poland tenth, with over seventeen thousand immigrants.[8]

Noncitizens make up one-quarter of all international patent applications from the United States, and college-educated immigrants have been found to be twice as likely to register patents as their U.S.-born counterparts. Furthermore, evidence shows that foreign-born university graduates are important contributors to U.S. innovation. Among people with advanced degrees, immigrants are three times more likely to file patents than U.S.-born citizens. Indian and Chinese immigrants and their descendants are also thought to be overrepresented among inventors, accounting for 14 percent of U.S. patents. The foreign-born make up 27 percent of the U.S. workforce with a doctoral degree, despite the fact that they only represent 13 percent of the U.S. population. It is mind-boggling to consider that it is the immigrant who is the source of our past, and potentially future, economic success.

Alexis de Tocqueville correctly observed this in his 1835 book, *Democracy in America*, in which he writes that the English government considered "New England as a land given over to the fantasy of dreamers, where innovators should be allowed to try out experiments in freedom." Freedom is the driver of prosperity, and "nowhere was this principle of liberty applied more completely than in the states of New England."[9]

Fast forward to today, and as Patricia A. Buckley, senior economic advisor to the U.S. Department of Commerce, explained before the House Judiciary Subcommittee on Immigration, "An important segment of the foreign-born are not in the United States to find a job—they are here to create jobs. . . . The high rates of entrepreneurship among the immigrant population contribute to the dynamic of the economy, fostering both investment and employment."[10]

Unfortunately, the United States' competitive advantage in the global marketplace has been slipping in recent years. In the past five years, we have fallen from first to seventh place in the World Economic Forums' Global Competitiveness Report. We no longer have the supply of talent to meet our current demands. The kind of talent that is driving the world's knowledge-based economy in the STEM fields is no longer in great supply in the United States.

At the same time, we are lacking in this talent pool, we are similarly deficient in other skill sets. America has lost six million manufacturing jobs in the last decade, yet today six hundred thousand jobs go unfilled because manufacturers cannot find workers with the right skills.

Possibly one reason many of these jobs go unfilled is because many Americans, unlike immigrants, are hesitant to move from their homes. Contrast the forces at work for immigration, where people must cross borders and cultures, to the migration of American citizens within the country. As a nation, the United States is often portrayed as restless and rootless. Census data, though, indicate that Americans are settling down. Only 11.9 percent

> Daniel Chu was born in Guizhou Province in China, but he came to the United States for high school and college. Prior to graduating from Penn State in 2013, he had some great opportunities in front of him. He had been offered an analyst position at the largest asset management firm in the United States and a developer position for Ryan Media Works, Inc., a tech startup focused on groups who have felt left behind by technology. Although accepting the analyst offer could have led to permanent residency, Chu chose to join the startup. He explains, "I have an interest and passion for entrepreneurship. As a recent graduate, I am at a point now where I am willing to take the risk. By joining the startup, I might be able to help create jobs." Chu further adds, "As corny as it might sound, I believe in the American Dream and I love this country. Like the many foreign-born entrepreneurs before me, I hope that my effort to create a business will make America a better place and help others live the American Dream. I just wish it were a less complicated process to stay and be a part of the United States' thriving startup community. Less red tape would enable me to focus more on my startups and less on bureaucracy."
>
> Chu had already previously cofounded another startup, Quipco, LLC, which makes clipboards for iPads and iPhones. All of Quipco's products are made in the United States for the purpose of creating jobs in the country.

of Americans changed residences between 2007 and 2008, the smallest share since the government began tracking this trend in the late 1940s, according to a Pew Social and Demographic Trends survey.

This survey found that most Americans have moved to a new community at least once in their lives, although a notable number—nearly four in ten—have never left the place in which they were born. Asked why they live where they do, movers most often cite the pull of economic opportunity. Stayers most often cite the tug of family and connections. Both the survey and Census data indicate that the biggest differences in the characteristics of movers and stayers revolve around geography and education.

Analysts say the long-term decline in migration has occurred because the U.S. population is getting older and most moves are made when people are young. Among all respondents to the Pew Research Center survey, 57 percent say they have not lived outside their current state; 37 percent have never left their hometown; and 20 percent have left their hometown but not lived outside their current state. As of 2009, only about 22 percent of Americans even had passports, while in many Western European countries the number is much higher, reaching 71 percent in the United Kingdom. These statistics clearly show that Americans have tended to stay close to home. Yet jobs do not grow homogenously. As different industries crop up in different places around the world, they need employees who are willing to make the transition and to move. In today's global community, the U.S.-born people are not leading when it comes to taking advantage of opportunities wherever they may arise.

Cue the eager immigrants: ready, willing, and able to take their turn to grab at that brass ring.

My parents were fortunate in qualifying for student visas to come to the United States to further their studies. Not only did they leave their native country, but also, while here, they lived both in Michigan, with its cold winters and industrial heritage, as well as Louisiana, with its swamps and Creole culture. They were one of the many immigrant pioneers of their day.

While my parents did not stay in the United States after their schooling, many foreign students do, and they in turn have a positive impact on the U.S. economy. Foreign students are often hardworking and entrepreneurial. They also help to build bridges between the United States and other countries, to bring global perspective, and to aid in U.S. innovation. Despite all of these benefits, U.S. immigration policy does not make it easy for students to stay, as it forces a large number of students to leave after graduation. In 2013, Mayor Bloomberg delivered Stanford University's commencement address. In the speech, he pointed out that 30 percent of the graduating class would have to leave the United States after their student visas expired—30 percent of the brightest minds at one of America's most elite universities. Bloomberg frankly stated, "We invite foreign students to study here, we subsidize the universities they attend (then) tell them to go somewhere else and work for one of our competitors. It's the most backwards economic policy you could possibly come up with."[11] In Bloomberg's eyes, a green card should be stapled to the diploma of every STEM graduate.

The United States should try to retain its international students. Having spent at least four years in the American school system, students have an idea of what being in the United States means and what opportunities are available to them. For a more explicit example, consider Yoon-shik Park, who came to the United States for graduate school. But Park did not leave the country after completing his studies at Harvard Business School. Quite the opposite happened; instead, he chose to start a family and a life in Massachusetts.

NOTES

1. Nikhil Joshi, "The Business Case for Immigration Reform Part 1: Low-Skilled Workers," *Business Forward.org*, April 2013, http://www.businessfwd.org/blog/body/BF_Immigration_Final.pdf (accessed October 23, 2013).

2. White House, "Building a 21st Century Immigration System," May 2011, www.whitehouse.gov/sites/default/files/rss_viewer/immigration_blueprint.pdf (accessed October 23, 2013).

3. Brookings Institute, "Brookings: Quality. Independence. Impact," http://www.brookings.edu (accessed July 8, 2013).

4. The Partnership for a New American Economy, "Open for Business: How Immigrants Are Driving Small Business Creation in the United States," August 2012, www.renewoureconomy.org/sites/all/themes/pnae/openforbusiness.pdf (accessed July 20, 2013).

5. Mark Koba, "How Immigrants Are Changing US Businesses," *CNBC*, September 4, 2012, http://www.cnbc.com/id/48646997 (accessed August 27, 2012).

6. Megan Slack, "By the Numbers: 44 Million," *White House Blog*, November 3, 2011, http://www.whitehouse.gov/blog/2011/11/03/numbers-44-million (accessed July 8, 2013).

7. Vivek Wadhwa, AnnaLee Saxenian, Richard Freeman, Gary Gereffi, and Alex Salkever, "America's Loss Is the World's Gain: America's New Immigrant Entrepreneurs, Part IV," Ewing Marion Kauffman Foundation, March 2009, www.kauffman.org/uploadedfiles/americas_loss.pdf (accessed July 1, 2013).

8. Fiscal Policy Institute Data Release, "What Kind of Businesses Do Immigrants Own? Detail by Country of Birth," June 2012, http://fiscalpolicy.org/wp-content/uploads/2012/06/immigrant-business-owners-by-country-of-birth-20120615.pdf (accessed August 27, 2013).

9. Alexis de Tocqueville, *Democracy in America* (Volume 1, Unabridged) (Stilwell, KS: Digireads.com Publishing, 2007).

10. Committee on the Judiciary, "U.S. Economy, U.S. Workers, and Immigration Reform," U.S. Government Printing Office, May 3, 2007, http://www.gpo.gov/fdsys/pkg/CHRG-110hhrg35117/html/CHRG-110hhrg35117.htm (accessed July 8, 2013).

11. Erin Durkin, "Mayor Bloomberg Blasts Immigration Policy to Stanford Grads," *New York Daily News.com*, June 17, 2013, http://www.nydailynews.com/new-york/mayor-bloomberg-blasts-immigration-policy-stanford-grads-article-1.1374798 (accessed August 14, 2013).

11

How Did He Get Here: Yoon-shik Park

Korean and American relations began in 1866, when the American ship USS *General Sherman* landed in Korea. Sixteen years later in 1882, diplomatic relations were formally established between the two countries through the signing of a treaty of peace, friendship, and commerce.[1] Just three years later, Philip Jaisohn, or Seo Jae-pil, left Korea as a political exile and became the first Korean citizen of America, where he became a medical doctor. After Japan was defeated in World War II, the U.S. Army military government, which controlled southern Korea, asked him to return to Korea to act as the chief advisor to the commanding general of the U.S. Army in South Korea. He was eventually asked to run for president of Korea, but he declined the nomination.[2] Today, Jaisohn's legacy lives on in Philadelphia in the form of the Jaisohn Memorial Foundation, which is a Korean center that provides medical, social, cultural, and educational aid to new Korean immigrants.

After Philip Jaisohn's immigration to the United States, Korea sent many more successful immigrants to America, even though immigration laws were not always in their favor. Between 1903 and 1905, over seven thousand Koreans immigrated to Hawaii as laborers for the Hawaiian Sugar Planters' Association. They were hired for the sole purpose of being cheap labor. The planters did, however, have a hard time convincing Koreans to immigrate. Consequently, missionaries were sent in, and nearly half of the recruited workers were Christian converts.[3]

Then, in 1905, Japan turned Korea into a protectorate and prevented any further emigration. Korea became a Japanese colony in 1910, thus extending to them the 1908 Gentleman's Agreement between Japan and the United States. This agreement allowed immigrant men to bring their wives to the United States, and between 1910 and 1924, eight hundred Korean women arrived in the United States. In this time period, Korean students also came to the United States to study or to work, including Syngman Rhee, who went on to become the first president of the Republic of Korea (South Korea) with U.S. military support after Korea was liberated from Japan.[4]

In 1920, the Korean American population numbered six thousand.[5] Then, the 1924 Nationality Origins Act completely prevented Asians from immigrating to America. The purpose of this act was to "preserve the ideal American homogeneity."[6]

After decades of this discriminatory policy, Koreans were once more allowed to immigrate to America with the passage of the McCarran-Walter Immigration Act in 1952. This act allowed Korea a quota of one hundred people who could immigrate each year. Finally, the Immigration and Naturalization Act of 1965 abolished immigration based on national origin.[7] This was the year Yoon-shik Park received the opportunity to move to America.

As the youngest son of Korean farmers, Park went on to exceed everyone's expectations. He excelled in scholastic activities, and in 1965, after finishing college in Korea, he was awarded the one full scholarship provided by his alma mater, Kyung Hee University in Seoul, to study in the United States.

At the time Park came to the United States, he was at the forefront of a new wave of immigration to the United States from non-European regions. By 1970, about seventy thousand Korean Americans lived in the United States.[8] He did not come to the United States as an immigrant like the bulk of Korean Americans, as he belonged to that privileged group of Korean young men and women who had the fortunate chance to study in America. Only after completing his advanced education in the United States did he decide to stay in this country to work and to raise a family.

By pursuing academics, he followed the long cultural tradition of Sa Nong Gong Sang (the societal hierarchy of scholar mandarins, farmers, artisans and manufacturers, and lastly merchants and traders) that had been part of his historical legacy for many centuries.

The Korean War began in 1950 with the invasion of the South of Korea by the North, and it lasted for three years. Infrastructure was heavily damaged, and at the time, South Korea had an underdeveloped, agrarian economy and was heavily dependent on foreign aid.[9] Due to the lack of foreign exchange reserves and the poor economic situation in Korea, the Korean government only allowed Korean students to leave the country to study abroad with a total of $50 in their possession. This was irrelevant to Park, as he only had $16 to his name.

Moving to Boston to continue his studies at Harvard Business School, he left his college sweetheart behind in Korea with the promise he would finish his studies within five years, after which they could be married.

At that time, there were few Korean immigrants in the area, but he did find a small group of compatriots through the local Korean church. The local church used the facilities of an American church for services each week in his mother tongue. At the end of his studies, he kept his promise, and his fiancé, Heawon, joined him in the United States. A local Korean minister married them in the Harvard University chapel.

Upon graduation with a doctorate in business administration, Park was offered a job with the World Bank in Washington, D.C., as an economist. In 1970, he and Heawon moved to Washington, D.C., and they had their first child, a son named Daniel. Park tells us that at this time there was only one Korean restaurant in the entire metropolitan Washington area (which was located in the basement of a hotel that has now become the Chinese Embassy), one Korean grocery store, and only one Korean immigrant church.

Meanwhile, back home, a military leadership took control of South Korea after angry students overthrew President Syngman Rhee. Although the government was autocratic and, at times, repressive, the economy experienced rapid growth from around 1961 to 1996, which came to be known as "the miracle on the Han River." Per capita income increased more than a hundredfold, and the economy grew about 9 percent annually.[10]

By the late 1970s, Dr. Park had become a well-known expert in international finance, and he was tapped by the founder and chairman of Samsung Group to return to Korea to serve as financial advisor. The perks of working in the private sector and especially for the largest multinational conglomerate in Korea were many. In addition, Korea began directing fiscal and financial policies toward consumer electronics in the 1970s, so it was an exciting and interesting time to work at Samsung.[11]

In the meantime, he and Heawon had two more children, a son, Jason, and a daughter, Joann, both of whom were born in the United States. The couple agreed that this career opportunity was too big to pass up, and so the family of five moved to Seoul. While he was experiencing incredible career growth, Park felt that his family life was not benefitting to the same degree. After two years, they decided to move back to the United States in order to offer their children the benefits offered by the richest, freest, and most advanced country in the world. By this time, Heawon and the children already thought of America as "home."

> A popular Korean word that many Korean immigrants live by is *anjŏng*. This term can be translated to mean "security" or "stability," and its meaning is often adopted by first-generation Korean immigrants. Korean immigrants who run small businesses usually do not set out to make millions of dollars but to achieve a modest, stable lifestyle; this ideal is at the center of anjŏng.[12]

Upon returning to the United States, Dr. Park entered full time into the professional life of an academic by taking a teaching position at George Washington University in Washington, D.C. He discovered a renewed sense of purpose interacting with bright young students from all over the world and felt that he had finally found his true calling.

As their children began middle and high school, Heawon, who had been an accomplished violin student at her university, found herself with more time on her hands and decided to pursue her realtor's license as a part-time hobby. She quickly realized she had natural business acumen and went on to become a successful real estate developer, with a substantial stable of commercial properties in her possession.

In the meantime, Park, in addition to being a beloved professor, was beginning to become a much-sought-after consultant, working with organizations such as the World Bank, Asian Development Bank, International Finance Corporation, Inter-American Development Bank, U.S. Agency for International Development (AID), U.S. Federal Reserve, U.S. Overseas Private Investment Corporation, U.S. Export-Import Bank, New York State Banking Department, Kuwait Institute of Banking Studies, and other private and public institutions around the world. He also found himself being consulted by a steady stream of Korean CEOs, cabinet ministers, and journalists. He assisted Lee Myung-bak, former CEO of Hyundai Engineering and Construction, in obtaining a visiting scholar position in Washington, D.C., before he went back to Korea to be elected as the mayor of Seoul and then the president of Korea. Between 1998 and 2009, Park also served as a member of the board of directors of Samsung Corporation in Korea. By now, Park was a scholar mandarin of the highest order.

By observing their parents, Daniel, Jason, and Joann learned the importance of education and hard work at a young age. In addition, Heawon ruled with an iron fist when it came to academics.

The eldest, Daniel, graduated from West Point and served five years in the military, including two years stationed in Korea, before he retired from military service as a captain. He went on to Harvard Business School, where he obtained his master's degree in business administration. He has had a successful career, starting out with McKinsey and Company, moving on to work with Target Corporation, and finally ending up at Amazon. He married a Caucasian American and is fielding inquiries about the timing of grandchildren from his eager parents.

The second son, Jason, went on to study economics and biology at Duke and has applied his education to his inherent business sense in assisting his mother in the real estate development business.

> The year 2003 was the centennial of the beginning of Korean immigration to the United States. On January 13, 2003, President George W. Bush issued a proclamation recognizing the centennial and commended Korean Americans for their "important role in building, defending, and sustaining the United States of America."[13]

The youngest, daughter Joann, went to MIT where she studied economics and graduated from Kellogg with her master's degree in business administration. She initially worked at JPMorgan before moving on to work at McKinsey and Company, and she is now the director of finance and strategy at the Texas Children's Hospital in Houston. She married a Chinese American dentist and recently gave birth to a baby girl, much to her parents' happiness.

The Parks have had a good life, both in and out of the United States. They have attained many professional and personal goals, raised three happy and successful children, and have had a positive impact in their local Korean immigrant church, all the while remaining indirectly involved in the affairs of their ancestral land.

To look at their family portrait, their faces do not convey the depth and breadth of their story and their contributions to life in the United States. Theirs is the classic tale of working hard, of taking full advantage of what their efforts have afforded them, of giving back to their adopted homeland, and of passing these values on to the next generation. The ripple effect of just these five people can be felt deep below the surface. Their story truly exemplifies the American Dream.

NOTES

1. Korean American Historical Society (KAHS), "1903–2003: A Century of Korean Immigration," May 27–June 20, 2003, http://www.kahs.org/news-centennial.html (accessed July 8, 2013).

2. National Association of Korean Americans, "In Observance of Centennial of Korean Immigration to the U.S.," http://www.naka.org/resources/history.asp (accessed July 9, 2013).

3. National Association of Korean Americans, "In Observance."

4. Korean American Historical Society, "1903–2003: A Century of Korean Immigration."

5. "Korean-American Population 1910–2010." *Korean-AmericanStory.org*. http://www.koreanamericanstory.org/index.php?option=com_content&view=article&id=199&Itemid=134 (accessed July 8, 2013).

6. "Milestones: 1921–1936—The Immigration Act of 1924 (The Johnson-Reed Act," U.S. Department of State, Office of the Historian, http://history.state.gov/milestones/1921-1936/ImmigrationAct (accessed July 8, 2013).

7. Korean American Historical Society, "1903–2003: A Century of Korean Immigration."

8. "Korean-American Population 1910–2010."

9. "South Korea: Economic and Social Developments," *Encyclopedia Britannica*, http://www.britannica.com/EBchecked/topic/322280/South-Korea/34997/Economic-and-social-developments (accessed July 8, 2013).

10. "South Korea: Economic and Social Developments."

11. "South Korea: Economy," *globalEDGEcom*, Michigan State University. http://globaledge.msu.edu/countries/south-korea/economy (accessed July 8, 2013).

12. Kyeyoung Park, *The Korean American Dream: Immigrants and Small Business in New York City* (Ithaca, NY: Cornell University Press, 1997).

13. National Association of Korean Americans, "In Observance."

12

The Bimodal Nature of Immigrants

As we saw earlier, immigrants in the workforce positively impact the U.S. economy through creating new jobs and fulfilling labor force deficits. These shortages are filled because there is little overlap between jobs often taken by the native population and those completed by immigrants. Whereas native borns typically have high school diplomas and bachelor's degrees, immigrants either typically do not have a high school diploma or they have graduate degrees.[1] Whereas native borns typically hold middle-skilled jobs, immigrants typically hold low- and high-skilled jobs.[2] There is certainly overlap, but overall, the bimodal nature of immigrants complements the education levels and skill sets of native-born Americans.

Additionally, immigrants and native borns both exercise their comparative advantages, which limits job competition in the areas of overlap. For example, low-skilled Americans are twice as likely to work in office or administrative positions; as native English speakers, they are more likely to possess strong communication skills.[3] Immigrants, on the other hand, have a comparative advantage in jobs that require physical strength and stamina. As such, they are twice as likely as low-skilled Americans to fill farming, fishing, and forestry jobs.[4] They are also often more willing to do work that is considered dirtier, more difficult, and more dangerous.

As previously noted, another factor limiting competition between American workers and immigrants is geography. While highly educated workers of both parties often move across the country for career opportunities, low-skilled workers are 67 percent more likely to never move out of the state in which they were born.[5] Low-skilled immigrants and low-skilled native borns, however, are not evenly spread across the United States. Immigrants live disproportionately in what are known as "immigrant gateway states": California,

Florida, Illinois, New Jersey, New York, and Texas.[6] Low-skilled Americans are distributed more evenly, with a higher concentration in the Southeast.

In a time when the baby boomer generation is retiring, there will be a need for over fifty million workforce substitutes from 2010 to 2030. Because there is a greater trend of Americans seeking higher forms of education, many native-born citizens will be overqualified for a large proportion of the jobs baby boomers leave. Thus, America will not be able to fill this workforce deficit without the help of immigrants.

Because of all these factors, foreign-born workers are already crucial to many of the United States' industries, fulfilling low-skilled jobs in the agriculture and food industry, the trucking and transportation industry, the construction industry, and the accommodation industry, among others. As reported by the Brookings Institution, "The U.S. education system does not create large numbers of low-skilled workers: In 2004, just 9 percent of native-born 24-year-olds were high school dropouts. Thus, low-skilled immigrants fill a gap in U.S. labor markets, and industries employing large numbers of low-skilled workers depend heavily on non-citizen immigrant labor."[7]

According to the Associated Press, in 2005 there was a deficit of twenty thousand truck drivers. But, with industry growth rates, the shortage has the potential to reach 110,000 drivers by 2014.[8] Another issue facing the industry is that many truckers are reaching retirement age, and few people are signing on as replacements. The previous estimate does not even account for the 219,000 drivers who are expected to retire during that time. Additionally, as the American Trucking Association found, there is an astounding turnover rate of current drivers hovering around 90 percent. Most likely, this turnover rate will only increase in future years, especially if the U.S. economy continues to reach healthier levels. The American Trucking Association reported that, "on average, trucking will need to recruit nearly 100,000 new drivers every year to keep up with the demand for drivers."[9] Therefore, many companies are advocating for immigration reform, as they see immigrants as an opportunity to replenish the shortage. Both a guest worker program and a pathway to citizenship for current illegal immigrants may help facilitate the deficit. In fact, legal immigrants already fulfill a proportional percentage of current drivers. As stated by the Associated Press, in 2005, Hispanics accounted for "an estimated one in seven of the nation's 1.3 million long-haul truckers." This percentage is equivalent to the proportion of Hispanics overall of the U.S. population.[10]

In addition to the trucking industry, low-skilled immigrants also fill jobs in the construction industry. As reported by the National Association of Home Builders, about 20 percent or 2.4 million of construction workers are immigrants. Of that 20 percent, over 50 percent are of Mexican descent, while an additional 25 percent arrive from other Latin American countries. Immigrant workers also often fill positions in the construction industry that are not favorable to native-born workers. For example, the top five occupations for foreign-born workers in the construction industry are construction laborers; carpenters; painters, construction, and maintenance; construction managers; and roofers; while the top five jobs for native-born workers are construction managers; carpenters; construction laborers; first-line supervisors/managers of construction trades and extraction workers; and electricians.

Despite immigrant involvement, the construction industry is still facing a labor shortage. According to a survey conducted by the National Association of Home Builders, "Construction trades with the most widespread and severe labor shortages are carpenters and roofers, with more than 50 percent of all builders consistently reporting either severe or some shortage of carpenters and more than 40 percent expressing concerns over availability of roofers."[11] It is important to note that, in these two areas, rates of employment for foreign-born workers are above average, therefore indicating their value to the industry. While immigration reform may increase the number of people available to work in the construction industry, it might be more of a detriment to the industry, as it has been found to hire undocumented workers. These workers are often paid much less than their legal counterparts, allowing contractors to keep building prices low. If reform is established and a large number of workers become legal, they will probably request a higher wage, thus increasing the costs of building. But this is up for debate, as making them legal will cause an increase in supply of potential workers, thus lowering the overall cost of projects.

With an estimated 53 percent of the agricultural workforce being fulfilled by undocumented workers, it is clear that the industry relies heavily on immigrants.[12] According to Immigration Impact, a project launched by the American Immigration Council to encourage rational conversation on immigration, the industry is currently facing a large worker shortage. As a result, farmers are losing thousands of dollars because their produce is rotting in the fields. Because of this, many are advocating for immigration reform that would legalize current undocumented workers and would provide a system to bring in future workers. For those who argue that immigrants are taking jobs from native-born citizens, a study by the Department of Agriculture found that this is not the case. In fact, immigrants have a positive impact on the industry. As reported by Forbes, "In 2012, the Department of Agriculture looked at the economic impact of cutting low-skilled immigrants by 6 million and found it would reduce Americans' wages by up to 0.6 percent, or about $90 billion."[13] Additionally, even during times of recession, there is still a shortage of American workers willing to work in the agricultural, food processing, and nursery-landscape industries. Moreover, immigrant workers help to establish additional jobs often filled by native-born workers. For a more explicit example, consider that "Texas AgriLife Research estimated that if federal and labor immigration policies were to result in the loss of just half of the 57,000 foreign-born dairy workers, an additional 66,000 workers would be lost due to the closure of some dairy farms, the resulting multiplier effect of fewer jobs in grain and fertilizer production, veterinary services, milk hauling, and other related service jobs"—totaling an economic loss of $11 billion. Not only would jobs be lost if immigrant workers were not present, but also the industry would have to move to other countries to sustain the demand of American citizens.[14] In addition to the agricultural industry, the food and restaurant industry also benefits from the presence of foreign-born workers. According to the Huffington Post, in certain food industries, over half of the employed workers are undocumented workers. Also, it has been found that the population growth rate is not sufficient to fulfill the employment needs of the restaurant industry. Because of this, many involved in the restaurant industry are advocating for immigration reform. As it stands, over one million workers employed in food services are foreign born, and over three hundred thousand workers employed in agricultural services are foreign born.[15]

Another industry in which immigrants are frequently employed is the hospitality industry. According to the Immigrant Learning Center, "Immigrants participate in the United States Leisure and Hospitality industry at a higher rate than the native-born as both workers and business owners."[16] Over 50 percent of maids, housekeeping cleaners, janitors, and building cleaners are foreign born. In addition to these occupations, immigrants frequently occupy roles as lodging managers, cooks, and dining room and cafeteria attendants or bartender helpers. Some studies have even shown that foreign-born workers fill 80 percent of entry-level roles in U.S. restaurants and hotels.[17] Additionally, it has been found that entrepreneurship levels in the accommodation industry are higher for foreign-born workers than they are for native-born people. Despite the recent recession and the presence of immigrants currently in the accommodation industry, it is facing a labor shortage. As the industry continues to grow at a predicted rate of 16.4 percent, according to the Bureau of Labor Statistics, even more jobs will need to be fulfilled. Presently, an estimated one of sixteen illegal immigrants work in the hospitality industry. For this reason, many in the accommodation industry are advocating for immigration reform, including the creation of a guest worker program. Also, many hope for a comprehensive, national reform because if policies vary by state, then large hospitality chains, such as the Marriott or the Hyatt, may face difficulty in hiring immigrants.

On the opposite end of the spectrum, many immigrants also fulfill industry needs in high-skilled professions, such as health care, high-tech manufacturing, information technology, and life sciences. Although many Americans do seek higher forms of education, not enough go into science, technology, engineering, and mathematics fields. As a result, many STEM employers look to immigrants to fulfill open positions. Additionally, Census data show that immigrants from India and Taiwan are the most highly educated of these immigrants. In addition, immigrants from the United Kingdom, China, Japan, Iran, and Germany tend to be better educated than native U.S. citizens. In 2000, less than a quarter of all native U.S.- and foreign-born residents held a bachelor's degree or higher, while 69.1 percent of Indian immigrants held such degrees, as did 66.6 percent of those from Taiwan and 42.7 percent from China. Immigrant groups from India, China, and Taiwan have a large presence within the U.S. engineering and technology workforce. Moreover, these groups are unique in terms of their educational and professional attainment. Census data reveal the median household income for foreign-born individuals living in the United States is $39,000, while Indian, Taiwanese, and Chinese foreign borns enjoy median household incomes of $69,000, $59,000, and $46,000, respectively.[18]

As the U.S. innovation industry continues to grow, the labor gap only widens: "A 2013 study shows that in the 100 largest metropolitan areas in the United States, 46 percent of job openings requiring significant STEM knowledge go unfilled for one month or longer."[19] Though there is a visa, H-1B, established to attract immigrants with STEM knowledge, the United States places a cap of sixty-five thousand people on it. Within the first week of the filing period for fiscal year 2014, this cap was reached. As a result, many businesses are unable to hire the talent they seek to remain competitive globally. Also, the lottery system established to determine who is allowed to immigrate does not properly account for the talent that could be gained. Because of this, many employers are advocating for immigration reform, which allows for a greater number of people to immigrate to the United States and to work in STEM fields. Additionally, as we saw earlier, this would have a positive impact on the U.S. economy, as studies have shown that wages of native-born employees have risen with the presence of foreign-born people working in STEM industries. Their presence has also led to the creation of additional jobs for people to occupy. At present, foreign-born workers already fulfill a large sector of high-skilled jobs. Over one million work in the health care industry, over 140,000 work in high-tech manufacturing, nearly 270,000 work in information technology, and over 40,000 work in life sciences.[20]

Industries, including information technology, biotech, nanotech, and robotics, will be the foundation of future economies and will desperately need higher-educated STEM employees. For the future of U.S. competitiveness and the successful development of future industries, the United States needs unrestricted access to this pool of high-potential immigrants.

NOTES

1. "Foreign-Born Workers: Labor Force Characteristics 2012," Bureau of Labor Statistics, U.S. Department of Labor, May 22, 2013, www.bls.gov/news.release/pdf/forbrn.pdf (accessed October 25, 2013).
2. "Foreign-Born Workers: Labor Force Characteristics 2012."
3. Audrey Singer, "Immigrant Workers in the U.S. Labor Force," *Brookings.com*, March 15, 2012, http://www.brookings.edu/research/papers/2012/03/15-immigrant-workers-singer#4 (accessed July 9, 2013).
4. Singer, "Immigrant Workers in the U.S. Labor Force."
5. "Under Siege: Life for Low-Income Latinos in the South," Southern Poverty Law Center, April 2009, http://www.splcenter.org/publications/under-siege-life-low-income-latinos-south/2-racial-profiling (accessed October 25, 2013).
6. Peter Whoriskey, "U.S. Manufacturing Sees Shortage of Skilled Factory Workers," *Washington Post*, February 19, 2012, http://articles.washingtonpost.com/2012-02-19/business/35444240_1_factory-workers-laid-off-workers-jobs (accessed July 9, 2013).
7. Singer, "Immigrant Workers in the U.S. Labor Force."
8. "Brookings: Quality. Independence. Impact." The Brookings Institute, http://www.brookings.edu (accessed July 8, 2013).
9. "U.S. Economy, U.S. Workers, and Immigration Reform," U.S. Government Printing Office, May 3, 2007, http://www.gpo.gov/fdsys/pkg/CHRG-110hhrg35117/html/CHRG-110hhrg35117.htm (accessed July 8, 2013).
10. "U.S. Economy, U.S. Workers, and Immigration Reform."
11. Natalia Siniavskaia, "Immigrant Workers in Construction," *NAHB Housing Economics.com*, http://www.nahb.org/generic.aspx?sectionID=734&genericContentID=49216&channelID=311 (accessed October 25, 2013).
12. The World Bank, "Global Economic Prospects 2006: Economic Implications of Remittances and Migration," November 14, 2005.
13. David Bier, "To Grow, the U.S. Economy Needs More Low-Skilled Immigrant Workers," *Forbes.com*, May 6, 2013, http://www.forbes.com/sites/realspin/2013/05/06/to-grow-the-u-s-economy-needs-more-low-skilled-immigrant-workers/ (accessed August 17, 2013).
14. Bier, "To Grow, the U.S. Economy Needs More Low-Skilled Immigrant Workers."
15. Bier, "To Grow, the U.S. Economy Needs More Low-Skilled Immigrant Workers."
16. The Immigrant Learning Center, "Immigrant Entrepreneurs and Workers in Leisure and Hospitality Businesses: Massachusetts and New England 2010," http://www.ilctr.org/promoting-immigrants/immigration-research/immigrant-entrepreneurs-and-workers-in-leisure-and-hospitality-businesses/ (accessed August 17, 2013).
17. The Immigrant Learning Center, "Immigrant Entrepreneurs and Workers in Leisure and Hospitality Businesses."

18. Vivek Wadhwa, AnnaLee Saxenian, Richard Freeman, Gary Gereffi, and Alex Salkever, "America's Loss Is the World's Gain: America's New Immigrant Entrepreneurs, Part IV," Ewing Marion Kauffman Foundation, March 2009, http://www.kauffman.org/~/media/kauffman_org/archive/researchreport/2011/6/americas_loss.pdf (accessed July 1, 2013).

19. Wadhwa, Saxenian, Freeman, Gereffi, and Salkever, "America's Loss Is the World's Gain."

20. Wadhwa, Saxenian, Freeman, Gereffi, and Salkever, "America's Loss Is the World's Gain."

13

The Lure of Clusters

A simple encounter in a coffeeshop can spark great ideas. The beauty of a cluster lies in the large number of interactions that otherwise would not occur between individuals residing within a cluster—because sometimes all it takes is a glimpse at an idea to make a connection that can change the world.

As described by Michael Porter, when business segments need high levels of specialization from various contributors, clusters of producers, suppliers, and training centers frequently arise. Examples include the nineteenth-century jute cluster in Dundee, Scotland, the diamond-cutting cluster in Surat, India, and the electronics cluster in Dongguan, China.

In the coming years, we will see clusters for the newest high-tech industries, such as biotechnology, nanotechnology, and shale oil and gas development. The United States was lucky to have Silicon Valley develop in California in the second half of the twentieth century, for it created jobs and made the United States the center for technological innovation. Immigration helped to fuel the cluster. From 1995 to 2005, immigrants founded 52 percent of the startups in Silicon Valley.[1] But there is no guarantee the next clusters will develop in the United States, especially with the current state of immigration laws. In addition, governments of countries all over the world are encouraging high-tech cluster formations in their own country through providing capital and infrastructure. While the federal budget has allocated $1.7 billion to the National Nanotechnology Initiative, Rusnano (Russia) and ChiNano (China) are also trying to establish nanotechnology powerhouses. Rusnano invested $1.1 billion in 2011 in the development of a nanoindustry,[2] and China has been developing a "Nano City" in Suzhou.

Money does not make discoveries; people do. While the number of engineering graduates in the United States is not small, the numbers abroad dwarf it. Every year, the United States graduates around 83,000 undergraduate engineers, while China graduates 600,000, and India graduates 350,000. In other words, for every one U.S. graduate, there are eleven graduates from China and India. There is debate as to the quality of Chinese and Indian engineers, but even if only 10 percent of the graduates are up to par with U.S. graduates, the numbers are still greater abroad. In addition, Mexico graduates 130,000 engineers and technicians a year from universities and specialized high schools.[3] Europe, on the other hand, graduates numbers more consistent with the United States. In 2007, France had fifty-five thousand engineering graduates, Poland forty-six thousand, and the UK forty-six thousand.[4] With a deficit of STEM workers in the United States, we will mostly need immigrants from countries with a large number of engineering graduates, such as China and India. Instead of making foreign engineers our competitors, we should encourage them to immigrate to the United States. The giants of Silicon Valley recognize the talent abroad and have spent millions of dollars trying to increase the number of H-1B visas. They know it is crucial to remaining competitive in a global economy.

The United States should make housing future high-tech clusters one of its quintessential economic goals. Doing so will allow the United States to remain the center for technological innovation and to remain an economic powerhouse. Our first step must be to attract highly skilled immigrants.

CASE STUDY: DETROIT'S AUTOMOBILE INDUSTRY

If we look back through American history, we can see that clusters and immigration have led to great economic prosperity. At the end of the nineteenth century, Detroit was only a second-tier commercial and industrial city. It was not until Henry Ford founded the Ford Motor Company in 1903 that the Motor City started on its path to become the center of America's economy. Not only did Ford create the modern assembly line and increase pay for industrial workers to five dollars a day, but he also recruited internationally. The immigrant workers at Ford represented over fifty nationalities and spoke over one hundred different languages. As a result, Detroit became one of America's most racially and ethnically diverse cities. According to Thomas Sugrue, a professor of history and sociology at the University of Pennsylvania, Ford "recruited skilled artisans from the shipyards of Scotland and England and blue-collar workers from the rural Midwest, as well as workers from Mexico and Lebanon, and African Americans from the city's rapidly growing population of southern migrants."[5]

Ford Motor Company went through great efforts to assimilate, or "Americanize," its immigrant workers. First, the company created the English Language School, where immigrants would spend six months reciting and learning daily life phrases. Upon graduating, immigrants participated in a ceremony called "The Pageant of the Ford Melting Pot," during which workers would symbolically climb into a melting pot wearing their national garb and come out wearing American clothing. The ceremony was so elaborate that the school's teachers would pretend to stir the pot with big, long spoons.[6]

Government support also helped the automobile cluster. Car companies realized that a national highway system would increase the demand for cars, so with this goal in mind, Detroit lobbied for such a system to promote car ownership. Eventually, the mutual benefits the car industry and the United States both received were so great that Charles Erwin Wilson, head of General Motors, made the statement, "For years I thought what was good for our country was good for General Motors, and vice versa." The quote is often misquoted as, "What's good for General Motors is good for the country." Wilson was the head of General Motors when President Eisenhower asked him to be the Secretary of Defense. As Secretary of Defense, he claimed that, if a situation arose in which he had to choose between the country and General Motors, he would choose the country. He also stated, however, that he truly believed such a possibility was inconceivable because the fates of the two were intertwined.

Other companies that grew alongside Ford and General Motors include Chrysler and Packard. By the 1950s, one out of every six working Americans worked directly or indirectly for the automobile industry. At its peak, Ford's River Rouge plant employed more than ninety thousand workers.[7] The economic prowess Detroit brought America was truly great. In addition, social scientists in the 1950s viewed the auto industry as a force that had the ability to end class conflict in America. Autoworkers were able to buy homes and to save money to send their children to school.[8] They were able to enter the middle class.

Eventually, Detroit began to deteriorate due to greater international competition, the oil crisis, and automation technology. Today, it is often portrayed as a city of empty buildings and high crime. All is not yet lost. In 2010, *Time* magazine published an article titled "Arab-Americans: Detroit's Unlikely Saviors." Thousands of Lebanese, Yemenis, and other Middle Easterners moved to Detroit as a result of Henry Ford's recruitment. During that time, a group of Iraqi Catholics, known as Chaldeans, made a home for themselves in Detroit. Today, both Muslim and Christian Middle Easterners can be found in the city. It has been estimated that at least two hundred thousand Middle Easterners live in the four-county region of southeastern Michigan. According to the article, "The Arab-American community in metro Detroit produces as much as $7.7 billion annually in salaries and earnings." Entrepreneurial in nature, Middle Easterners have started more than fifteen thousand businesses in the metro area. When Nafa Khalaf, cofounder of Detroit Contracting, was asked about the future of Detroit, he responded, "You want to know if Detroit has a future? Ask us Arabs. We believe in this place."

Though it is admirable that the Arab American community holds faith in Detroit, the city has declared bankruptcy. The only way to rejuvenate it is to reestablish the cluster or to promote another cluster, similar to the way Boston refocused its attention from textile manufacturing to the high-tech computer industry. Now, Boston has refocused once again and has become one of the leaders in biotechnology.

Clusters require a large workforce and government encouragement and support, such as the U.S. nationwide road systems investments. In the case of Detroit, immigrants helped to fill the workforce needs. They helped to build America's once greatest industry. Even now, at a time when most have little faith in the fate of the city, immigrants are trying to help it get back on its feet.

CASE STUDY: SILICON VALLEY

In 2013, Silicon Valley held its breath while Congress debated immigration reform. The leaders of Silicon Valley wanted a greater slice of the world's high-tech labor pool pie. They spent millions in a super PAC to try to increase the number of foreign-worker visas.

According to Adam Thierer, of the Mercatus Center for Politics at George Mason University, "High technology companies are among the fastest growing lobbying shops in Washington."[9] The supply of H-1B visas is not nearly high enough for the number demanded. Mark Zuckerberg, founder of Facebook, believes American companies will lose their competitive edge if they do not begin to employ more immigrants. In a *Washington Post* op-ed, he writes, "In a knowledge economy, the most important resources are the talented people we educate and attract to our society. A knowledge economy can scale further, create better jobs, and provide a higher quality of living for everyone in our nation."[10] Professor Dan Schnur of the Jesse M. Unruh Institute of Politics at the University of Southern California, puts it more bluntly: "If you are a tech company, immigration is not a social issue, not a cultural issue, not a moral issue—it is a bottom-line issue."[11]

AnnaLee Saxenian, dean of the School of Information at the University of California, Berkeley, has researched the role of immigrants in Silicon Valley for over a decade now. In 1999, she found that in the previous two decades, immigrants made up one-third of Silicon Valley's scientific and engineering workforce. In 1998, Chinese and Indian engineers in the region alone operated businesses that generated $16.8 billion in sales and provided 58,282 jobs. They accounted for a quarter of the technology businesses in Silicon Valley at the time. In 2005, 52.4 percent of the startups in the region had at least one key founder who was an immigrant. A study conducted in 2012 and published in a Kauffman Foundation paper, however, found that 43.9 percent of the startups in Silicon Valley at that point were immigrant founded.[12] The significant 8 percent drop may indicate a potential change in the attitude of immigrants in coming to the United States and remaining here.

In 2007, a study titled "Intellectual Property, the Immigration Backlog, and a Reverse Brain-Drain" predicted that, if the foreign-born visa problem was not addressed, reverse brain drain would occur. With a decade wait time for permanent residence visas, immigrants are bound to get frustrated and decide to either return home or to move to another country.[13] According to "America's Loss Is the World's Gain: America's New Immigrant Entrepreneurs, Part IV," "for the first time in decades, the growth rate of immigrant-founded companies has stagnated, if not declined."[14] This observation should cause policymakers to raise red flags. Zuckerberg and other Silicon Valley leaders recognize the problem. Will the United States ultimately be able to remain technologically and economically competitive? The Silicon Valley cluster and its technologies need continuous product and service improvements to continue its success in the face of global competition and to prevent the fate of the Detroit automobile industry. It cannot achieve this goal without highly skilled immigrants.

TECHNOLOGICAL REVOLUTIONS

Global tectonic is a phrase I have used to identify "the process by which developing trends in technology, nature, and society slowly revolutionize the business environment of the future."[15] In 2005, Erik Peterson, now director of A. T. Kearney's Global Business Policy Council, and I identified twelve global trends that will shape the future of society and business. These trends range from governance to knowledge dissemination to urbanization. In *Global Tectonics: What Every Business Needs to Know*, we stress that CEOs and managers must prepare for the changes that these global tectonics will bring because those that do not will fall behind. Among the trends we identified were biotechnology and nanotechnology.

With the rapid growth in these two fields, we can expect a life science and a nanotechnology cluster to form somewhere in the world within the coming years. So add on the issue of the formations of a life science and a nanotechnology cluster to the potentially struggling Silicon Valley, and the United States will be challenged to remain the technological leader of the world, unless it hosts significant portions of these clusters.

In 2012, ManpowerGroup released the results of its seventh-annual Talent Shortage Survey. The survey found that 49 percent of U.S. employers had a hard time filling mission-critical positions within their organizations. On the other hand, the survey found that only 34 percent of employers globally were facing the same problem. Over 1,300 U.S. employers were surveyed, and they reported the hardest positions to fill were those in skilled trades, engineering, and IT. They had a hard time due to "lack of available applicants, applicants looking for more pay and lack of experience."[16] Both a life science and a nanotech cluster would require engineers. Life science would in particular require IT staff to develop the much-needed area of bioIT. If the United States is already having a hard time filling these positions, how will it fill the high workforce demand of a cluster? It is simple economics. Supply must increase, and to do so, a greater number of immigrants must be added to the available labor pool.

Furthermore, we learned earlier that for every foreign STEM graduate student who remains in the United States, 2.62 secondary jobs are created. In addition, for every high-tech job created in a metro area, five long-term secondary jobs outside of the high-tech sector are created, as well. Two of the five are professional jobs, and three of the five are service industry jobs.[17] Hosting a cluster would be the greatest stimulus package we could receive.

LIFE SCIENCE CLUSTER

The Human Genome Project, which began in 1990, completely mapped the human genome after thirteen years of work and $4 billion. Today, about a decade later, a genome can be mapped in just fifteen minutes for under $1,000.[18] The field of life science has made huge strides in the last few decades. The discoveries made can be used to diagnose and treat disease. Gene therapy will allow mutated genes, which cause disease, to be replaced with engineered healthy genes. In addition to the health benefits, the area of genomic medicine is projected to generate $350 billion worth of economic activity and millions of jobs.[19]

In the July–August 2012 issue of the *Harvard Business Review*, John Sviokla, a principal at PwC Consulting; Dietrich A. Stephan, a board member of the Personalized Medicine Coalition; and I wrote an article about the imminent emergence of a life science cluster. Titled "Why Life Science Needs Its Own Silicon Valley," the article recognizes the benefits of a life science cluster and the need for government support in developing the cluster. As stated in the article, "The genomics cluster will include multinational corporations, research institutions, scientists, students, investors, related industries, and start-ups that haven't been imagined yet." A life science cluster would bring jobs and prestige to the city that hosts it. After much analysis, we determined that the United States, the United Kingdom, and Canada are well positioned to host the cluster. We also recognized the window of opportunity for hosting the cluster will only be open for so long, and whichever nation succeeds will receive a great economic boost and head start in the field.

No one really knows how to start clusters or why they occur where they do. The software cluster that grew in Seattle was likely a result of the city being the birthplace of Bill Gates. We believe, however, that bioIT and government support will be instrumental in the development of a life science cluster.

First, genomic medicine is data driven, so for genome studies to become widely useful, bioIT must be further developed. Researchers should amass a database of genomic data, including information in areas such as disease outbreaks, family history, and environmental exposures. The U.S. Department of Veterans Affairs is currently collecting blood samples and health and lifestyle information from veterans through the Million Veteran Program. The goal of the program is to help researchers learn how genes affect health.[20] Perhaps this program will play the same role for the genomic medicine cluster as the U.S. nationwide highway did for Detroit's automobile cluster. Unfortunately, IT personnel is one group of workers the United States is strongly lacking, as discovered by the ManpowerGroup. As it turns out, immigrants disproportionately specialize in information technology. Immigrants represent 16 percent of America's workforce but 23 percent of the information technology industry.[21] Additionally, immigrants are on average more educated in the fields of IT and life science.[22] For a life science cluster to develop in the United States, we will need the help of immigrants. We will need IT experts to develop databases that can hold vast amounts of genomic data while remaining secure and easily accessible to researchers.

Second, governmental support could kick-start the development of a cluster. Governments have the capital and influence needed for research and development projects too large for individual companies. In addition, government can provide infrastructure conducive to cluster growth and incentivize companies to reside in certain areas through tax incentives. For example, Vancouver is home to many companies in the movie industry because of the British Columbia Film and Television Tax Credit program. Returning to the previous point, governments could help promote or even develop the genomics database that will be necessary for the success of a life science cluster.

If America has what it takes to develop a genomics cluster, then the United States could simultaneously create a new industry ecosystem that alters the course of medicine and bolsters the country's economy.

NANOTECHNOLOGY CLUSTER

Nanotechnology is another field of science that has developed rapidly over the last few decades. According to Roco, Mirkin, and Hersam in *Nanotechnology Research Directions for Societal Needs in 2020*, "Between 1990 and 2008, 17,600 companies from 87 countries were involved in nanotechnology publications and patent applications."[23] Nanotechnology is the study of matter at the nanoscale, which is about 1 to 100 nanometers. A nanometer is a billionth of a meter. With the invention of the scanning tunneling microscope in 1981, we gained the ability to see and eventually to control individual atoms. Why was this critical? Because quantum effects take over at this scale. Properties, such as melting point, fluorescence, and electrical conductivity become size dependent. Nanotechnology essentially allows each and every atom to be put in its most efficient place.

Previously unimaginable inventions have come out of nanotechnology. Through metamaterials, we have almost achieved invisibility. A metamaterial is an artificially created matter that bends light around it. To the human eye, an object covered in a metamaterial appears invisible. In June 2013, Stanford made a breakthrough in creating invisibility through the use of optical metamaterials. Previous efforts only allowed invisibility within a limited range of optical wavelengths and, therefore, colors. A Stanford research team, however, has designed a material that can bend nearly all wavelengths of light visible to the human eye.[24] Other nanotech breakthroughs include the discovery of graphene, the best heat-conducting material known to man, new cancer treatments, and energy-generating shirts. Penn State researcher John Badding and his team have developed the first fiber-optic solar cell. The fibers are thinner than human hair and can produce electricity. The U.S. military has already begun to invest in the fiber, which can power small electronics for soldiers in the field.[25]

In 2009, there was $254 billion worth of products using nanotechnology in the market.[26] By 2015, global nanotech industry output is predicted to reach $2.4 trillion.[27] It is no wonder that Jack Uldrich and Deb Newberry referred to nanotechnology as "an iceberg that threatens to sink even the 'unsinkable' companies." Nanotechnology will come to change the business landscape, and the United States should aim to be at the front of the wave.

A nanotechnology cluster is bound to form soon. Nanotechnology knowledge is known to be highly tacit, which means that distance limits knowledge diffusion.[28] Tacit knowledge is not easily spread written down or verbally, as it is best transferred face to face. Consequently, nanotech researchers and companies will tend to clump together, and investors will know where to locate themselves. Currently, the American cities with the most nanotech institutions are Boston, San Francisco, San Jose, and Raleigh. But since the U.S. National Nanotechnology Initiative was created in 2000, nations everywhere have also started their own national nanotech programs. If we look at spending by countries in purchasing power parity, we find that China spent more in funding nanotechnology than the United States did in 2011.[29] In absolute terms, the United States still spent the most. But the fact of the matter is, the race for nanotech domination is on. According to Cientifica, which monitors the emerging technology landscape, the United States, China, and Russia are the most competitive when it comes to nanotechnology. After taking the quality of scientific institutions, capacity for innovation, and funding into account, these three countries are the most likely to win the race.[30] Like the life science cluster, the window of opportunity to develop a nanotechnology cluster will only be open for so long, and whichever country succeeds will gain a significant advantage in the field. In 1983, Soete and Dosi observed about emerging microelectronics, "The switch from an old technological paradigm to a new one [opens] dramatic new possibilities of change in the international structure of supply, the relative position between countries and the pattern of international competitiveness."[31]

If the United States would like this head start, it must implement immigration reform now. A Lux Research survey in 2007 found that out of twenty-six U.S. companies asked, 60 percent of them believed they would face a nanotechnology labor shortage. Nanotech is not so much an industry but rather a general-purpose technology, and so the jobs required to sustain a cluster range from manufacturing to research and development. Nanotechnology has been at the initial stages of the technology, development, and assimilation curve, so for a while now, nanotech has been research heavy and has relied on the work of scientists. Yet the trend is beginning to shift, as more products incorporate nanotechnology, and workers of all skill levels will be needed.

Noela Invernizzi, a fellow with the Science and Technology Innovation Program, has researched the effects of nanotechnology on labor. While she admits it may still be too early to analyze changes in labor, she believes this area must be looked at, and some changes can already be observed. Her results, published in the *Journal of Nanoparticle Research*, found nanotech is moving toward manufacturing. The manufacturing she is talking about is advanced manufacturing, which requires high technical and computer aptitudes. This shift will require more engineers and more machinists/machine operators, if we wish to keep manufacturing within the United States. These are two jobs that U.S. companies had a hard time filling, as reported by ManpowerGroup.

In 2007, a group of scientists, mostly from the University of Illinois–Springfield, researched the barriers to nanotechnology commercialization. They reported a story about how there are Nanosolar shingles for homes but a lack of installers for the shingles. Thus, we will also need more skilled trades workers because a good portion of nanotechnology falls into the energy realm, and buildings and homes will need workers to install the more energy-efficient products. Due to a shift away from vocational training, the United States is also greatly lacking skilled trades workers. Training a new generation of workers to adapt to our technological advances will take time, and by then, the United States may have lost the first-mover advantage.

As for the research and development of nanotechnology, our lower numbers of STEM graduates could be problematic down the road. In addition, many nanotech employees and scientists are foreign nationals, and as a result, they are often not allowed access to federal labs, further lowering potential scientific innovation.

To house the nanotechnology cluster, the United States must encourage immigrants with the relevant skills to come here. We should not only increase the H-1B cap, but we also should encourage skilled trades workers to immigrate to America. With government support in reformed immigration laws and capital investments in infrastructure, the United States could bring home the nanotech cluster.

OTHER REVOLUTIONARY FIELDS

Life science and nanotechnology are just two of many possible high-tech clusters that could form in the years to come. Others include shale oil and shale gas, robotics, 3D printing, defense-related technologies, and information technology, and even new fields of multimedia and entertainment. The rate of technological development in these fields has been astounding. As diverse as these fields are, a common thread tying them together is the need for experts in the STEM fields.

To house any of the above clusters, we will need immigrants to fill many of the STEM positions. We need to encourage foreign students to remain in the

United States after graduation and raise the H-1B cap. In addition, we should consider changing some of the laws regarding foreign nationals working in the United States.

An example lies in the U.S. defense industry. World military spending in 2012 was $1.7 trillion, and U.S. military spending accounted for 39 percent of it.[32, 33] While U.S. military spending decreased in 2012, China and Russia, the second and third largest spenders after the United States, increased their military spending.[34] A defense cluster already exists in the United States, but we are putting it at risk by completely restricting noncitizen immigrants from working in our military-industrial complex. We developed this blanket rule to prevent potential threats to our national security, but implementing this rule is indeed a threat to our national security. It further aggravates the labor shortage for our major defense contractors, such as Lockheed Martin and Northrop Grumman, and it limits the talent pool available to these defense contractors. Given the labor shortage, it would make more sense to allow noncitizens to work in certain designated areas with appropriate supervision.

Another high-tech cluster that affects national security is the shale oil and shale gas cluster. Within the last seven years, with new technological advancements, it was discovered that the United States holds substantial deposits of oil shale. According to the Energy Information Administration, the deposits hold an estimated fifty-eight billion barrels of potentially recoverable oil[35]—enough to meet U.S. oil demand at current rates for another 250 years. In 2012, the International Energy Agency reported that the United States is projected to surpass Saudi Arabia in total oil production by 2020, making it the world's largest oil producer. In other words, the reserve deposits will allow the United States to become energy independent.

While Americans constitute less than 5 percent of the world's population, they consume 26 percent of the world's energy. In addition, they account for about 25 percent of the world's petroleum consumption, making the United States the world's largest petroleum consumer. Consider the fact that in 2012, the United States imported around 40 percent of the petroleum it consumed. Some 28 percent of the imported petroleum came from Canada, 13 percent from Saudi Arabia, 10 percent from Mexico, 9 percent from Venezuela, and 5 percent from Russia.[36] Energy independence will alter U.S. foreign policy as the U.S. policy has long been based on the belief of a growing scarcity of oil. The Energy Information Administration reported that the "U.S. could become completely independent of imports from outside of North America by 2020."[37]

Furthermore, the reserves in place, such as the Eagle Ford, the Bakken, and those in the Permian Basin, also contain high volumes of natural gas.

The large potential resource volumes reported for shale oil and gas have generated comparably large expectations for increased future oil and gas supplies in both the United States and the rest of the world. These expectations include the substitution of domestic gas for imported oil and the use of domestic gas as a cleaner or safer alternative for coal- and nuclear-generated electricity. Shale natural gas in the form of compressed and liquefied natural gas is becoming more viable as a fuel option as technological developments are made. The United States could go even further than energy independence and begin exporting gas.

The shale deposits have caused natural gas prices in the United States to remain around $3.45 mmBtu (one million British thermal units), while gas prices have been $8 to $9 in Europe and $16 to $19 in China and Japan. As a result, major industries are returning to the United States to benefit from the cheap gas, yet we need the skills for this dramatic turnaround in energy-intensive industries.

But energy is only one component of the potential of shale oil and gas. The U.S. plastics-producing industry is increasingly shifting away from oil-derived naphtha (which is a major ingredient in making both gasoline and ethylene used for plastics production), choosing instead to run plants on the gases butane or propane. It is also investing billions in plants that run on ethane, made from cheap shale gas. The U.S. plastics industry is now expanding for the first time in decades, as factories are able to cut production costs and to compete on a global scale. According to the association of American Fuel and Petrochemical Manufacturers, three years ago, U.S. companies used oil-derived naphtha 50 percent of the time and shale gas ethane 50 percent of the time to produce ethylene. Today, U.S. companies use naphtha 20 percent of the time and ethane 80 percent of the time. This ratio is set to tip even further over the next six years as companies, including Dow Chemical and Exxon Mobil, are planning $25 billion worth of new projects, which will mainly run on shale gas.

With this newfound energy source, we need scientists and engineers to develop the safest ways to draw the gas and oil out of the ground as well as to develop efficient ways in which the energy can be stored and used. Yet we are currently turning away some of the world's energy experts as a result of our H-1B limits. Last year, I met a bright, young expert in the area of shale oil and gas named Mohammed, who questioned remaining in the United States because of visa difficulties. That was one of the moments during which I realized just how great the opportunity cost of our immigration laws is.

Now, let me share with you the story of Mohammed.

NOTES

1. Vivek Wadhwa, AnnaLee Saxenian, Richard Freeman, Gary Gereffi, and Alex Salkever, "America's Loss Is the World's Gain: America's New Immigrant Entrepreneurs, Part IV," Ewing Marion Kauffman Foundation, March 2009, www.kauffman.org/uploadedfiles/americas_loss.pdf (accessed July 1, 2013).
2. Vladislav Putilin and Anatoly Chubais, Rusnano Annual Report 2011, en.rusnano.com/upload/images/normativedocs/RUSNANO_AR2011_ENG.pdf (accessed July 1, 2013).
3. William Booth, "Mexico Is Now a Top Producer of Engineers, But Where Are Jobs?" *Washington Post*, October 28, 2012, http://articles.washingtonpost.com/2012-10-28/world/35498580_1_mexico-city-president-enrique-pe-a-nieto-engineers (accessed July 24, 2013).
4. Vera Erdmann and Tanja Schumann, "European Engineering Report," *Institut der deutschen Wirtschaft* Köln, April 2010, www.vdi.de/uploads/media/2010-04_IW_European_Engineering_Report_02.pdf (accessed July 20, 2013).
5. Thomas J. Sugrue, "Motor City: The Story of Detroit," *Gilder Lehrman American History*, March 2007, www.gilderlehrman.org/history-by-era/politics-reform/essays/motor-city-story-detroit (accessed July 8, 2013).
6. "Transcript: Henry Ford," *American Experience*, WGBH, PBS, http://www.pbs.org/wgbh/americanexperience/features/transcript/henryford-transcript/ (accessed July 8, 2013).
7. Sugrue, "Motor City: The Story of Detroit."
8. Sugrue, "Motor City: The Story of Detroit."
9. William La Jeunesse, "Silicon Valley Banks on Immigration Bill for Access to Foreign Workers," *Fox News*, June 24, 2013, http://www.foxnews.com/politics/2013/06/24/silicon-valley-banks-on-immigration-bill-for-access-to-foreign-workers/ (accessed July 8, 2013).
10. La Jeunesse, "Silicon Valley Banks on Immigration Bill."
11. La Jeunesse, "Silicon Valley Banks on Immigration Bill."
12. Wadhwa, Saxenian, Freeman, Gereffi, and Salkever, "America's Loss Is the World's Gain."
13. Wadhwa, Saxenian, Freeman, Gereffi, and Salkever, "America's Loss Is the World's Gain."
14. Wadhwa, Saxenian, Freeman, Gereffi, and Salkever, "America's Loss Is the World's Gain."
15. Fariborz Ghadar and Erik Peterson, *Global Tectonics: What Every Business Needs to Know* (University Park, PA: The Penn State Center for Global Business Studies, 2008).
16. ManpowerGroup, "ManpowerGroup Annual Survey Reveals U.S. Talent Shortages Persist in Skilled Trades, Engineers and IT Staff," Manpower US Pressroom, http://press.manpower.com/press/2012/talent-shortage/ (accessed July 9, 2013).
17. "Rebuilding Local Economies," Immigration Policy Center, http://www.immigrationpolicy.org/just-facts/rebuilding-local-economies (accessed August 9, 2013).

18. Erika Check Hayden, "Nanopore Genome Sequencer Makes Its Debut," *Nature*, February 17, 2012, http://www.nature.com/news/nanopore-genome-sequencer-makes-its-debut-1.10051 (accessed July 31, 2013).

19. Fariborz Ghadar, John Sviokla, and Dietrich A Stephan, "Why Life Science Needs Its Own Silicon Valley," *Harvard Business Review Magazine* July–August 2012, http://hbr.org/2012/07/why-life-science-needs-its-own-silicon-valley/ar/1 (accessed July 9, 2013).

20. Ghadar, Sviokla, and Stephan, "Why Life Science Needs Its Own Silicon Valley."

21. Audrey Singer, "Immigrant Workers in the U.S. Labor Force," *Brookings.com*, March 15, 2012, http://www.brookings.edu/research/papers/2012/03/15-immigrant-workers-singer#4 (accessed July 9, 2013).

22. Singer, "Immigrant Workers in the U.S. Labor Force."

23. M. C. Roco, C. A. Mirkin, and M. C. Hersam, *Nanotechnology Research Directions for Societal Needs in 2020*, September 2010, http://www.wtec.org/nano2/Nanotechnology_Research_Directions_to_2020/ (accessed October 28, 2013).

24. Brian Dodson, "Metamaterials Breakthrough Could Lead to the First Wide-Spectrum Optical Invisibility Cloak," *Gizmag*, June 12, 2013, http://www.gizmag.com/metamaterials-wide-spectrum-optical-invisibility-cloak-stanford/27813/ (accessed July 9, 2013).

25. Sebastian Anthony, "The First Flexible, Fiber-Optic Solar Cell That Can Be Woven into Clothes," *ExtremeTech.com*, December 7, 2012, http://www.extremetech.com/computing/142755-the-first-flexible-fiber-optic-solar-cell-that-can-be-woven-into-clothes (accessed July 9, 2013).

26. Mihail C. Roco, Chad A. Mirkin, and Mark C. Hersam. "Chapter 13 Innovative and Responsible Governance," In Nanotechnology Research Directions for Societal Needs in 2020, WTEC, 2010, www.wtec.org/nano2/Nanotechnology_Research_Directions_to_2020/Nano_Resarch_Directions_to_2020.pdf (accessed December 15, 2013).

27. "Global Nanotechnology Industry Output Expected to Reach $2.4 Trillion by 2015," Yahoo! Finance, http://finance.yahoo.com/news/Global-Nanotechnology-iw-3399006244.html (accessed December 15, 2013).

28. Andrea Schiffauerova and Catherine Beaudry, "Canadian Nanotechnology Innovation Networks: Intra-Cluster, Inter-Cluster and Foreign Collaboration," *Cairn.info*, http://www.cairn.info/revue-journal-of-innovation-economics-2009-2-page-119.htm (accessed July 9, 2013).

29. Tim Harper, "Global Funding of Nanotechnologies and Its Impact," July 2011, *cientifica*, cientifica.com/wp-content/uploads/downloads/2011/07/Global-Nanotechnology-Funding-Report-2011.pdf (accessed July 1, 2013).

30. Harper, "Global Funding of Nanotechnologies and Its Impact."

31. Noela Invernizzi, "Nanotechnology between the Lab and the Shop Floor: What Are the Effects on Labor?" *Journal of Nanoparticle Research* 13 (2011), http://cms.springerprofessional.de/journals/JOU=11051/VOL=2011.13/ISU=6/ART=333/BodyRef/PDF/11051_2011_Article_333.pdf (accessed October 28, 2013).

32. Anup Shah, "World Military Spending," *Global Issues.org*, May 2, 2011, http://www.globalissues.org/article/75/world-military-spending (accessed July 5, 2013).

33. Shah, "World Military Spending."

34. "New SIPRI Data on Military Expenditure—World Military Spending Falls, but China, Russia's Spending Rises," *SIPRI Fact Sheet 2013*, April 15, 2013, http://www.sipri.org/media/pressreleases/ (accessed July 31, 2013).

35. Edward McAllister and Timothy Gardner, "UPDATE 3-Rise in Shale Oil Boosts Global Crude Supply Estimate—U.S. EIA," *Reuters.com*, June 10, 2013, http://www.reuters.com/article/2013/06/10/global-shale-idUSL2N0EM1KM20130610 (accessed July 31, 2013).

36. "How Dependent Are We on Foreign Oil?" *U.S. Energy Information Administration*, July 13, 2012, http://www.eia.gov/cfapps/energy_in_brief/foreign_oil_dependence.cfm?featureclicked=3 (accessed July 31, 2013).

37. David Blackmon, "The Texas Shale Oil and Gas Revolution—Leading the Way to Enhanced Energy Security," *Forbes.com*, March 19, 2013, http://www.forbes.com/sites/davidblackmon/2013/03/19/the-texas-shale-oil-gas-revolution-leading-the-way-to-enhanced-energy-security/ (accessed July 10, 2013).

14

A Day in the Life

The airline allows me priority boarding due to my frequent business flyer status, so while waiting for them to process and to start loading the rest of the passengers, I open my iPad to check my email before the flight crew clamps down on electronic devices. Even with being "randomly" searched on all three legs of my trip so far, I congratulate myself on having anticipatively arrived with more than enough time before take off.

It has been an awful week. The stock market dropped yet again, sending my investments into a tailspin, and I had to correct fifty-four exams for my graduate course Global Strategy Formulation and Implementation (although I have to admit that receiving the school's Best Teacher Award ameliorates the tedium). And now I have a new worry: my board meeting with Nason Medical Centers revealed we are being investigated by Medicare and the Justice Department.

As the passengers start to file in, I quickly flip over my computer bag embellished with the Pennsylvania State University logo. I dread having to discuss Jerry Sandusky and his sentence on forty-five counts of serial pedophilia with yet another person.

Fortunately for me, across the aisle two thirty-something-year-old women, who are much more likely to be interested in reading their fashion magazines than in having a discussion with a global business consultant, are stowing their carry-on bags.

People-watching has become an occupational hazard in my traveling lifestyle, and so I continue to let my eyes scan the oncoming trail of people, some of whom are frequently cross-referencing their paper tickets to find their designated seats. The typical assortment of business travelers wind their way down the aisle, some, like me, carrying their suit jackets so they do not get wrinkled, others neatly dressed in polo shirts with cell phone holders attached onto their belts. A few young families stumble along, trying to corral their youngsters to the dreaded glances of other passengers.

The line filing onto the plane goes in stops and starts, as the dexterity of each passenger to heave his or her belongings up into the closest available overhead bin is challenged. During one such lull in the procession, the two women across the aisle from me take particular notice of one individual passenger. The straightening of their spines and subtle nudging between them alert me to the fact that a man of some attraction is approaching our row. Looking down the line, I notice the person of their attention, a thirty-something-year-old man who is the prerequisite tall, dark, and handsome.

The sigh of regret is almost audible when he stops at our row and instead of filling the empty seat next to them, turns toward me and motions that he is to occupy the seat on my right. I smugly stand to allow him to pass into my row. After he slides past me, I buckle myself in and say "hello" to him with a smile. He returns my greeting with an audible reply and similarly busies himself with his seat belt.

I go back to my tasks, while the plane personnel continue their typical loading sequences. Trying to hurry before we are asked to turn off our electronic devices, I email approval of my budget report for the Center for Global Business Studies at Penn State University, hoping that my funds will not be cut again this year.

I download the board report detailing the investigation by Medicare and the Justice Department in order to go through it in more detail and to catch up on all the attachments prepared for board member review. After starting in on all the legal jargon, I quickly decide to put it aside to go over it once I get home. Somehow I will have to fit this into the already jammed-pack summer I have ahead of me.

This year I won't be taking a vacation, as my sixteen-year-old twins, John and Anna, need my help in improving their 1800 SAT scores if they ever hope to get into a decent school. Compared to when I was growing up, it is becoming more and more difficult to motivate them. When I was in high school, I attended regular classes in American schools overseas and then spent my summers repeating the same topics in school in Iran with the students who had flunked that year. I had to endure twelve months out of the year schooling, and they resent that they have me tutoring them in math for an hour each day while a professional tutor comes to the house every morning to go over the English portion of the SATs. Obviously, this is not what their friends are doing over their summer.

Pulling out from my bag the current draft pages of an upcoming presentation, I feel my new neighbor surreptitiously glancing over at my printouts.

The title, "America and the Iranian Political Reform Movement—delivered before Congress and the House Foreign Affairs Committee," printed in bold at the top of each page, must have caught his eye, as he breathes out an, "Oh."

As I glance up at him, he says, "What an interesting topic. Are you from Iran?"

I put the page down, realizing this is going to be the start of a conversation, and say, "Yes, I was born there, but have lived most of my life here in the States. Where are you from?"

"Beirut, Lebanon," he replies.

"Oh, I went to an English teaching boarding school in Beirut; I think in 1960, 61, I was in 8th and 9th grade. I have very fond memories of Lebanon." As it turns out, I went to International College, a preparatory high school for the American University of Beirut, and so did he.

His face lights up as he replies, "So do you speak Arabic?"

"No, not really. I can only understand just a little bit. Besides, I wouldn't suggest that we start speaking in Arabic together on an airplane!" I say with a conspiratorial smile.

He laughs knowingly and glances briefly past me to the two young women who apparently have not given up hope of some kind of connection.

I shift the conversation back to more mundane topics and ask, "So do you live here in the U.S. now or . . .?"

"Yes, I am a student at Stanford."

"What are you studying?"

"Petroleum Engineering. I was just in Ohio doing some on-site research for my PhD thesis in shale oil and gas."

I practically turn in my seat. "Really? I did my thesis on the evolution of OPEC strategy when I was at Harvard Business School. And now I do a lot of executive education for Saudi Aramco."

With my experience in the oil industry and his background in the shale oil and gas industry, we start discussing the potential of oil imports to the United States being displaced by domestic unconventional shale oil and gas production. It is a hot topic right now, and I am pleased to find someone with real insight to bounce ideas off.

Meanwhile, as our conversation turns to the vagaries of oil and natural gas production, its history and future, the flight attendant comes by with offers of our choice of beverages. It soon becomes clear that this man is a highly sought-after expert in his field, as he tells me about the global competition in evaluating the many shale oil and gas reservoirs.

"So what are your plans for after graduation?" I ask, impressed with his knowledge and experience.

"Well, I would ultimately like to stay in the U.S. and continue to work in the industry, but I am not sure if I will be able to get a work visa to allow me to stay. I do have two offers in Australia, where it is easier to get a visa, but that would be my fallback position."

Our plane has landed, but I am still intrigued by this man. "I am Fariborz, by the way," I say, holding out my hand.

"Mohammed," he replies.

The two women across the aisle must have given up hope now that I have been monopolizing his attention, and so they quietly exit the plane.

I have a connecting flight to make in two hours to State College, and I ask Mohammed if this is his final destination.

"No, I'm catching a plane back to San Francisco."

Finding out that his flight leaves thirty minutes after mine, I ask him if he would like to grab a cup of coffee with me.

"I would really like that, however," and here he breaks eye contact, "I must say *Asr* [afternoon prayers] when we land. Would you mind? We could meet after I am finished?"

"Of course, that is fine." This could be interesting, I think to myself.

Placing both of our carryons beneath the table, we settle in with our black coffees.

I begin by asking, "So if you already have two job offers in Australia, why would your first choice be to stay in the U.S.?"

"Well I do have a one-year job offer here in the U.S., but I am concerned that at the end of that year, without the assurance of an H-1 visa, that I will be exactly in the same place I am right now. Also, it has always been my dream to live in America. That is one of the reasons I came here to get my PhD, along with hoping it would lead to a job so I could stay. There are many more opportunities here than in Australia. Even though I know that I have two really good offers there, along with knowing that I would be able to get a visa, I just feel that it is in America where I can make the biggest career moves. Also, I have come to appreciate a lot of the American culture . . . okay, so not everything, but I have made some really good friends here in university and in the local Lebanese community . . . I feel like I have adapted well here in the U.S.—I shaved my beard so that I wouldn't stand out as much on campus and have made a few American friends in my program. Unlike my roommate who has refused to shave, I think I can still practice my religion and be a good 'American.'"

"You are . . . Shiite?" I hazard, based upon his Lebanese background.

"Yes."

I tread tenderly, "Did you feel like your beard had been a problem . . .?"

"Well, I thought about it after another Muslim student decided to shave his beard last year. It was much easier for him to fit in with the other American researchers in his program after he shaved it off. He still practices his religion though."

"I understand," I replied with a nod.

I never saw Mohammad again, and I'm not sure where he ended up going after he graduated, but if it is Australia, or any other country besides the United States, that would be disappointing to me and a shame for the United States as a whole.

15

Prejudice Exists, But So What?

Although the United States is a nation built by immigrants, throughout its history, its people have often held prejudice against the newcomer. Despite the time period, there remains at least one group of people that becomes the target of discrimination.

European immigrants to the United States never faced the extreme prejudice that people of other nonwhite races experienced—from the anti-Asian laws of the 1800s to the Jim Crow laws designed to deny basic freedoms to African Americans in the nineteenth and twentieth centuries.

One group that faced brutal treatment because of geopolitical events was the more than one hundred thousand Japanese Americans whose freedom, rights, and property were stripped from them by order of President Franklin D. Roosevelt after Japan attacked Pearl Harbor in 1941, marking the United States' entry into World War II. The United States also went to war that year against Germany and Italy, but other than requiring them to recite a loyalty oath, the government never felt the need to intern German and Italian Americans.

It was only decades later, in 1988, through an act of Congress signed by President Ronald Reagan, that the government apologized for this dark and disturbing chapter in American history. Meanwhile, although thousands of Jews had been admitted into the United States under the combined German-Austrian quota from 1938 to 1941, the United States did not pursue an organized and specific rescue policy for Jewish victims of Nazi Germany until early 1944.

While some American activists sincerely intended to assist refugees, serious obstacles to any relaxation of U.S. immigration quotas included public opposition to immigration during a time of economic depression, xenophobia, and anti-Semitic feelings in both the general public and among some government officials. Once the United States entered World War II, the State Department practiced stricter immigration policies out of fear that refugees could be blackmailed into working as agents for Germany.

> Upon graduation from Yale with a PhD in 1884, Norwegian Thorstein Veblen was unable to obtain an academic job, partly due to prejudice against Norwegians and partly because most universities considered him insufficiently educated in Christianity, as most academics at the time held divinity degrees. He went on to be one of the founders of The New School and coined the phrase *conspicuous consumption*.
>
> In his 1919 work, "The Intellectual Pre-Eminence of Jews in Modern Europe," his position was that many Jews were caught between two worlds, detached from traditional Judaism and Jewish communal life, yet accepted grudgingly (if at all) by their host societies. Their marginality made them skeptical of conventional ideas and stimulated creativity that led to intellectual eminence and, often, economic success. Other social scientists have generalized Veblen's approach, linking marginality to creativity for immigrants, pariah groups, and groups that accept society's goals but are blocked from reaching them through conventional means.

Immigration restrictions were still in effect in the United States after the war, and legislation to expedite the admission of Jewish displaced persons (DPs) was slow in coming. In 1948, following intense lobbying by the American Jewish community, Congress passed legislation to admit four hundred thousand DPs to the United States. Nearly eighty thousand of these, or about 20 percent, were Jewish DPs. By 1952, some 137,450 Jewish refugees (including close to one hundred thousand DPs) had settled in the United States. The amended 1948 law was a turning point in American immigration policy and established a precedent for later refugee crises.

The 1960s brought a significant shift in U.S. immigration policy that had previously served white Europeans predominantly. Under the 1952 Immigration and Nationality Act, countries such as Japan and China had strict quotas systems, whereas immigrants from northern and western European countries were allowed to make up 85 percent of all immigrants.[1] President Kennedy, in setting out to overhaul the law in 1963, called it "nearly intolerable."

"The law was just unbelievable in its clarity of racism," said Stephen Klineberg, a sociologist at Rice University. "It declared that Northern Europeans are a superior subspecies of the white race. The Nordics were superior to the Alpines, who in turn were superior to the Mediterraneans, and all of them were superior to the Jews and the Asians."[2]

> **Benjamin Franklin in "Observations Concerning the Increase of Mankind, Peopling of Countries, etc.," 1751**
>
> Why should Pennsylvania, founded by the English, become a Colony of Aliens, who will shortly be so numerous as to Germanize us instead of our Anglifying them, and will never adopt our Language or Customs, any more than they can acquire our Complexion.

The 1960s were also a time of great ideological shifts within society. During this decade, young people began to revolt against the conservative norms of the time, creating a counterculture that sparked a social revolution throughout much of the Western world. It began as a reaction against the conservatism and social conformity of the 1950s and the U.S. government's extensive military intervention in Vietnam.

The civil rights movement occurring at the same time includes noted legislation and organized efforts to abolish public and private acts of racial discrimination against African Americans and other disadvantaged groups. So within this context, Congress passed the revamped policy after Kennedy's assassination. As President Johnson signed the Immigration and Naturalization Act in 1965, he declared it would "not reshape the structure of our daily lives or add importantly to either our wealth or our power." But he could not have been more wrong because the unintended consequence of the law, as is often the case with laws, was to significantly change America's demographics. This was due to two provisions: One gave priority to family reunification; the other gave preference to professionals with skills in short supply in the United States.

"Congress was saying in its debates, 'We need to open the door for some more British doctors, some more German engineers,'" Klineberg said.[3] It seems that nobody considered that there were going to be Egyptian doctors, Indian computer programmers, and Chinese engineers, all who would be able, for the first time, to immigrate to America because the act had abolished national origins quotas.

Despite the appearance of a call for radical social change within the United States, the new act was not met with much favor. In a 2006 report by National Public Radio, Karen Narasaki, head of the Asian American Justice Center, said the new law was not popular with the public. "It was not what people were marching in the streets over in the 1960s," she said. "It was really a group of political elites who were trying to look into the future. And again, it was the issue of, 'Are we going to be true to what we say our values are?'"

Then, with the closing of the decade, a backlash to the monumental social changes occurred, ultimately leading to a transformation of American society.

While one segment of society—liberal to moderate, mostly urban and suburban—embraced the change, another segment—mostly conservative and religious—viewed the changes as abhorrent. Unlike the liberals and moderates, they did not view the social and political movements as progress toward a better nation, but rather they considered it as anti-American, contrary to American ideals, and instigated by foreign influences or "outside agitators."

Some of those who reacted against the changes were known as "the silent majority," a term Richard Nixon, elected president in 1968, used to build a conservative voting base of support. They decried the campus unrest, the antiwar protests, and the challenges to authority; they protested the proliferation of pornography that appeared in movie houses and magazine racks across the nation; they rallied against U.S. Supreme Court decisions such as *Engel v. Vitale*, which ruled organized prayer in public schools as unconstitutional and declared the government had "taken God out of the classroom." They demanded a return to what they believed was normal American life, something that existed in the 1950s. Conservative columnists such as George Will championed such views, dismissing the movements in the 1960s as nothing more than drugs and thoughtless federal welfare policies, which create a culture of victimization.

Though the country was split between the conservatives who wished to return to the 1950s and the liberals who led the 1960s charge, both groups of people largely seemed unconcerned with foreign affairs. The two oceans that separate the United States from most of the world, the Atlantic and Pacific, gave many Americans a feeling of security. They believed these vast waters kept their enemies, real and imagined, from their shores, even though intercontinental ballistic missiles waiting in Soviet silos should have disabused them of such naive notions. These great oceanic barriers did not isolate them from attack, but it did allow them to isolate their thinking about the rest of the world. Unlike people in countries where close borders require some degree of identification and a more than superficial knowledge of your neighbors, many people in the United States felt little need to better understand what was going on in other countries.

With Americans questioning social and political values and the country's place as a great nation, by 1970, the nation began to turn into itself. Despite some initial backlash, the socially progressive values that began in the 1960s, such as increasing political awareness and political and economic liberty of women, continued to grow.

But by the end of the 1970s, America's confidence and the image it had of itself as a beneficent power and leader of freedom was shattered by events in Southeast Asia and the Middle East. The Vietnam and Yom Kippur Wars, the Lebanese civil war, the Iranian Revolution, and the Arab-Israeli conflicts,

> Rabbi Menachem Mandel:
>
> Intolerance lies at the core of evil. Not the intolerance that results from any threat or danger. But intolerance of another being who dares to exist. Intolerance without cause. It is so deep within us, because every human secretly desires the entire universe to himself. Our only way out is to learn compassion without cause. To care for each other simply because that "other" exists.[4]

in addition to an economic recession due to an oil crisis resulting from the oil embargoes of the Organization of Arab Petroleum Exporting Countries, all contributed to a sense of malaise. It certainly did not help that the U.S. people also saw their first president resign over the Watergate scandal.

The 1980s were an era of tremendous population growth around the world, with rates of natural increase close to or exceeding 4 percent annually in a number of African, Middle Eastern, and South Asian countries. In the United States, immigrants made up one-third of the population growth, marking the greatest change in population since the early part of the twentieth century. Nearly six million arrived, bringing the total number of foreign-born people to almost twenty million. The largest percentages of arrivals came from Mexico and Asia, with Eastern Europeans trailing behind.

This time period also saw great social, economic, and general change, as wealth and production migrated to newly industrializing economies. As economic liberalization increased in the developed world, multiple multinational corporations associated with the manufacturing industry relocated overseas. America was starting to look like a different place.

"International newcomers accelerated the extraordinary growth in the West," according to "Immigrant Tide Boosts Population," a December 1990 article in the *Washington Post*. "At the same time, newcomers from abroad replaced a rapidly departing native-born populace in a band of states stretching across the Midwest and Northeast, stemming or reversing what could have been devastating population losses."[5]

Meanwhile, developing countries across the world faced economic and social difficulties, as they suffered from multiple debt crises, requiring many of these countries to apply for financial assistance from the International Monetary Fund (IMF) and the World Bank. Partially because of this, many people from these countries tried to immigrate to America through both legal and illegal means.

During this time, legal immigrants did not concern Americans as much as illegal immigrants did. In an attempt to mitigate the problem of illegal immigration, the 1986 Immigration Reform and Control Act (IRCA) established a process for employers to verify an applicant's eligibility to work in the United States. But the new law did not stop fraudulent documentation or employers choosing to ignore the law for cheap labor. IRCA also created a pathway through which undocumented immigrants residing in the United States since January 1, 1982, or working in agriculture for ninety days in a one-year period beginning on May 1, 1985, could eventually obtain citizenship.

Though most Americans were chiefly concerned with undocumented immigrants, all immigrants in general were dimly viewed by Americans, some of whom criticized U.S. policies for contributing to a lower "quality" of immigrant, one who lacked skills and education and preferred welfare to work.

"More and more of America's unskilled workers are immigrants," wrote George J. Borjas, an economics professor, in a 1990 *Wall Street Journal* op-ed. "Immigrants accounted for just 12 percent of all high school dropouts (persons with less than a high school education) in the U.S. labor force in 1975. By 1985, the proportion of high school dropouts who were immigrants had almost tripled—to 32 percent."[6]

A national survey taken in 1986 by *CBS News* and the *New York Times* found only 8 percent of respondents supported an increase in immigrants, according to social historian Joel S. Fetzer, author of *Public Attitudes toward Immigration in the United States, France, and Germany*. "U.S. data suggests that Americans view immigrants in general with very lukewarm affection," Fetzer wrote. "The American mass public's view on immigration policy appears equally ambivalent, if not outright anti-immigration."[7]

Yet the general public was not the only one to strike up concerns with immigration. Although Reagan's administration was responsible for IRCA, which arguably granted amnesty for illegal immigrants, it "often framed unauthorized immigration as an issue of national security."[8] And clearly national security was one of President Reagan's main priorities, as he was responsible for establishing a military buildup during the 1980s to thwart the Soviet Union. This buildup consequently raised fears it could lead to nuclear war between the two superpowers. Late in the decade, though, changes occurred quickly that calmed concerns. Mikhail Gorbachev came to power in the Soviet Union. He ended economic aid to Soviet satellites; then he and Reagan agreed to remove all intermediate nuclear missiles from Europe. A year later, they signed a treaty to remove all medium- and short-range nuclear missiles.

The pace of historic change picked up speed in 1989, a year that became one of the most significant in modern history: Soviet troops withdrew from Afghanistan. Poland became independent, followed by Hungary. The Berlin Wall crumbled. And the communist governments in Czechoslovakia, Bulgaria, and Romania fell; some quietly, others, like Rumania, brutally. The Soviet empire was no more. It was a dizzying year, and Americans now had new hope and confidence for the future. Their optimism had been renewed. The national economy had boomed, and jobs appeared plentiful and well paying, although real wages were actually declining.

As fast and vast as the changes occurring were, many Americans were not ready to embrace them. Nostalgia for a past believed to have been simpler rippled throughout the country. This sentiment was only heightened by the rugged cowboy image President Reagan promoted of himself, his vision of a simpler America—one that was happy at home and distant from the rest of the world and its problems. Now, a conservative-embracing society found security in that vision.

In keeping with the image Reagan projected, Americans, in many respects, remained emotionally disengaged with the rest of the world. Despite rapid developments in computer technology, and in particular information technology—making the world smaller and faster, hyperdriving the pace of life, Americans did not often communicate or collaborate with people from other countries. Telecommunication had, as social scientist John Thompson noted, eliminated a sense of context. "The advent of telecommunication thus resulted in the uncoupling of space and time," Thompson wrote in *The Media and Modernity*. "It became possible to experience events as simultaneous despite the fact that they occurred in locales that were spatially remote."[9]

Although many Americans largely dismissed the rest of the world, their attitude did not stop foreigners from desiring to immigrate to the United States. The record-high immigration rates of the 1990s, of more than thirteen million people entering the country, was comprised of about half from Latin America and many from Asia. Yet the new influx was of former Soviet citizens. Immigrants also continued a trend that began in the 1970s of concentrating in six destination states: California, New York, Texas, Florida, New Jersey, and Illinois. By 2000, more than two-thirds of the country's foreign-born population lived in these states.

As a more diverse group of people immigrated, however, American demographics continued to change, which also consequently ushered in a change in attitude. Though white Europeans were still a majority in the country, they seemed to become a less dominate ethnic group, as American culture and media began to embrace different races and cultures. America was no longer a melting pot. It was a soup swirling with flavors that sought to complement each other.

If change went into hyperdrive in the 1980s, it went into light speed in the 1990s, as computers dominated the home and office; cell phones started to replace landlines in homes; and the Internet reduced the globe to the size of a monitor screen. Even though technology was helping to smash old notions about simplicity in life and relationships, there were many Americans who still resisted change. Some of them blamed foreigners and projected that blame onto immigrants, legal and illegal, for the loss of a job that was sent overseas by a company or a corporation seeking to cut labor costs and improve profit margins on their inability to get a job. According to *New York Times* journalist Thomas Friedman, thirty-five years ago, it was clearly better to be a "B" student in Bethesda than a genius in Bangalore, but that has now started to change. This change sparked even greater discontent for anyone living in America who could be identified as a "foreigner." A pamphlet "Facts Have Faces," issued in the mid-1990s by the National Council of Churches, stated, "A majority of this nation [is] of immigrant origin, yet a 1993 poll revealed that 60 percent of Americans believe immigration is bad for the country. What's happening? A troubled economy, the end of the Cold War and abiding racism contribute to a resurgence of anti-immigrant sentiment. This mentality is not new. Throughout our history, those already here feared new arrivals might threaten their jobs, security, and safety."[10]

The Gulf War drew Americans' attention to the people of the Middle East like no other event, including the Iranian hostage crisis, had before. Entering into the lexicon were terms such as *jihad*, as the media and political leaders focused on the region's culture and religion, in part to assuage fears and concerns about Muslims, a faith that few Americans ever considered or deeply understood.

Because of this, one group that left many Americans fearful or at least distrustful was immigrants of Middle Eastern origin. The ongoing dispute between Israel and its neighbors, as well as the Persian Gulf War, helped create an image of an enemy in the minds of many people who easily revert to tribalism in search of that security. That image was a Middle Eastern Muslim male. The 1993 car bombing of the World Trade Center, which killed six and injured more than one thousand people, reinforced that image because most of the perpetrators were from that region's countries.

Two years later, when a truck bomb destroyed the Alfred P. Murrah Federal Building in downtown Oklahoma City, Oklahoma, killing 168 people, including 19 children, and injuring 680, the first reaction was it was the work of Middle Eastern terrorists. In fact, Americans began to stigmatize, to persecute, and to scapegoat anyone who appeared to be Arab or Muslim, according to Edward T. Linenthal, author of *The Unfinished Bombing: Oklahoma City in American Memory*. As stated in the book,

> Many residents of Oklahoma City of Middle Eastern descent or African-American Muslims bore the brunt of the nation's initial rage at "Muslim

terrorists." KFOR television's coverage of the bombing informed viewers that a member of the Nation of Islam had taken credit for the bombing. They cautioned it might be a prank call, but repeated the "story" throughout the day's coverage, with one report noting that similarities with the World Trade Center bombing were "eerie."[11]

The TV station also mistakenly identified an Iraqi man who was a citizen of Oklahoma City as being one of the bombers, Linethal wrote. Yet despite being cleared by the FBI—and even when it became unequivocally clear the bombers were two white Americans—the man "was subject to public harassment and lost his job."

Despite the contributions of Arab Americans to academics, business, the arts, and famous Americans known for their Muslim faith—Muhammad Ali and Kareem Abdul-Jabbar, for example—many Americans held suspicious or negative views of Arab Americans. Many Americans remained stunned that two white U.S. Army veterans, one from Michigan and the other New York, had plotted and carried out what was, at the time, the worst terrorist attack on American soil.

As time went on, however, the bombings at the World Trade Center and Oklahoma City soon became a memory for many Americans, who were distracted by the country's prosperity. They turned their attention to stock portfolios and mutual funds and to buying bigger homes and bigger vehicles with gas prices low enough to make a sports utility vehicle an affordable luxury. Dot-com companies were starting up and making fortunes; serious-minded business writers were predicting the Dow would reach thirty-six thousand shortly. By decade's end, moneymaking fever seemed to grip the nation.

The turn of the century was just around the corner, and so were events that would challenge the American system of politics and government, would change Americans' views of their place in the world, and would, once again, bring fear and loathing of foreigners and immigrants. It seems that no matter the time period, there always remains at least one group of people (which changes depending on what is happening socially and politically) who becomes the target of prejudice and discrimination.

THE NEW ENEMY

After the September 11 terrorist attack, the same sentiment that lead to the internment of loyal Japanese Americans aimed its wrath at anyone dark-skinned and dark-haired, whether Muslim or Sikh, no matter if he or she was a citizen or was born in the United States.

> Fear often makes people intolerant or at least quick to judge, and at times to judge wrongly. Such was the misfortune of a Muslim dentist from Texas, Dr. Al Badr Al-Hazim, who was wrongly arrested as a terrorist shortly after the attacks of September 11, 2001, made front-page news.
>
> The *Philadelphia Daily News* ran his photo on the front page with this headline: "The Devil Among Us." Al-Hazim was later found to be completely innocent of the charges. Yet that failed to make the front pages.
>
> The attacks that day put America under great stress, largely because of a lack of understanding about the geopolitical state of the Middle East and American policy regarding that region. Islam became a scapegoat by an uninformed society that viewed the religion—not the individuals responsible for the attacks—as extreme and violent. Yet despite instances such as Dr. Al-Hazim, a Saudi native, who was detained for two weeks before the FBI released him, Americans generally viewed most Middle Easterners with tolerance.
>
> Al-Hazim believed this as he waited in his cell, reading the Quran. As he told a newspaper reporter afterward, he turned to Allah for guidance in that dark time. "He wants me to be patient, and he wants me to forgive," he recalled. "I will be patient, and I will forgive."

Particularly targeted were those who wore the customary clothes of their culture or, heaven forbid, had a beard. The anger and suspicion toward Middle Easterners that exploded after 9/11 began brewing in the 1970s with the Arab states' oil embargo in 1973 to 1974, which impacted not only the American economy but also Americans' driving habits. This sentiment continued through the first attack by a Muslim extremist on New York City's World Trade Center in 1993.

In the aftermath of 9/11 and the accompanying economic upheavals, anti-immigrant sentiment flared not only against Muslims in general (and Americans of Middle Eastern heritage) but also against illegal aliens, in particular Mexicans. The anti-immigrant lobby grew potent enough that it was able to secure political and financial support for a wall now being erected along the border between Mexico and the United States.

Despite the obstacles and challenges immigrants of all creeds, colors, and race have faced over the centuries, they have more often than not managed to overcome and to often find opportunity in their new country; many have successfully assimilated, becoming leaders in government and captains of industry, helping to create even greater economic and political opportunities for all Americans. Americans are now less and less identified by a single race or religion and more identified as a nation of grand diversity; an element that has proven to be its strength, not its weakness. It's doubtful this nation of immigrants would acquiesce to a wall replacing its Golden Door.

The lesson that history teaches us is that, while it is important to acknowledge prejudice and redress where necessary, successful integration for an immigrant requires that he or she persevere in spite of it—something immigrants have managed to do amazingly well.

I like to think of my own story and how, despite the additional barriers placed along the way because of my heritage, I "got over it." Many of the issues I encountered ended up coming to a legal head, starting with a professor I was completing a research project for while I was a student at Harvard. When his project failed to get published, and he learned that I was also working on another project that had gotten positive notice, he launched an internal investigation. I was eventually exonerated of any wrongdoing, but I was completely unprepared for the manner in which conflict was dealt with in a legal arena in the United States, and so I had seen no need for legal representation.

My case is not unique. Most immigrants, especially those who have recently come to America, rarely revert to lawsuits. Oversees, lawsuits are not nearly as frequent. As evidence, consider the fact that though the United States' population only accounts for 5 percent of the world's population, it has 50 percent of the world's lawyers.[12] Additionally, 25 percent of people who are incarcerated reside in U.S. prisons. Thus, because immigrants are largely unused to the widespread prevalence of lawyers, they do not think to hire one. Moreover, when confronted with a potential legal battle, many immigrants feel they will lose anyway, so they choose not to engage when possible. Clearly, the United States' legal system may not be as supportive for immigrants as it is for native borns. This is particularly the case for undocumented immigrants, who are unprotected by legal services. As Grace Meng, a researcher for the U.S. program at Human Rights Watch, wrote, "Undocumented immigrants have long been afraid of government officials, but that fear is now translating into a fear of the justice system. Immigrants avoid going to court in communities from Fresno to Rochester, even to pay traffic tickets or to help a family member with translation, because Immigration and Customs Enforcement agents like to hang out by the courthouse."[13]

Decades later, when the U.S. government decided to downgrade Intrados' status and reduce an already awarded contract, my reaction this time was to respond legally. However, after years of fighting its decision, I decided to walk away from this David-and-Goliath legal battle and settle the case. Frequently, U.S.-government-initiated lawsuits seem more like legalized extortion, even to U.S. companies and individuals, so you can imagine how immigrants feel about court dealings against government agencies.

But this wasn't the last of my experiences with U.S. litigious society. As a board member of Nason Medical, I had to undergo yet another investigation, this time by Medicare. While the claim was that we had improperly filled out forms, we had followed the instructions given to us by Medicare's local office. But these instructions turned out to be incorrect, and this ultimately had no bearing on the outcome. Thus, we had to spend over a million dollars in legal fees and pay a penalty fine, which was much smaller than the legal expenses and all the costs associated with the documents the government subpoenaed.

What's even more incredible about government health services is that if you underbill, you lose the chance to recuperate your mistake. But if your error is in overbilling—even if it is just a quarter of a percent of invoices (a rate applauded by any other industry)—you are dragged through the mud with highly intrusive audits that cost a fortune. You cannot even obtain credit for any underbilling, which may often be greater in total amount than the overbilling. No wonder our medical system is such a mess! It is this kind of behavior that frightens doctors and providers of health services. Many immigrants feel they will be treated in a similar vein by our justice system and by the courts. Immigrants are thus reluctant to go to court and often even have to learn that going to court is an option. Native borns, on the other hand, do not hesitate to hire a lawyer and go to court.

I wish I hadn't had to, but I once again gathered myself up and got over it.

RACIAL PROFILING

Efforts by U.S. law enforcement officials meant to curtail illegal immigration have one significantly adverse effect: racial profiling. Many immigrants living in the United States, both legally and illegally, have become victims of racial profiling by law enforcement officials. Essentially, the criteria used by most law enforcement officials is the question: "Does he/she *look* illegal?"

A 2012 survey by the Southern Poverty Law Center found that 47 percent of respondents knew someone who was treated unfairly by the police as the result of an effort to enforce immigration laws.[14] The most common complaint was that Latinos were pulled over for minor traffic offenses—or no offense at all. This number increased to 55 percent in Alabama and 60 percent in Georgia.

In a recent study by the Pew Hispanic Center, nearly one in ten Hispanic adults (8 percent of native-born U.S. citizens and 10 percent of immigrants) reported that in the past year they had been pulled over by police or other authorities with questions about immigration status.[15] Additionally, police checkpoints in predominantly Latino neighborhoods are frequent. Data provided by the city of Albertville, Alabama, showed that 73 percent of the vehicles seized and impounded from roadblocks were owned by drivers with Latino surnames. Census data for the small city in north Alabama show that Latinos make up only 16 percent of its population. Because many southern places charge hefty fines for driving illegally, these checkpoints can be a profitable revenue source for local governments. Fines can vary from hundreds to thousands of dollars, and many states can inflict jail time, as well. Some local laws permit police to seize a driver's vehicle and to fine the owner for the number of days it is in their possession. Also, a number of jurisdictions use minor traffic offenses as an excuse to bring immigrants into deportation proceedings.

According to the ACLU, Hispanics are "more than three times as likely to be searched during a traffic stop," demonstrating an obvious racial disparity.[16] The ACLU argues that it is important to note that in previous reports Hispanic drivers were less likely to actually be harboring contraband. In more recent reports, the Justice Department has not included a racial breakdown in these numbers.

In April 2012, the Arizona legislature passed SB 1070, which was considered one of the strictest anti-illegal immigration laws in history. This law was mostly known for measures that increased the occurrence of racial profiling. Under this law, if police have "reasonable suspicion" about a person's immigration status, they are afforded the opportunity to verify it.[17] In other words, anyone who looks like an immigrant must show documentation of immigration.

Not only have Hispanics been the target of racial profiling but also they are increasingly subjected to bias-motivated crimes. Particularly in the Southwest, where anti-immigrant sentiments have historically been quite prominent, Latinos have been targeted as the source of social and economic issues. In some instances, often because they were perceived as criminals, Latinos have even faced harassment and deportation.[18] Many Americans assume that most Latino or Hispanic immigrants are more than likely illegal. "An Associated Press poll from 2010 found that 61 percent of people said that Hispanics face significant discrimination."[19] Seven out of ten immigrant Latinos indicated that discrimination is a significant barrier that keeps Latinos from succeeding in the United States, while less than half (49 percent) of their native-born counterparts indicated this feeling.

Racial profiling and discrimination, however, are not problems only experienced by Hispanic immigrants. Following the terrorist attacks of September 11, 2001, people of Arab descent experienced an unprecedented level of racial profiling, with law enforcement officials citing "national security" as the compelling interest that allows for such racial profiling. For example, one program, Operation Front Line, "allows federal law enforcement authorities to target immigrants and foreign nationals for investigation in order to detect, deter, and disrupt terrorist operations."[20] In 2003 President Bush, through an executive order, issued rules forbidding federal agents from using race or ethnicity in their habitual investigations.[21] The order, however, was mainly a public relations statement, as thousands of exemptions could be imposed.

According to "Muslims Report Rising Discrimination at Work," an article published in the *New York Times*, "although Muslims make up less than 2 percent of the United States population, they accounted for about one-quarter of the 3,386 religious discrimination claims filed with the Equal Employment Opportunity Commission last year."[22] Additionally, Arab immigrants are frequently accused of crimes with which they have no affiliation. The hate crimes following September 11, which included murder and beatings, were directed at Arabs solely because they shared or were perceived as sharing the national background of the hijackers culpable for assailing the World Trade Center and the Pentagon.

Antiterrorism policies of airline passenger profiling, in particular, have disproportionately affected Arabs and Muslims. As stated in an article from *PBS*, "Some have been taken off planes or not allowed to board because of their ethnicity. Anti-terrorist programs and policies that single out people of Arab descent have also contributed to creating negative bias in the public eye, not to mention fear of the police and hesitation to report hate crimes among Arab Americans."[23] On numerous occasions, I have been searched "randomly" going through security on an airplane trip. Though this may seem absurd and unfair, the immigrant learns to tolerate and understand it. The point still remains—you should get over it.

NOTES

1. "Gathering and Interactions of Peoples, Cultures, and Ideas: A Brief Timeline of U.S. Policy on Immigration and Naturalization," *The Flow of History*, http://www.flowofhistory.org/themes/movement_settlement/uspolicytimeline.php (accessed July 10, 2013).

2. Jennifer Ludden, "1965 Immigration Law Changed Face of America," *National Public Radio*, May 9, 2006, http://www.npr.org/templates/story/story.php?storyId=5391395 (accessed August 27, 2013).

3. Ludden, "1965 Immigration Law Changed Face of America."

4. "Intolerence: Based on Letters and Talks of the Rebbe, Rabbi M. M. Schneerson," *Chabad.org*, http://www.chabad.org/library/article_cdo/aid/150549/jewish/Intolerance.htm (accessed October 29, 2013).

5. Barbara Vobedja, "Immigrant Tide Boosts Population: Decides Gainers, Losers among States, Regions," *Washington Post*, December 31, 1990, http://news

.google.com/newspapers?nid=1310&dat=19901231&id=u0JWAAAAIBAJ&sjid=i-oDAAAAIBAJ&pg=4916,8134841 (accessed October 29, 2013).

6. George Borjas, "Immigrants—Not What They Used to Be," *Wall Street Journal*, November 8, 1990, http://www.hks.harvard.edu/fs/gborjas/publications/popular/WSJ110890.htm (accessed October 29, 2013).

7. Joel S. Fetzer, *Public Attitudes toward Immigration in the United States, France, and Germany* (Cambridge, UK: Cambridge University Press, 2000).

8. Joseph Nevins, "Ronald Reagan and Comprehensive Immigration Reform," *North American Congress on Latin America*, November 15, 2012, http://nacla.org/blog/2012/11/15/ronald-reagan-and-comprehensive-immigration-reform (accessed July 10, 2013).

9. John Thompson, *The Media and Modernity: A Social Theory of the Media* (Stanford, CA: Stanford University Press, 1995).

10. "The City (La Ciudad)—Teachers Guide," *PBS.org*, http://www.pbs.org/itvs/thecity/resources1_8_print.html (accessed October 29, 2013).

11. Edward T. Linenthal, *The Unfinished Bombing: Oklahoma City in American Memory* (New York: Oxford University Press, 2003).

12. Conrad Black, "Conrad Black, 'Flight of the Eagle,'" *Book TV.org*, http://www.booktv.org/Watch/14688/Book+TV+Interview+Conrad+Black+Flight+of+the+Eagle.aspx (accessed July 10, 2013).

13. "Rebuilding Local Economies," *Immigration Policy Center*, http://www.immigrationpolicy.org/just-facts/rebuilding-local-economies (accessed August 18, 2013).

14. "Under Siege: Life for Low-Income Latinos in the South," *Southern Poverty Law Center*, April 2009, http://www.splcenter.org/get-informed/publications/under-siege-life-for-low-income-latinos-in-the-south (accessed July 9, 2013).

15. "Under Siege: Life for Low-Income Latinos in the South."

16. "Department of Justice Statistics Show Clear Pattern of Racial Profiling," *American Civil Liberties Union*, April 29, 2007, http://www.aclu.org/racial-justice/department-justice-statistics-show-clear-pattern-racial-profiling (accessed July 9, 2013).

17. Tim Cohen and Bill Mears, "Supreme Court Mostly Rejects Arizona Immigration Law; Gov Says 'Heart' Remains," *CNN Politics*, June 26, 2012, http://www.cnn.com/2012/06/25/politics/scotus-arizona-law (accessed July 7, 2013).

18. Ricardo A. López, "We Must Stop the Negative Immigratio Rage!" *Latino Opinion*, http://www.latinoopinion.com/category/prejudice-and-discrimination/ (accessed July 15, 2013).

19. Alan Fram, "Poll Finds Discrimination against Hispanics Is High," *Seattle Times*, May 20, 2010, http://seattletimes.com/html/nationworld/2011916375_biaspoll21.html (accessed July 15, 2013).

20. "End Racial Profiling," *The Leadership Conference on Civil and Human Rights*, *civilrightsdoc.info*, www.civilrightsdocs.info/pdf/discrimination/racial-profiling-and-counterterrorism-w-banner-final-4-15-12.pdf (accessed July 8, 2013).

21. Eric Lichtblau, "Bush Issues Federal Ban on Racial Profiling," *New York Times*, June 17, 2003, http://www.nytimes.com/2003/06/17/politics/17CND-PROF.html (accessed July 9, 2013).

22. Steven Greenhouse, "Muslims Report Rising Discrimination at Work," *New York Times*, September 23, 2010, http://www.nytimes.com/2010/09/24/business/24muslim.html?pagewanted=all (accessed October 29, 2013).

23. "Caught in the Crossfire: Arab Americans," PBS: Public Broadcasting Service, http://www.pbs.org/itvs/caughtinthecrossfire/arab_americans.html (accessed August 23, 2013).

16

Sticking to Your Own May Work, But It's Not Easy

With the nation's first law to restrict free immigration enacted in 1882, due in part to a post–Civil War economic decline, the Chinese, hemmed in by legality and intolerance, gathered in urban areas and created "Chinatowns." Here they did business with one another, forming communities that allowed the Chinese to prosper. Chinatowns sprang up in cities across the country, from New York to San Francisco, linked by a continental network.

"A Chinatown served as a safe haven and second home for Chinese immigrants," according to Library of Congress history. "It also was a good place to do business: The shops and factories in a Chinatown were almost exclusively Chinese-owned, and would hire Chinese workers when many non-Chinese businesses would not."

The Chinese weren't the first to create such towns. Early European immigrants to this country, the Germans, Irish, and Italians, also faced discrimination. They initially huddled in vast neighborhoods in cities that in some instances were ghettolike. These groups rose up the economic and class ladders only because within those neighborhoods, they formed their own societies with vibrant economies and a strong, hardworking business class. These neighborhoods have largely dissipated over the last century because these groups have assimilated into the mainstream due to the creation of suburban communities and internal U.S. migration.

As these European communities dissipated, other communities rose, and we can still see ethnic community protection today. We see this behavior in places such as Los Angeles, which has the largest population of Persians outside of Iran, with some eight hundred thousand first- and second-generation immigrants, and has garnered the moniker of "Tehrangeles." In addition, Los Angeles has the largest Korean American population in the country and

> Herman and Bettina Linder of Vienna Austria arrived in Providence, Rhode Island in 1939, having fled at Herman's father's insistence.
> Upon arrival in the United States, they went to relatives, who provided them some money and then—in what was a network of relatives in the new country—sent them to an uncle in New York, who offered further assistance for a good start in the United States.
> The couple settled in Philadelphia. Herman took a job in a clothing factory, which was a step down from running his father's Vienna liquor store and haberdashery that he would have eventually inherited. Bettina went on to work in a high-end woman's dress shop.

is home to a large Koreatown, which began developing in the early 1970s. By the early 1990s, the Los Angeles Koreatown covered an estimated five-hundred-block area. The entrepreneurial spirit of Koreans and their hope of achieving the American Dream fueled the growth of Koreatown.

> Korean immigrants have been successful as entrepreneurs and small business owners in the United States thanks to a centuries-old underground money-lending system known as *kye*. Kye (pronounced "keh") allows individuals within the Korean community to borrow money, regardless of their ability to access traditional bank loans. In kye, people join together and contribute money, usually ranging from $200 to $500 a month, into a communal pot, with the total money being dispersed to those who need it most on a rotating basis; the monthly kitty can reach several thousand dollars. Kye allows Koreans to access startup capital quickly and is considered by many to be at the heart of Koreans' entrepreneurial success in the United States. Trust and social pressure are two of the backbones of kye, as there are no official documents that members sign to engage in the program. Usually members are familiar with one another, either from church or other means, fostering honesty and security in the lending system.

Unlike at the turn of the century, though, the invisible walls of these neighborhoods keeping immigrants in and Americans out have largely disappeared. The process of throwing off legal segregation in the United States lasted through much of the 1950s, 1960s, and 1970s, when civil rights demonstrations resulted in public opinion turning against enforced segregation. Regardless, de facto segregation persists in varying degrees today. The contemporary racial segregation seen in America in residential neighborhoods has been shaped by public policies, mortgage discrimination, and redlining, among other things.

Rejecting the movement toward integration of the 1960s, black power activist Malcolm X considered himself a black man of African decent, who had the misfortune of being an American citizen. As he once declared: "Being born here in America doesn't make you an American."

Malcolm X didn't realize he had embraced something that was at that time possible only in America: the reinvention of one's life story. Caste and class rules in the rest of the world keep people in their places. But America has singularly allowed many the opportunity to recast themselves on their own terms, reframe their successes and failures, and have second, or even third, acts.

My own career trajectory goes from working with a fellow Iranian in Boston, Massachusetts, renovating and managing properties, to starting The Computer Emporium with an Egyptian, Canadian, and an American, to now sitting on the Board of Directors of Westfield Insurance in Ohio and Nason Medical Centers in South Carolina and becoming accepted by the "good old boy network."

As many immigrants have proven, it is possible to remain in your ethnic enclave and carve out a small place for yourself. However, this is not the picture that the American Dream outlines. The more difficult path is the one the vast majority strives for—that of successful assimilation. You cannot do this unless you eventually venture out of the small, safe haven that the immigrant community provides. To become American, you must assimilate.

17

Assimilation Is Critical

When people think of the culturally diverse United States, the idea of a melting pot has historically come to mind. After all, it is a nation born of immigrants and founded on notions of equality and freedom for every person. Recently, however, people have begun to question this analogy, endeavoring to establish a new association: the salad bowl. Some argue that the United States is no longer made up of a number of cultures blended together to create one unique culture, and it is instead made up of a number of distinct cultures unified purely by laws and government. And with the debate over immigration reform already underway, whether immigrants actually assimilate has been a major point of contention.

Many conservatives argue that the new wave of immigrants makes little to no effort to become a part of American culture, favoring instead their own heritage and cultural roots. Others, though, assert that today's immigrants are just as integrated as in prior years. These people point to studies that show second-generation immigrants tend to supersede their parents socioeconomically, continue to remain enthusiastic about the United States' potential success, and identify as being American by the third generation.

Yet how does one really determine how integrated an immigrant is into American culture? The concept of assimilation is complicated and multidimensional, as it is inherently wrapped up in "questions of identity, belonging, and the very essence of being American," as explained by an article published by the *Christian Science Monitor*.[1] Moreover, because assimilation must be measured over a period of time, it is difficult to assess the degree to which the new wave of immigrants have assimilated—which is precisely the group of people that would be most affected by a conceivable immigration reform.

Those are not the only barriers people face, however, when attempting to determine whether immigrants have assimilated into the United States. Conditions of immigrants' integration may not be the same today as they were in the nineteenth and early twentieth century, as questions of the effects of race and discrimination have been brought to the forefront. When Congress passed the Nationality Act of 1965, it opened the doors to a wave of new immigrants, including Africans, Latin Americans, and Asians, who had previously been denied access by an immigration quota system that favored northern Europeans.[2] Because of this, the immigrant population—which hovers around forty million, according to the 2010 U.S. Census—is incredibly diverse.[3] This inherently makes determining the rate of assimilation even more challenging. As explained by the Migration Information Source,

> One of the most difficult tasks in gauging group differences in the completeness of assimilation involves figuring out how much race and ethnicity—rather than other factors—affect economic mobility. Immigrants who become "racialized" and are treated as disadvantaged racial or ethnic minorities may find their pathways to economic mobility and assimilation blocked because of racial/ethnic discrimination.[4]

Though early Irish and Italian immigrants were initially discriminated against as inferior races, they were eventually seen as white by the sheer fact that their skin color was not black. Academics, however, are still debating whether Latin Americans and Asian Americans, who make up the majority of the new wave of immigrants, will be considered "white." More specifically, as reported by the *Christian Science Monitor*, "Today, census data show, 12 million immigrants come from Mexico and 10 million hail from South and East Asia. Almost 4 million come from the Caribbean, while 14.5 million come from Central America, South America, the Middle East, and elsewhere."[5] As such, many are currently unsure of the impact discrimination has on new immigrants' ability to assimilate.

Despite these difficulties, studies have been conducted to ascertain the degree to which immigrants have assimilated. With the help of the Manhattan Institute of Policy Research, Jacob Vigdor, a public policy professor at Duke University, used Census data beginning in 1900 to track the assimilation progress of immigrants. Through creating an index that calculated the statistical difference between native-born Americans and immigrants, Vigdor was able to measure assimilation in three categories: civil, cultural, and economic. According to his findings, Latin Americans have the most difficult time assimilating, especially civically and economically. On a whole, however, people who came to the United States are more integrated than those who ended up in European countries, but less so than those in Canada. Other studies have reportedly found that some Latin Americans have experienced assimilation difficulties. As told by a *New York Times* article, "A 2002 study [by the Public Policy Institute of California], for instance, reported that despite 'improvements in human capital and earnings' for second-generation Mexican immigrants, the third generation still 'trails the education and earnings of the average American,' and shows little sign of catching up."[6] This potentially could be the result of the economic status of many Mexicans while immigrating. Because many come from poverty, they often settle in communities plagued by insufficient schools and limited job growth, thereby inhibiting their ability for upward mobility.

Other studies, such as the ones recently completed by the Pew Research Center, have found that second-generation Hispanics, along with Asian American second-generation immigrants, are generally more integrated than their parents. As reported by the *Christian Science Monitor*, both groups outperform their parents economically, have friends and family of different ethnicities, and are "twice as likely to say they consider themselves to be a 'typical American.'"[7] Additionally, more so than the general public, they value hard work, strive for career success, and are optimistic about the future of the United States. About 90 percent of second-generation Hispanics and Asian Americans also say they have the ability to speak English at least "well."

Not all studies, however, have reported positive results overall. For example, results from a recent Hudson Institute study, which used data from a Harris Interactive survey, "led the researchers to conclude that 'America's patriotic assimilation system is broken.'"[8] Whereas 81 percent of native-born citizens believe schools should focus on American citizenship rather than on ethnic pride, only 50 percent of foreign-born citizens support this. The study also found that 85 percent of native-born citizens consider themselves to be American citizens over "citizens of the world," compared with 54 percent of the foreign-born population. In an age of increased globalization, however, viewing oneself as a citizen of the world may potentially be beneficial. Though some argue it decreases one's likelihood of holding allegiance to a particular nation, thinking globally does not necessarily equate to abandonment of patriotism. Rather, it recognizes that there has been a shift in how different countries increasingly interact with one another. This gives people who view themselves as global citizens an advantage because they recognize their ability to perform in the global market and to be export oriented, allowing for the possibility of future job growth as well. As explained in an article on *Inside Higher Ed*, "On a practical level, global citizenship provides a concept that can create bridges between the work of internationalization and multicultural education. Although these efforts have different histories and trajectories, they also share important goals of cultural empathy and intercultural competence."[9] Yet in the Hudson Institute study, there was also a difference in twenty-three percentage points in the belief that English comprehension is "very important for the future of the American political system."[10] Based on these findings, among other reported statistics, researchers determined that an extensive "patriotic gap" exists in America between the native-born and foreign-born populations.

These results have led people to question whether the United States is doing enough to help immigrants integrate into their new communities. A *New York Times* article published in 2012 reported, "This year, the Department of Homeland Security plans to spend a measly $18 million—far less than a tenth of 1 percent of its budget—on helping immigrants assimilate. Meanwhile, states with large immigrant populations are cutting the budgets of community and state colleges, precisely where immigrant students predominantly enroll."[11] Not only do immigrants often feel a lack of support from the government, but they also face issues from the general public.

> "Nativists take the position that they don't want any immigrants at all—they want to build fences," [Alejandro] Portes [who developed the theory of "segmented assimilation" in the 1990s] says. "The other position is to turn [immigrants] into Americans as quickly as possible—this is forced assimilation. . . . The problem is that the first generation cannot be turned into Americans instantly. And the attempt to do so is often counterproductive. It creates fear and alienation, it denigrates the culture and language of immigrants themselves, and it denigrates it to their kids."[12]

This in turn can lead to the potential for "downward assimilation," which is when immigrants find solace in gang culture. Though one may think those who immigrate to the United States as refugees receive an abundance of aid, in fact, it, too, is rather limited. According to the *Christian Science Monitor*, refugees receive "about seven months of cash assistance and help in connecting to a job, housing, and most of the public benefits available to US citizens." Yet these people, especially the children, are often already troubled and need the most help in finding footing in a completely new cultural arena.

Because of the limited resources provided, some people have argued for an immigration reform effort that focuses more attention on assimilation processes. As research shows, having immigration integration policies in place can yield beneficial results. "For example, research by Richard Florida and Charlotta Mellander found that nations which focus more on immigrant integration have higher levels of economic competitiveness, are more innovative, and have higher rates of entrepreneurship."[13] Recently, the Migrant Integration Policy Index measured the United States against thirty other countries on its immigration and integration policies. Overall, the United States ranked ninth, scoring 62 out of the possible 100 points. The study reported, "This overall ranking is good, especially when the lack of national integration policy is taken into account. Unpacking the meaning of this score, however, demonstrates that the United States can and should think much more carefully about how we welcome and encourage new immigrants."[14] According to *Politico*, a political news source, many conservatives would like to see an assimilation policy that supports "patriotic principles instead of programs related to workforce training, and access to health care, legal help and youth education, which they argue sound more like entitlements."[15] Nonetheless, currently, no official policy is intact to help all immigrants assimilate into the United States.

WHEN ASSIMILATION DOESN'T OCCUR

As argued previously, proper assimilation, though difficult to measure, is crucial for an immigrant's success. History has even shown us that, when people fail to assimilate, it is not only a detriment to themselves but also to society at large. Both the Boston Marathon bombings and the 1992 Los Angeles riots perfectly illustrate this claim.

Marked as the worst terrorist attack since 9/11, the Boston Marathon bombings occurred on April 15, 2013. Two pressure-cooker bombs exploded near the finish of the marathon on Boylston Street in downtown Boston. Three people lost their lives, and two hundred eighty more were injured because of the bombs. Following the attack, the two suspects, the Tsarnaev brothers, fled the scene, and a citywide manhunt ensued. The elder brother, Tamerlan Tsarnaev, twenty-six, was killed by police gunshots, and the younger brother, Dzhokhar Tsarnaev, nineteen, was later caught hiding in a boat in Watertown. Dzhokhar has since been taken into custody, treated in the hospital, and recently pleaded not guilty—though he previously admitted to federal agents that he played a role in the bombings. He also cited U.S. military involvement in Afghanistan and Iraq as being the motivation for the attack, which came days after an attack in Afghanistan for which the Afghan government blames the CIA. Though a conclusion has not been reached, other possible motivations include: opposition to the American drone strikes in Pakistan, opposition to the Kyrgyz government's cooperation with the Americans, and opposition to the Russian government's cooperation with the Americans.[16] According to an article published in the *New York Times*, "The portrait investigators have begun to piece together of the two brothers suspected of the Boston Marathon bombings suggests that they were motivated by extremist Islamic beliefs but were not acting with known terrorist groups—and that they may have learned to build bombs simply by logging onto the online English-language magazine of the affiliate of Al Qaeda in Yemen."[17]

Both brothers legally immigrated to the United States when they were young. The eldest, Tamerlan, came with his two sisters a year after his parents and younger brother, Dzhokhar, immigrated to the United States in 2002. Before the children were born, the parents left dangerous Chechnya, a small region in Russia historically stricken by Islamic uprisings fueled by separatist wars. The family first arrived in Kyrgyzstan, where Tamerlan was born in 1986. In 1993, Dzhokhar was born. The family eventually left Kyrgyzstan for the mainly Muslim region of Dagestan in Russia. Less than a year later, in 1994, the parents and Dzhokhar made it to the United States as refugees, fleeing political persecution. A year later, at the age of sixteen, Tamerlan joined his family in Massachusetts. The family did not arrive to the United States equipped with knowledge of the English language, but by the time Dzhokhar enrolled at Cambridge Rindge and Latin School in 2007, he barely even retained his accent.[18] He seemed to seamlessly integrate into the school's culture, both academically and athletically. As a novice, he joined the school's wrestling team, quickly gaining ranks within the team and being elected captain. Upon his graduation in 2011, he won an academic scholarship for college. Accounts from his classmates, teachers, and coaches reveal that Dzhokhar was quite popular, yet despite having numerous friends, no one really knew about his personal life. No members of his family ever showed up to any of his matches, and when he was asked about his past, he deflected questioning by simply stating he was Chechen and had lived in Russia.[19]

Like his younger brother, Tamerlan appeared to initially assimilate into the United States well. Shortly after arriving, he registered with USA Boxing, the organization that runs amateur boxing in the United States. After winning a fight in a local boxing tournament, Tamerlan reportedly told the *Lowell Sun* newspaper in Massachusetts that he liked the United States because it offered more job opportunities than Russia did.[20] In 2008, Tamerlan apparently became incredibly involved in religion under the possible influence of a family friend, a change that caused some friction in the household. According to a *New York Times* article, Dzhokhar was "irritated" by his brother's newfound devotion; nonetheless, he still looked up to him as his older, wiser brother, especially when their father returned to Russia. A year later, a photograph of Tamerlan training appeared for a university magazine story; the caption, a quote from Tamerlan, read: "I don't have one American friend. I don't understand them."[21] According to Cambridge police department records, that same year, he was also arrested for allegedly assaulting his girlfriend. In the years following, he married Katherine Russell and cared for their toddler, while Katherine worked as a home health aid. Starting in 2011, their mother, Zubeidat, also became more devout, and Tamerlan began to pray five times a day. Both were reportedly influenced by a family friend named "Misha" to become more religious.[22] According to an article published on *Huffington Post*, a client of Zubeidat reported that during one of her services, Zubeidat began quoting a conspiracy theory, which she said her son also believed, that 9/11 was staged by the U.S. government as a way to convince people to hate Muslims.[23]

Tamerlan's history became even more concerning when in early 2011, Russia asked the FBI to look into Tamerlan's activities. As reported by *CNN*, "'The request stated that it was based on information that he was a follower of radical Islam and a strong believer, and that he has changed drastically since 2010 as he prepared to leave the United States for travel to the country's region to join unspecified underground groups,' the FBI said in a statement."[24] But by the summer of 2011, the FBI had concluded that no terrorism activity could be found, so in 2012, Tamerlan left for Russia. It is unclear what Tamerlan did while in Russia, though some have speculated he used the time to be instructed by Chechen rebels. Six months later, Tamerlan returned to the United States, but it remains uncertain whether he made other trips to Russia. Soon after his arrival back in the States, Tamerlan created a YouTube channel featuring videos with footage of the Imarat Kavkaz group, "the most potent militant Islamist group in the north Caucasus, which includes Chechnya and Dagestan," according to CNN.[25] Another video showcases jihadist leader Abu Dujana, who had ties to Imarat Kavkaz and was killed by Russian security services. Tamerlan also submitted an application for U.S. citizenship on September 5, 2012, prompting further investigation by federal law enforcement agencies in 2013. The Islamic Society of Boston reported that during the same time frame, Tamerlan vocally disrupted a preacher's sermons twice, challenging the preacher's convictions. After the second interruption, leaders of the mosque told Tamerlan he was not allowed to attend if he continued to interject during sermons. Tamerlan chose to remain quiet.

Meanwhile, Tamerlan's brother, Dzhokhar, graduated from the Cambridge Rindge and Latin School and began college at the University of Massachusetts in 2011. During his freshman year, he started a Twitter account, tweeting statements that "sometimes revealed a young man more troubled and blunt-spoken than he seemed in person," according to an article published in the *New York Times*.[26] Though on September 11, 2012, he was granted American citizenship and appeared happy about it, "the previous March, he had written 'a decade in america already, I want out,' followed in April by 'how I miss my homeland #dagestan #chechnya.'"[27] Although Dzhokhar did not appear to be as outwardly devout as his brother, *CBC News* did find a social networking site page where he lists Islam as his worldview and has several videos about Islam.[28] Thus, despite an outward appearance of being able to fit into

American society, Dzhokhar seemed to harbor feelings of anger and isolation. According to Jean-François Ratelle, who studies Chechen radicalism and lived in the Republic of Dagestan to conduct research, "the brothers seemed to be not well integrated into American society, especially Tamerlan. Often, he said, young people turn to radical Islam to find answers or a society and peer network that accepts them."[29]

But the Boston Marathon bombings are not representative of the first time in U.S. history when immigrants have struggled to assimilate into American culture. Edward Chang, a professor of Asian American studies at the University of California, Riverside, immigrated to Los Angeles, California, in 1974. Settling in Koreatown, he came with his family in hope of obtaining the American Dream. He was there to witness the 1992 riots that ensued, following the release of the four Los Angeles Police Department officers who beat Rodney King. Yet that was not the only event that could have fueled the riots. On March 16, 1991, a fifteen-year-old girl named Latasha Harlins was shot and killed by Soon Ja Du, who accused Harlins of attempting to steal a bottle of orange juice from her store. Though Du was convicted of voluntary manslaughter, she was able to walk away with probation after posting a $250,000 bail.[30] As Angela Oh, the spokesperson for the Korean community during the riots, told National Public Radio, "The visual was a woman walking out of court having just completed a case in which a teenager has been shot and killed, right? So the ire was really intense at that moment. . . . My belief is that that was the spark."[31] During the riots, fires destroyed a significant portion of Los Angeles; however, Koreatown was hit hard as a result of poor black-Korean relations. Many Koreans were killed, and their businesses and homes were diminished to nothing. Chang said the riots marked a turning point for many Koreans, who realized the inherent problems in having isolated themselves. In fact, he told NPR, "Prior to 1992, Korean immigrants considered themselves Korean. . . . But after 1992, they began to call themselves Korean-Americans."[32] As a result, many Koreans became more active members of the community, attempting to lessen discrimination and embrace multiculturalism. Businessman Chris Lee also said, "I think we are much more accepting, which I think is a first step toward becoming assimilated into this country."[33] Clearly, what happened in Koreatown is another example of how vital proper assimilation is.

NOTES

1. Stephanie Hanes, "Immigration: Assimilation and the Measure of an American," *Christian Science Monitor*, July 7, 2013, http://www.csmonitor.com/USA/

Society/2013/0707/Immigration-Assimilation-and-the-measure-of-an-American (accessed July 24, 2013).
    2. Hanes, "Immigration: Assimilation and the Measure of an American."
    3. Hanes, "Immigration: Assimilation and the Measure of an American."
    4. Susan K. Brown and Frank D. Bean, "Assimilation Models, Old and New: Explaining a Long-Term Process," Migration Information Source, October 2006, http://www.migrationinformation.org/feature/display.cfm?id=442 (accessed July 24, 2013).
    5. Hanes, "Immigration: Assimilation and the Measure of an American."
    6. Ross Douthat, "When Assimilation Stalls," *New York Times*, April 27, 2013, http://www.nytimes.com/2013/04/28/opinion/sunday/douthat-when-the-assimilation-of-immigrants-stalls.html?_r=0 (accessed July 24, 2013).
    7. Hanes, "Immigration: Assimilation and the Measure of an American."
    8. Hanes, "Immigration: Assimilation and the Measure of an American."
    9. Kris Olds, "Global Citizenship—What Are We Talking About and Why Does It Matter?" *Inside Higher Ed.com*, http://www.insidehighered.com/blogs/globalhighered/global-citizenship-%E2%80%93-what-are-we-talking-about-and-why-does-it-matter (accessed July 24, 2013).
    10. John Fonte, "New Hudson Study: America's Patriotic Assimilation System Is Broken," *Hudson Institute*, April 8, 2013, http://www.hudson.org/index.cfm?fuseaction=publication_details&id=9569 (accessed July 24, 2013).
    11. Dowell Myers, "The Next Immigration Challenge," *New York Times*, January 11, 2012, http://www.nytimes.com/2012/01/12/opinion/the-next-immigration-challenge.html (accessed July 24, 2012).
    12. Hanes, "Immigration: Assimilation and the Measure of an American."
    13. "The Migrant Integration Policy Index," *Immigration Policy Center*, http://www.immigrationpolicy.org/just-facts/migrant-integration-policy-index-mipex-iii (accessed July 24, 2013).
    14. "The Migrant Integration Policy Index."
    15. Tarini Parti, "'Assimilation' a Flash Point in Immigration Debate," *Politico.com*, June 10, 2013, http://www.politico.com/story/2013/06/assimilation-a-flash-point-in-immigration-debate-92469.html (accessed July 24, 2013).
    16. John J. Xenakis, "World View: Chechnya, Kyrgyzstan, and Analysis of the Boston Bombers," *Breitbart*, April 20, 2013, http://www.breitbart.com/Big-Peace/2013/04/19/20-Apr-13-World-View-Generational-analysis-of-Boston-Marathon-bombings (accessed July 24, 2013).
    17. Michael Cooper, Michael S. Schmidt, and Eric Schmitt, "Boston Suspects Are Seen as Self-Taught and Fueled by Web," *New York Times*, April 23, 2013, http://www.nytimes.com/2013/04/24/us/boston-marathon-bombing-developments.html?pagewanted=all&_r=0 (accessed July 24, 2013).
    18. Michael Wines and Ian Lovett, "The Dark Side, Carefully Masked," *New York Times*, May 4, 2013, http://www.nytimes.com/2013/05/05/us/dzhokhar-tsarnaevs-dark-side-carefully-masked.html?pagewanted=all&_r=0 (accessed July 24, 2013).
    19. Wines and Lovett, "The Dark Side, Carefully Masked."

20. "Timeline: A Look at Tamerlan Tsarnaev's Past," *CNN.com*, April 22, 2013, http://www.cnn.com/2013/04/21/us/tamerlan-tsarnaev-timeline (accessed July 24, 2013).

21. "Timeline: A Look at Tamerlan Tsarnaev's Past."

22. David Caruso, Michael Kunzelman, and Max Seddon, "Zubeidat Tsarnaeva, Mother of Boston Marathon Bombing Suspects, Says She's Just Someone Who Found Deeper Spirituality," *Huffington Post*, April 28, 2013, http://www.huffingtonpost.com/2013/04/28/zubeidat-tsarnaeva-mother-boston-marathon-bombing-suspects_n_3176009.html (accessed July 24, 2013).

23. Caruso, Kunzelman, and Seddon, "Zubeidat Tsarnaeva, Mother of Boston Marathon Bombing Suspects, Says She's Just Someone Who Found Deeper Spirituality."

24. "Timeline: A Look at Tamerlan Tsarnaev's Past."

25. "Timeline: A Look at Tamerlan Tsarnaev's Past."

26. Wines and Lovett, "The Dark Side, Carefully Masked."

27. Wines and Lovett, "The Dark Side, Carefully Masked."

28. "Family of Accused Bombers Divided over Allegations," *CBSnews*, April 19, 2013, http://www.cbc.ca/news/world/story/2013/04/19/boston-marathon-bombing-suspect-profile.html (accessed July 24, 2013).

29. "Family of Accused Bombers Divided over Allegations."

30. Karen Grigsby Bates, "How Koreatown Rose from the Ashes of L.A. Riots," *NPR: National Public Radio*, April 27, 2012, http://www.npr.org/2012/04/27/151524921/how-koreatown-rose-from-the-ashes-of-l-a-riots (accessed July 24, 2013).

31. Bates, "How Koreatown Rose from the Ashes."

32. Bates, "How Koreatown Rose from the Ashes."

33. Bates, "How Koreatown Rose from the Ashes."

18

Next Generation, and the Next, and the Next

By the time George Washington became our first president, his family had deep Virginia roots, but his great-grandfather, who never returned to England and died on his plantation in 1677 at age forty-six, was known as John Washington, "the immigrant." He had come to America as the second master on a two-sailed ketch, after Oliver Cromwell's cohorts—on charges that he was a "malignant royalist" and a drunk—had stripped his reverend father of his parish.

My own wife's fifteenth great-grandfather, Isaac de Turk, came to this country from Germany in 1708, and when he died nineteen years later, his tombstone was inscribed with only the date and "Joseph the immigrant."

President John F. Kennedy's great-grandfather Patrick came to the United States from Ireland in 1848, leaving behind a country in the suffering throes of the crippling potato famine. Patrick Kennedy was a cooper—a maker of wooden casks, barrels, buckets, tubs, butter churns, and other such items. His son Patrick "P. J." Joseph Kennedy became a prominent Boston businessman and eventually a powerful politician.

But it was P. J.'s grandchildren who would see unprecedented success; two became U.S. senators, and one became the thirty-fifth president of the United States, a milestone for all Catholics.

In 1963, President John F. Kennedy, who admired his heritage, traveled to Ireland's southeast coast, to the place where his great-grandfather set out for America more than a century earlier, and he told the residents of New Ross: "When my great-grandfather left here to become a cooper in East Boston, he carried nothing with him except two things: a strong religious faith and a strong desire for liberty. I am glad to say that all of his great-grandchildren have valued that inheritance."

As time progresses, it also accelerates, and nowhere can this be seen in more clarity than in the assimilation and acceptance of President Barack Hussein Obama II. Born in Hawaii to a highly educated Kenyan father and an American mother, President Obama has written that "the opportunity that Hawaii offered—experience a variety of cultures in a climate of mutual respect—became an integral part of my worldview, and a basis for the values that I hold most dear." His multicultural experience is what the American experience was for the Europeans who initially immigrated here, and it is now the experience of the non-Europeans.

Obama's presidency opens another door of opportunity for Americans of non-European descent. The future bodes well for Hispanics, Latinos, blacks, and Asians who may seek the nation's highest office. Now anyone, regardless of race, creed, color, or gender, truly can become president, though certainly for any individual it will require great political skill, fortitude, and tenacity.

Obama possesses such qualities, but his presidency is more than just a continuation of the immigrant narrative. It serves as another link to the world at large. Where the presidencies of George Washington and John F. Kennedy connected America to England, Ireland, and in general, Europe, Obama's connects the nation to Kenya and, on a larger scope, Africa and Indonesia, the homeland of his stepfather and where Obama once lived as a child.

Perhaps, considering his heritage, family, and life experiences, Obama is a connection to the world at large. This link is something that he shares with immigrants, who owe part of their success to this trait since time immemorial.

Because parents and children acculturate in different ways and at different rates, immigrant parents and children increasingly live in different cultural worlds. Immigrant parents often understand little of their children's lives outside the home. For immigrant children, it can be difficult to live with the expectations and demands of one culture in the home and another at school.[1]

The world is becoming more and more diverse, with immigration continuing to have a significant role in the growth of the nation. Pew Research Center data show that in recent decades, "Immigration's importance increased as the average number of births to U.S.-born women dropped sharply before leveling off." Nearly one in five Americans will be an immigrant in 2050, compared with one in eight today, but by 2025, Pew states, "The immigrant, or foreign born, share of the population will surpass the peak during the last great wave of immigration a century ago."[2]

The children of the prior wave of immigration founded such household names as McDonald's, Disney, Bose, Ford, and General Electric. We are currently riding the recent wave of the likes of eBay, Yahoo!, Google, PayPal, Zappos, and Amazon, and it is important that we plan a future that takes advantage of the next potential wave.

> Steve Ballmer, CEO of Microsoft, was born in Detroit. Bill Gates and Paul Allen, the founders of Microsoft, were both born in Seattle. However, the birthplace of the next CEO of Microsoft could very well be Zimbabwe or India.
>
> According to the *Seattle Times*, Paul Maritz, a Zimbabwe native, and Satya Nadella, an India native, are strong contenders for the position. Both are engineers who have the technical and business background needed to succeed as the chief executive officer of Microsoft.[3] With generally stronger technical backgrounds, immigrants could become many of America's future business leaders.

One surprising characteristic unites the majority of America's top high school science and math students: their parents are immigrants. While only 12 percent of the U.S. population is foreign born, 70 percent of the finalists in the 2011 Intel Science Talent Search competition were the children of immigrants, according to a National Foundation for American Policy analysis. While former H-1B visa holders comprise less than 1 percent of the U.S. population, 60 percent of the finalists had parents who entered the United States on H-1B visas, which is generally the only practical way to hire skilled foreign nationals.

As history has proven with George Washington, John F. Kennedy, and Barack Obama, it will be the children and grandchildren of today's immigrants who will go on to lead our nation.

NOTES

1. "Crossroads: The Psychology of Immigration in the New Century," American Psychological Association, Presidential Task Force on Immigration, www.apa.org/topics/immigration/immigration-report.pdf (accessed July 1, 2013).

2. Jeffrey S. Passel and D'Vera Cohn, "U.S. Population Projections: 2005–2050," *Pew Hispanic.org*, February 11, 2008, http://www.pewhispanic.org/2008/02/11/us-population-projections-2005-2050/ (accessed July 9, 2013).

3. Brier Dudley, "Ballmer's Biggest Success Was Out of the Spotlight," *Seattle Times*, August 24, 2013, http://seattletimes.com/html/businesstechnology/2021682849_brierballmerlegacyxml.html (accessed August 27, 2013).

19

How Did She Get Here: Otessa Ghadar

My oldest daughter, Otessa Marie Ghadar, was born in 1982, just outside of Washington, D.C. She was the only grandchild for my parents, and for more than thirteen years, she was our only child, until her younger twin siblings were born.

She was a bright and sociable child who excelled at almost everything she put her hand to. We were fortunate to live in the nation's capital because we had access to the best schools, and she grew up there, surrounded by the children of diplomats and political leaders from around the world.

It was during this time that I read an article that outlined the academic rigors and achievements of children in China. I made her read the article and tried to impress upon her that these were children she would eventually be competing against for opportunities. So, at ten years old, she interned during the summer at my company, Intrados, where in addition to being our "copy girl," she had to learn Lotus 1-2-3.

It wasn't until I took a position at Penn State University, nestled in Happy Valley, Pennsylvania, that she seemed to struggle. There, with a name like "Otessa Ghadar," she first stood out for more than her accomplishments. Her seventh-grade year in public school presented one particularly difficult adjustment, and it soon became clear that she needed to be in a more cosmopolitan setting. It was decided that Choate Rosemary Hall would be the best solution, and so she went to boarding school until high school graduation.

She went on to study at Columbia University in its School of Engineering and Applied Science, one of approximately only three hundred other students admitted, and she took up majors in theoretical physics and mathematics. She managed to excel, and her aptitude in the applied sciences was readily apparent. We were all very proud of her achievements and felt confident in the security of her future job prospects.

It wasn't until the end of her sophomore year that she told us she was switching over to Columbia's School of Arts to major in film studies. This news felt like something akin to watching someone go through a midlife crisis, seeing him or her act out on unfulfilled fancies to his or her ultimate demise and ruination.

While I had strayed from the original path my parents had set before me of becoming a medical doctor, I still stayed on an academic path that held the promise of opportunity, if I continued to work hard. I had no idea how she expected to succeed in a career in the film industry. In an arena where talent and hard work guarantee nothing, I was terrified for her future options.

However, she was adamant in her choice. While she was exceptional in physics and mathematics, she assured me that pursuing this path would never make her happy. So, at the age of nineteen, her bright engineering career veered off its well-intentioned course.

She did indeed thrive in her film studies and even went on to get her master's degree in this area. She was finally in her element. It was here that she started to write about Lis and me having to flee Iran during the revolution. She says she was drawn to it, as even though our story had some foreign elements, it was still a quintessentially American narrative about the fruits of risk taking and hard work. Writing about your parents, however, is a tricky topic, and so during this time, she turned to writing small vignettes about her memories of coming of age and of self-discovery in 1990s Washington, D.C.

These turned into her MFA thesis for graduate school and a web series starting in 2007 called "Orange Juice in Bishop's Garden." She is a pioneer of the web series format, and the show is now going into its seventh season, with viewership in over 140 countries around the world. She has received many accolades and honors for her work, including being a three-time LA Web Fest Winner, a Telly Award Winner, named Filmmaker of the Month by the D.C. Government Office of Film, and a Webby Official Honoree.

While initially her change in focus seemed "weird," as she calls it, she was able to see the potential of an entire new industry. She says,

> I saw it first and took a chance—and ended up being right. I have become (while not a big money-maker), a captain of industry in my field, a renowned authority, and a prestigious top name in this cool and cutting-edge growth industry. My path and passion were directly influenced by the bold and admirable choice I saw [my dad] and mommy make with both The Computer Store and Intrados. And incidentally, my "arts" field of new media is so firmly entrenched in tech-

nology, that I make constant use of my math and science training. New Media is truly a marriage of art and technology. So as much as my path seemed to diverge back in college, if we scratch the surface, we find indeed that it is not so very different after all.

It has been interesting, and at times surprising, to me to watch her progression growing up as a second-generation immigrant. While every parent sees a bit of themselves in their children, upon reflection, there are some unique characteristics I can only attribute to that common immigrant-pioneering ethos.

In 2009, Otessa started 20/20 Productions, a "new media" company, where she continues to serve and to define the industry. The advent of this field can be traced back to the democratization of information that allowed people to take advantage of the Internet to produce a grassroots globalization, centered on people rather than on the flow of capital. New media allows for users to establish relationships and to experience a sense of belonging that transcends traditional temporal and spatial boundaries. It changes continuously because it is constantly modified and redefined by the interaction between users, emerging technologies, and cultural changes. We only need to look to the Middle East to see how new media has been used as a tool for sweeping change.

Otessa recently added academic author to her list of credits, with her publication of the first-ever new media textbook for twenty-first-century students, titled *The Wild West of Film*. The irony of the title, considering our immigrant path, is not lost on me. With the publication of *The Wild West of Film*, new media will finally have a book about its field. As Otessa says,

> There is not one yet. No one has done it! I am the first! And I am the first to fill a great need. Again, this can-do attitude and sense that if something does not exist, you yourself should go out and do it (and not just complain about the lack). . . . This is something I credit to the immigrant initiative and mind-set, and I credit [my dad] in particular. If ever something did not exist or was lacking, [my dad] always said to me: "Well, then why don't you do it? Don't wait for someone else. If there's a need or a hole, get cracking on fixing or filling it."

As Otessa has exemplified, the next generation works hard but goes its own way into new fields and interests. This is also reminiscent of the first generation of immigrants. The can-do spirit and drive to complete hard work does remain with at least the next generation.

The Viewpoint of an Immigrant's Spouse

Lis de Tuerk Ghadar has a unique perspective on immigration, not only as a native-born American married to an Iranian immigrant, but also because she became an immigrant to Iran for a period of time. She is also the mother of second-generation immigrant children, Otessa, Anna, and John, born into a mix of family cultures.

Of her own experience of emigrating to Iran before the revolution, she describes a time of incredible family closeness and support, respectful curiosity on the part of strangers, and an enriching dichotomy of cultural traditions existing alongside Western ideals. Her exposure to a culture that at that time celebrated a broader spectrum of viewpoints than that to which she had been accustomed was eye-opening and unexpected.

Looking back on her time in Iran and then her eventual return to the United States in 1979, she recognizes that no matter how much exposure one has, or acclimating one does, one can never eradicate one's culture. She saw this with herself in Iran, when she would be reminded to respect certain cultural differences and act accordingly, and she saw this with her husband, Fariborz, upon his final immigration back to the United States.

Some of the particular challenges one faces in an intercultural marriage are that it is not easy to view the other person's different perspective as cultural, rather than just a difference of opinion. Eventually accepting this she believes has led her to become more understanding of others, while her experience of living in another culture has ultimately made her a better person overall.

She has no regrets about choosing to take on some significant life issues, but she is instead optimistic that this force of curiosity and acceptance that she sees in their grown children will echo and ripple out to others. She firmly believes that it will be easier for her children by the time they are her age because of the exposure they have had growing up as participants in these two cultures. It would seem that curiosity, respect, openness, and acceptance will be part of the very powerful legacy that this intercultural family will leave behind.

20

Old Country Is Old

Just as the decision to immigrate involves a cost-benefit analysis for the individual immigrant, the experiences of the countries involved can similarly be captured as a calculation of risk to reward. There are three parties involved in every act of international migration: the migrant himself, his country of origin, and his country of destination. Each of these parties has its own distinct and often conflicting interests in the process. What is good for the immigrant may not be good for his home or host country; the home and host countries gain and lose in different ways.

Is emigration good for the immigrant's country of origin? The answer lies in an analysis of who the immigrant is, where he goes, and what he does there.

BENEFITS

Immigration can serve an important safety-valve function for a "sending" country by relieving that country of some of its inhabitants, thus reducing the pressure on resources, particularly in densely populated and impoverished regions.

Immigration of certain demographic groups in society can relieve pressure on labor markets and ease intergenerational tensions. Countries with large youth/working-age populations experience downward pressure on wages, especially among unskilled laborers, if labor supply significantly exceeds demand. Unemployed youth populations are politically destabilizing as well, and their home countries often welcome their migration.

Immigrants perhaps benefit their home countries most when they send home a portion of their wages to family and friends or make investments in their countries of origin. By some estimates, remittances comprise double the amount of foreign aid that developing countries receive and up to 30 percent of some poor countries' total GDP. Remittances that are made through formal banking channels from immigrants living in developed countries back to their developing homelands have, by some estimates, quadrupled over the last two decades, from $60 billion in 1990 to $240 billion in 2007. Other estimates put the current figure closer to $318 billion or nearly $1 billion per day. Millions more in remittances are made through informal channels.

Both the countries of origin and the destination generally encourage remittances. Destination countries benefit from fees on banking transactions incurred in sending the money home. It has also been shown that remittances nurture ties between immigrants and their home communities that serve as a "safety net." When immigrants fall on hard times in their host countries, they are often able to depend on relatives and connections back home instead of becoming reliant on public welfare.

Immigrants living in the United States send the most money back home, with $42 billion leaving the country in 2006, of which $25 billion of it went to Mexico (formal banking channels only).

Remittances can be so significant that origin countries encourage migration. The *Times of India* reports that twenty million Indians working and living abroad have made India the largest single recipient of remittance flows; India receives $27 billion remitted from various countries, which comprises one-tenth of total global remittances.

It has been found that the poorer the immigrant, the more likely he is to send remittances. The majority of remittances to developing countries come in small increments from unskilled laborers. Remittances are less volatile than foreign aid or investment and tend to actually increase during times of global economic hardship.

When large immigrant communities form in wealthy and influential nations, they form a powerful diaspora, which can advocate for the interests of their countries of origin in the host country and in the international community.

Benefits negotiated by and made possible through this diaspora can include investment, aid, preferential trade policies, and even political pressure for reform in the home country. For instance, the Chinese diaspora in the West has spearheaded business deals and agitated for Communist Party reforms in China. Perhaps the most prominent example is the Jewish immigrants in the United States through their lobbying efforts, which result in substantial influence on U.S. policy. In addition, American Jews provide Israel financial support through investments from both the government and private companies.

When immigration is temporary or circular, or when immigrants maintain close ties to their home countries, valuable exchanges of ideas are facilitated, and the country of origin benefits from the immigrant's experiences in a more modernized society.

COSTS

The primary cost associated with emigration for the country of origin is the "brain drain," or the loss of some of its brightest citizens.

When immigrants are skilled and/or highly educated, the sending country experiences not only the loss of that worker and his contribution to society, but also the investment made in his education or training and the potential for him to mentor and teach others. Considering making an international move requires some financial solvency and entrepreneurship from anyone, even unskilled workers who emigrate are a loss to their country of origin.

The effect of "brain drain" is acute in many developing nations where doctors and nurses are in short supply locally because they have been so heavily recruited to make up for shortfalls in developed countries such as the United States.

PBS Frontline/World's Barnaby Lo has reported that the United States is expected to have a deficit of eight hundred thousand to one million trained nurses by the year 2020, and the American government actively recruits medical personnel all over the world with special visas. Lo goes on to note that because the nursing shortfall is so extreme and the recruitment so lucrative, many trained engineers, teachers, and even doctors in places such as the Philippines, India, and South Africa are abandoning their careers to enter nursing school with an eye toward emigration. In the Philippines alone, a study by the country's former Secretary of Health found that "80 percent of all government doctors have become nurses or are in nursing schools. There are roughly 9,000 doctors-turned-nurses and 5,000 of all these medical practitioners are now working abroad."[1] The public health and economic effects of this trend are potentially devastating to developing countries.

Not only are financial successes and talents transferred to the recipient country, but also potentially valuable political assets are, as well. When the best and brightest leave, they take potential reformist energy and acumen with them.

So we can see that whether an immigrant's decision to relocate hurts or helps his country of origin is highly subjective and situational. Countries of origin usually have little say over the matter, unlike the immigrant (if he is acting voluntarily) or the recipient country (to the extent that it can enforce its legal restrictions on immigration). Rarely, and only in highly repressive regimes, are people prevented from voluntarily leaving their country. The country of origin is thus largely a passive actor in the immigration equation.

Some developing countries have experimented with tying financial assistance for in-country education with promises to students to stay at home for a period of years after graduation; others have tried financial grants to study abroad with promises of return. But these measures are difficult to enforce and have been met with limited success.

For example, Iran lost over one million people after the revolution, many of whom where highly educated and trained. As a result, the nation's economy suffered, totaling a loss of around $30 to $40 billion.[2] According to Migration Information Source, over 45,000 Iranians immigrated to the United States alone just before and during the revolution, while over 150,000 more immigrated during the following decade. Moreover, as stated by Migration Information Source,

> Because the second wave [after the Revolution] included large numbers of professionals, entrepreneurs, and academics, it accelerated the "brain drain." . . . According to the Ministry of Culture and High Education, right before the revolution and subsequent closure of all universities in 1980, there were 16,222 professors teaching in Iran's higher education institutions. When the universities reopened in 1982, this figure had plummeted to 9,042.[3]

Though many Iranian immigrants had originally planned to return, in many cases, they have yet to make their way back to Iran. And as time passes, it becomes increasingly unlikely that they will, in fact, return. Even years after the revolution, reportedly the brain drain continues to occur in Iran at higher levels because of the country's inability to satisfy the needs of its citizens, especially those who are highly educated. The Migration Information Source further reported that the government is trying to establish efforts such as creating additional jobs to mitigate the problem, but the "results of these efforts have not yet materialized."[4]

Though Michel Amsalem is not Iranian, he, along with his family, was forced to immigrate as a result of political and social unrest in his home country, Algeria. And like many of the Iranians who left as a result of the revolution and did not return, Amsalem has no future plans to return home. But when Amsalem initially left Algeria, he did not head directly for the United States. His eventual life in the United States has involved multiple moves in different countries.

NOTES

1. Barnaby Lo, "Philippines: Have Degree, Will Travel. Where Have All the Nurses Gone?" *PBS.org*, December 18, 2007, http://www.pbs.org/frontlineworld/rough/2007/12/philippines_hav.html (accessed October 30, 2013).
2. Shirin Hakimzadeh, "Country Profiles: Iran: A Vast Diaspora Abroad and Millions of Refugees at Home," Migrations Policy Institute, September 2006, http://www.migrationinformation.org/feature/display.cfm?ID=424 (accessed July 9, 2013).
3. Hakimzadeh, "Country Profiles: Iran."
4. Hakimzadeh, "Country Profiles: Iran."

21

How Did He Get Here: Michel Amsalem

Michel Amsalem was born in Oran, Algeria, in 1947, into a family that had been granted French citizenship by Napoleon III, who, on a trip to Algeria in the 1860s, stayed with Amsalem's family. His surname means "people united" in Hebrew, and his family proudly traces its Sephardic Jewish roots back to fourth-century Algeria, before the Arab invasions. At the beginning of the sixteenth century, his mother's family settled in Morocco, after being chased from the Iberian Peninsula by the Spanish Inquisition. His mother's maiden name, Maïmaran, in fact means "never converted" in Portuguese. A census taken on June 1, 1960, showed there were 1,050,000 non-Muslim civilians in Algeria at that time, or 10 percent of the total population, including 130,000 Jews.

As a result of their centuries-long stay in Algeria and Morocco, Jews were fully integrated in the local society and culture, even though they lived somewhat separately. That changed markedly after France took over these two countries, in 1830 for Algeria and at the beginning of the twentieth century for Morocco. Jews were much quicker than Muslims to assimilate into French culture, to learn French, and to take advantage of the French education system. In the 1870s, all Algerian Jews were granted French citizenship by the "Décret Crémieux," an act sponsored by the then-French minister of justice Adolphe Crémieux, which further separated them from the Muslim pre-French population. As a result, by the middle of the twentieth century, Jews identified much more with the French than with the local Muslim population.

This, together with the anti-Semitism that was then grabbing the Arab world, ended up making their continued stay in Algeria impossible, once the country gained its independence from France in 1962 after a protracted war. Within a matter of months, practically all Jews and most other non-Muslims were airlifted out of Algeria. Most of them went to France, a country of which they had the nationality and spoke the language, yet they were culturally very different. A number went to Israel and Canada; very few went to the United States. Because Amsalem's father worked for the French government, his family went to France and settled in Paris, leaving behind everything they owned. So at age fifteen, Amsalem ended up in a boarding high school in Paris. The integration was difficult due to the heated atmosphere that had surrounded the Algerian war and to the cultural differences, but it was helped by the large number of Jews and Christians who had just left all three North African countries to resettle in France.

After completing high school, college, and graduate school in France, Amsalem came to the United States in 1971 as a student in the MBA program of Columbia University, financed by a scholarship from the French government. He went on to Harvard in 1972 for his doctorate in business administration, financed this time by an American scholarship. While Amsalem was a graduate student at Harvard, he started consulting for the World Bank, which offered to finance his research on technology choice in developing countries and its impact on employment and capital usage. Later on, in 1975, while he was completing his thesis work, the International Finance Corporation, the private sector arm of the World Bank, offered him a position as economist for the Africa region.

In 1976, Amsalem brought his sister, Annie, who by then had completed her studies in dentistry, to Boston University to do a specialization in periodontics. In 1979, despite being offered a teaching position at Boston University School of Dentistry, she was forced to return to France because of her inability to secure a resident visa. Though she opened a successful practice in Paris, she never gave up on her dream of moving to the United States, and she entered the citizenship lottery faithfully every year.

Amsalem met his soon-to-be wife, Tammy, at the World Bank. The daughter of an American diplomat, she was born in Mexico and grew up in France and the USSR. A mathematician by trade, she worked on the economic forecasting models developed by the World Bank. They married in 1979 and moved to New York, where Amsalem had been offered a position as a professor at Columbia University's Graduate School of Business, and Tammy enrolled as a graduate student in public health.

The next seven years were spent at Columbia. During that period, Amsalem published a book (MIT Press) and a number of articles and monographs, and he was awarded several prizes for excellence in teaching. Meanwhile, their first child, Arielle, was born, followed, two years later, by their son, David. In 1985 Citicorp asked Amsalem to start its Structured Finance Department. Coming after the 1982 emerging markets debt crisis, the department was to be in charge of developing all of Citibank's fee-based business in developing countries. Amsalem spent five years at Citibank, which he describes as among the most exciting of his career given the level of creativity, both in the organization and in the market, in trying to solve the damning financial problems then faced by developing countries and investors in these countries.

At the beginning of 1991, at a time when the emerging markets financial crisis was easing and opportunities were growing exponentially, Citibank went into its own financial crisis due to the collapse of the U.S. real estate market. Amsalem then left Citibank with a group of colleagues to start the investment bank for Latin America and Eastern Europe, Banque Indosuez. He moved his family, including his youngest daughter, Judith, born in 1990, first to Paris and then to London, seeing in this move an opportunity to give his children a bilingual and bicultural education.

The same year, after fifteen years, his sister's tenacity paid off, when she received a letter from the U.S. Immigration Service announcing that she had been selected in the immigration lottery and was granted a residency visa. She immediately sold her practice in France and moved to Boston.

Though successful on their own, the operations of this new investment bank were, by the mid-1990s, seriously impaired by the impact of a deep French real estate crisis. This, together with his desire to give his children, by then bilingual, an American education, led Amsalem to move his family back to New York at the end of 1995.

Upon his return to the United States, Amsalem partnered with venture capitalist Alan Patricof to launch Patricof Emerging Markets. He headed this venture until it was sold together with the other investment banking/merchant banking operations of the Patricof group to Bank of New York in 1999. At that time he also resumed an academic activity, teaching courses in business strategy as an adjunct professor in the Executive MBA program at Columbia University.

Following a short-lived partnership with an old colleague from Bank Indosuez in launching a hedge fund focused on the financing of small and microcap listed companies in the high-technology area, Amsalem launched his own fund in the same field in 2002. He manages this family of funds through their management company, Midsummer Capital, to this date, although he is in the process of passing on this management responsibility to the senior staff working with him.

His three children have given Amsalem a unique perspective on his own immigration, first to France, and finally to the United States. While they all have benefited from their experience living in France and from being bilingual and bicultural, their approach to life is clearly American, and their present status in life is the result of the opportunities offered by this country.

After graduating from New York University Tisch School of the Arts, his daughter Arielle is an Emmy-award-winning film editor of feature-length documentaries and television series; his son, David, is a medical student at Vanderbilt University; and his daughter Judith is a graduate of Cornell University in Environmental Studies and is working for the Environmental Law Institute in Washington, D.C. All three are, by now, trilingual; all three went to Hebrew school in New York; and all three firmly consider themselves to be "American," though they all share a strong international "bent."

While Amsalem talks wistfully about his birthplace in Algeria, he quickly adds that his country, as he knew it, has disappeared like a number of other countries, such as Syria, Iran, Egypt, and Lebanon, which have been buffeted by war and sectarian violence and where an element of society has been eliminated. He believes that the United States' strength is its diversity and its tolerance, allowing so many different people, many of them "refugees" from other countries, to develop their particular skills and to contribute them to the common good. He hopes the virtues of tolerance and respect ultimately win out over intolerance and bigotry.

> *A Certain People: American Jews and Their Lives Today* by Charles Silberman, 1985:
>
>> American Jews are committed to cultural tolerance because of their belief, one firmly rooted in history, that Jews are safe only in a society acceptant of a wide range of attitudes and behaviors, as well as a diversity of religious and ethnic groups.

The message he has passed onto his children, in addition to a strong emphasis on the value of education, is that the onus for their future is squarely on them. The example is clear: America gives most an opportunity to forge their own path, and those who take advantage of such an opportunity ultimately succeed.

22

Can You Go Home Again?

A significant number of students and others who are in the United States studying technology, science, and engineering, and who would absolutely love to work here, are going to have to go back home. The fact is we're driving a chunk of people out of the country who have skills very much in demand.

These immigrants are the same ones who will be instrumental in developing the future-oriented industries vital for the United States to lay claim to in order to have continued global economic success. Future-oriented industries that form clusters, such as nanotechnology, biotechnology, robotics, and shale oil and gas, will be nurtured somewhere around the world, and if we don't allow the potential innovators in these industries to remain in the United States, we cannot expect to be a default leader in the competition of global economies.

Case in point: Each year the United States provides four hundred thousand visas to foreign-born students to study at American colleges and universities, and then our current immigration laws force them to leave the country upon graduation, thereby becoming our competition.[1]

For the Harvard Class of 2016, foreign citizens, U.S. dual citizens, and U.S. permanent residents together make up more than 19 percent of the class, representing eighty-six countries. So what are their options after graduating?

Currently there are more than a million temporary workers and students in the skilled-worker immigration categories waiting for a yearly allocation of 120,000 permanent resident visas.[2]

Indian and Chinese immigrants who had worked or received their education in the United States and had returned to their home country were asked to rate why they had initially decided to come to the United States.

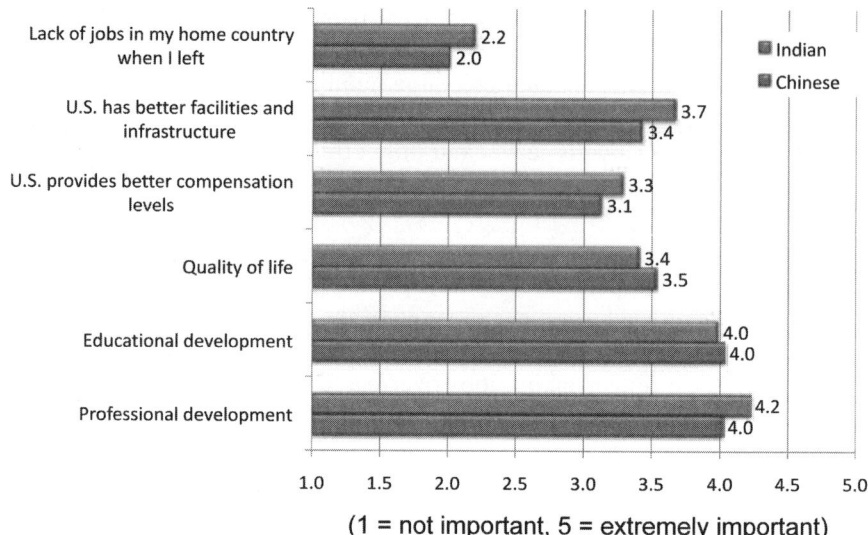

Average Rating of Factors Contributing to Decision to Migrate to the United States
Vivek Wadhwa, AnnaLee Saxenian, Richard Freeman, Gary Gereffi, and Alex Salkever, "America's Loss Is the World's Gain: America's New Immigrant Entrepreneurs, Part IV," Ewing Marion Kauffman Foundation, March 2009, www.kauffman.org/uploadedfiles/americas_loss.pdf.

The table above illustrates that the type of motivation for their coming to America was certainly one of betterment of themselves, which would in turn have enriched our society.

Virtually every industrialized country will be confronted with a significant labor shortage, particularly in the knowledge sectors. This is exacerbated by aging (retiring) populations and low birthrates, particularly in Japan, Germany, the Netherlands, and Scandinavia. Japan hasn't responded to it; the population is homogenous and xenophobic, and even though its population peaked in 2006, in terms of allowing immigration or encouraging it, it's just not part of the country's makeup. Europe is also in a decidedly negative position. Its nation-states, with their homogeneous (or at best two culture states, think Switzerland), have a built-in knee-jerk reaction to immigration and the foreigner in general. Because Europe has such a different history than the United States, which was founded by immigrants, countries there are even less inclined to accept those who are culturally, ethnically, or religiously different than themselves. Immigration, therefore, remains a politically touchy subject and a rallying cry for extremist parties, due to issues with integration into these relatively insular societies. To boost their birthrates, European nations have implemented policies that reward families who have children via tax incentives and increased maternity leave. But it is doubtful that these policies will suffice to staunch Europe's population decline.

Germany has been somewhat more open, particularly after World War II, when it lost a generation of young men. In 1961, it signed a labor recruitment agreement with Turkey, encouraging large numbers to immigrate as (mainly unskilled) guest workers. However, they were viewed only as guests who were expected to eventually leave, and little effort was made to successfully integrate them into society.

The companies that suffer the most from this are the smaller leading-edge companies in science, technology, and innovation, companies that really rely on brainpower. According to "Tech Firms Go Abroad to Hire," published in *USA Today*, there has been a recent surge in these companies hiring abroad because the United States no longer provides the best brainpower. These companies are no longer taking jobs overseas for cheaper labor, like some may speculate; rather, they are looking for brighter talent.[3]

A study by Roger Marting and Richard Florida found that creative jobs requiring highly skilled talent have grown from 10 percent of the economy to more than 30 percent. Filling these creative opportunities represents a new economic opportunity. While talented immigrants created 52 percent of Silicon Valley's companies, today many are leaving thanks to immigration policies that have made it harder to stay in the United States.

A further shift toward Thomas Friedman's comparison of the historical change in options for the "B" student from Bethesda and the genius in Bangalore is that, nowadays, if you are that genius in Bangalore, "you no longer need to emigrate to innovate."

For example, former chief data officer at Yahoo!, Usama Fayyad, came home to Jordan convinced there was enough raw material to create an Arab "Silicon Wadi." He is now a part of Oasis500, an Arab-owned high-tech accelerator, looking to nurture four hundred new startups in Jordan.

Experts are even seeing a new trend in which ambitious American children of immigrant parents are returning to their country of origin because they see greater opportunities abroad.[4] Those countries are seeing immigration as an integral part of their national economic strategy and have responded by making employment, investment, visa, and tax incentives available to those who make the move. However, this is a phenomenon best suited to the younger generation, as it is doubtful that many fifty-plus-year-old immigrants would be equipped to deal with this new occurrence.

My own original return to my native country was at the age of about seven years old. My parents had finished their university studies, and so along with my sister, the four of us took a freighter from Louisiana to Casablanca. We were unable to afford better transport, as the currency situation in Iran meant that we were only able to rely upon what my parents had been earning by working, while my father was also attending school.

The culture shock of that trip got incrementally greater each stop we made. I had become quite Americanized by this point, and leaving the southern United States and arriving in Casablanca presented a whole different landscape of people, sights, and smells. From here we went to Beirut, which was quite untouched by the Western world at that time, and then onward by car to Tehran. I was now fully down the rabbit hole.

While we had been in the United States, our social circle consisted of the four of us, and a few other international students. Now, back in Tehran, we were immediately welcomed into a large extended family that had an active social and cultural life.

I can still fondly recall the monthly gatherings at my grandmother's beautiful house. As the matriarch, she would invite the local Mullah over in order to say prayers (Rouzeh khanney), and it would turn into an all-day family event.

On the floors were large rugs and various smaller ones scattered on top. Huge cushions and pillows were neatly arranged in order to facilitate conversation. There was a beautiful silver samovar with a set of Iranian teacups, along with rice cookies or sweets. The men were separate, chanting, while the women, dressed in their black chadors, were crying. The children were given free reign to play all over the garden, and after the Mullah left, refreshments were consumed, connections reestablished, and contacts made.

This picture is unlikely to exist today in the same way it did for me back in the 1950s. While there are still cultural differences quite apparent today, the likelihood that there will be a common cultural lexicon upon which one can draw makes it all the easier for an immigrant to reacclimate back into his or her society.

However, for immigrants who have been here for a few years and to some extent have assimilated into the U.S. culture, returning to the old country may have a romantic attraction, but the reality is much different. Both the immigrants and their countries of origin have evolved in different ways. There are often new political environments, loyalties, and cultures, and while returning may seem ideal on the surface, it is in fact difficult, for many immigrants have already assimilated into an entirely different culture.

My return to Iran is impossible, for Iran has changed. It is less Western, more religious, and much more repressive. Heawon Park also faces a similar situation; she has become an Americanized woman of Korean decent. The younger generation and the graduating students, who have arrived more recently, however, see their country of origin as one without many changes. They, therefore, might have a much better chance of actually returning.

Now that the United States is no longer the only place where talented people can put their skills to work, there should be a wakeup call that immigrants have a plethora of never-before-seen options at their disposal. Brain drain no longer occurs in only one direction; the United States cannot afford to rest on her past laurels.

NOTES

1. "Building a 21st Century Immigration System," *White House*, May 2011, www.whitehouse.gov/sites/default/files/rss_viewer/immigration_blueprint.pdf (accessed July 1, 2013).

2. Vivek Wadhwa, AnnaLee Saxenian, Richard Freeman, Gary Gereffi, and Alex Salkever, "America's Loss Is the World's Gain: America's New Immigrant Entrepreneurs, Part IV," Ewing Marion Kauffman Foundation, www.kauffman.org/uploadedfiles/americas_loss.pdf (accessed July 1, 2013).

3. John Shinal, "Tech Firms Go Abroad to Hire," *USA Today*, June 5, 2013, http://usatoday30.usatoday.com/MONEY/usaedition/2013-07-05-Silicon-Valley-not-waiting-for-US-immigration-reform_ST_U.htm (accessed August 18, 2013).

4. Kirk Semple, "More U.S. Immigrants' Children Seek American Dream Abroad," *New York Times*, April 15, 2012, http://www.nytimes.com/2012/04/16/us/more-us-children-of-immigrants-are-leaving-us.html?pagewanted=all (accessed July 8, 2013).

23

Lessons for the Next Generation

Children of immigrants to the United States learned from watching their parents work hard at making something of their lives in a country offering a chance to succeed. Many of them carried on to achieve great things, like my daughter Otessa, Zbigniew Brzezinski, and Yoon-shik Park and their respective children. They did so in part to give something back to the country that allowed them and their parents the chance for a better life.

I have seen this phenomenon at work in different levels within my own family. While my parents mainly associated with fellow Iranians and relatives, my sister and I made friends with and each married outside our nationality. I married an American, and my sister married an Egyptian. My three children are even one more step removed from the life and roots of their Iranian heritage. My oldest daughter, Otessa, a successful independent

> As an immigrant from Mexico who worked the farm fields and ranches across the western United States for nearly thirty years before retiring back in his homeland, Jesus Silva and his offspring typified the American immigrant experience.
>
> Silva came to the United States in 1952, invited by the government under the labor-seeking Bracero Program. It began during World War II and continued in the postwar era, when America needed the help of immigrant laborers during an era of tremendous economic and population growth.
>
> He had earned enough to spend his senior years in relative prosperity in Pajacuaran, Mexico. He owned his home, modest though it was compared to the homes he would see in the United States. But his Mexican-born children chose to remain in America, where they raised families and where their families went from being laborers in the fields with little education to employees of companies determined to see their children enter college in order to enter a professional field, such as law or medicine.

filmmaker (who went back to being called Otessa when she went to college), is engaged to an Uruguayan American. While my parents thought that my career endeavors in the computer industry were crazy and doomed to failure, my initial reaction when Otessa changed from being a science major at Columbia University to filmmaking was incredulity and skepticism. However, it has been her hard work and determination that has made her successful in her career, just as it was in my sister's and mine.

Regardless, it is difficult to imagine that I could have achieved as much as I have today without the impact of various mentors along the way and the U.S. mind-set of itself being the land of opportunity. Besides the importance of education and hard work my parents instilled, I can identify key individuals whose influence and advice were crucial to my success. The first was Dr. Richter at Ursinus College, without whom I would never have been encouraged to set my sights on MIT and Harvard. Dr. Stobaugh of Harvard nurtured my academic interests, and Minister of Commerce Kazem Khosroushahi in Iran took me under his wing when I needed guidance. Then there was Abdullah Jumah at Saudi Aramco, who recognized my drive to help educate the next generation of leaders, and he has continued to consult with me on their yearly senior management identification process since 1979. And lastly, William A. Schreyer, Chairman Emeritus of Merrill Lynch, took a chance on a driven immigrant and granted me the first endowed chair with his name.

Because I was able to recognize how critical this mentorship was to my success, I, too, have taken it upon myself and consider it my duty to mentor youth I have met throughout my life. Through acting as a consultant and through teaching at various universities, I have encountered thousands of students, managers, and executives whom I hope to have inspired. In particular, I remember Babak, who went on to work for Exxon; Hamed, an IT guru for the financial sector; Nimrata, who is a manager at Dell's supply-chain operations; Krishna, who joined Westfield in the actuarial area; Holly, who is developing apps in Canada; and Baljit, who is a famous economic development expert. And the same can be said for many immigrants who chose education and thus were mentors to many—such as Yoon-shik Park, who teaches at George Washington University; Michel Amsalem, who taught at Columbia University; and Zbigniew Brzezinski, who teaches at SAIS. All of us hope that we have done our part to help the next generation excel and contribute to society in their own way.

While the winds of ignorance and intolerance still buffet America today, within the last thirty years more Americans, particularly the younger generations, have come to embrace diversity, viewing it as America's strength, not its weakness.

For the first time since 1994, when the Chicago Council Survey first asked the question, only a minority (40 percent) of Americans consider a large influx of immigrants and refugees a "critical threat" to the United States. And fewer now than ever recorded in these surveys (53 percent) say that "controlling and reducing illegal immigration" is an important foreign policy goal for the United States.

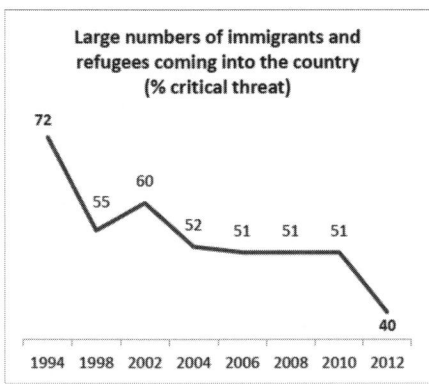 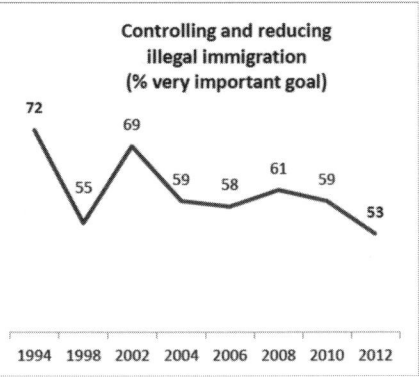

Chicago Council Survey Results
Dina Smeltz, "Foreign Policy in the New Millennium," 2012 Chicago Council Survey, www.thechicagocouncil.org/files/Studies_Publications/POS/Survey2012/2012.aspx.

A new federal immigration program, known as Deferred Action for Childhood Arrivals, opened on August 15, 2012, after being put in place by the Obama administration. It protects eligible immigrants from deportation and allows them to apply for a work permit. Among other criteria, applicants must provide documentation showing they arrived in the United States before they were sixteen years old, are under the age of thirty-one, and have lived continuously in the United States for the past five years. But the program doesn't offer legal residency or a path to citizenship, and participants must reapply for authorization every two years.

Within two months of the start of the new program, about 180,000 young illegal immigrants applied for the two-year reprieve from deportation. Thus far, 4,591 cases have been approved, according to the Department of Homeland Security.

For the first time since the question was asked in 2002, the 2012 Chicago Council Survey found more Americans support keeping immigration at present levels (42 percent) than favor decreasing them (37 percent). This is a striking change in opinion from ten years ago when six in ten Americans favored decreasing immigration levels. While still relatively low, the proportion of Americans supporting an increase in legal immigration levels over the past ten years has more than doubled, from 7 percent in 2002 to 18 percent today.

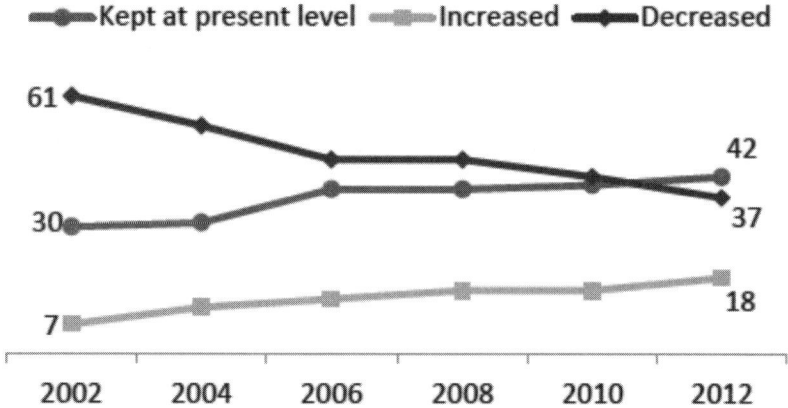

American Opinion on Immigration Level
Dina Smeltz, "Foreign Policy in the New Millennium," 2012 Chicago Council Survey, www.thechicagocouncil.org/files/Studies_Publications/POS/Survey2012/2012.aspx.

New York Times Washington bureau chief David Leonhardt writes that today's generation gap is wider than it has been since the 1960s, and that,

> beyond political parties, the two have different views on many of the biggest questions before the country. The young not only favor gay marriage and school funding more strongly; they are also notably less religious, more positive toward immigrants, less hostile to Social Security cuts and military cuts and more optimistic about the country's future. They are both more open to change and more confident that life in the United States will remain good.

One striking illustration of the young, and specifically the immigrant, being open to change is Iranian immigrant Babak Parviz and German immigrant Sebastian Thrun of Google X. They have recently revealed Project Glass, futuristic eyewear that is like a computer screen overlaid on the real world.

What second-generation Russian immigrant and Google cofounder Sergey Brin started, they are taking into a whole other realm. It is no accident that they are involved in the next big thing (nanotechnology and biotechnology), and in addition to this project, partner Thrun is also developing unmanned robotic cars that drive more safely. They each have that common immigrant combination: a risk-taking spirit and a strong work ethic.

Many of today's young immigrants are finding careers in completely new industries and fields. The "app" economy barely existed five years ago, yet in that same time frame, it has spawned 470,000 new jobs. These new fields generate the need for talent with new skills.

Yet by 2018, the number of working Americans fifty-five years or older will have increased by 5.8 percent over the past decade, while only 12.7

percent of the labor force will be aged sixteen to twenty-four.[1] This means that the United States will be required to maintain an aging workforce that works well into the retirement years. According to a report by the Center for Strategic and International Studies, in an aging workforce, "employees may become less adaptable and mobile, innovation and entrepreneurship may decline, rates of savings and investment may fall, public-sector deficits may rise, and current account balances may turn negative. All of this threatens to impair economic performance."[2] In other words, we need to remember that learning and refreshing one's skill set must become a lifelong endeavor.

The lessons I take as I look back and even as I look forward to my own children and their immigrant peers are ones of remembering to never lose the fire. The world no longer consists of protected markets and stagnant populations. The only way to succeed is to take a lesson from this immigrant book: work hard and take risks.

NOTES

1. John Hagel III, John Seely Brown, and Duleesha Kulasooriya, "The 2011 Shift Index: Measuring the Forces of Long-Term Change," *Deloitte Center for the Edge* 1 (2011): 17.

2. Richard Jackson and Neil Howe, with Rebecca Strauss and Keisuke Nakashima, *The Graying of the Great Powers: Demography and Geopolitics in the 21st Century* (Washington, DC: Center for Strategic and International Studies, May 2008).

24

Blueprints for Policymakers

Immigration is central to the story of the United States, and figuring out how to do it right in the twenty-first century is both critically important and politically loaded to the point in which rational debate is impossible: case in point, nobody knew for sure whether candidate Herman Cain's proposal for an electrified fence on the Mexican border was a joke.

In the pursuit of tight borders, current U.S. immigration policy turns away potential contributors to our economic strength. Open borders are not an option for any sovereign nation of significant size. At the same time, periods of intense nativism in U.S. history have spurred extremely restrictive policies. As history should show conclusively, the cost of barring potential entrepreneurs is high. Former Citibank CEO Walter Wriston once commented about money that "capital goes where it's wanted, and stays where it's well treated," but in a global economy that runs on ideas, talent, and hard work, the statement holds even more true for brainpower.

U.S. students' rapidly declining interest in STEM is even more portentous. The United States accounts for only 4 percent of the total engineering degrees awarded globally, while Asia accounts for 56 percent of the degrees granted.

Technology-based industries tend to create large numbers of high-paying jobs and to generate large volumes of high-margin exports. Worse still, even the most staid industries are being forced to become technology industries. The future of automobiles, we are told, is in new fuel-efficient, self-driving designs. Even utilities are being forced to go high tech, with the need to move to clean coal and renewable energy sources and to build and to manage smart infrastructures. Hopefully, factors such as growing interest in biotech, nanotech, robotics, sustainability, and new education incentives and programs (such as those that encourage math and science education) will increase domestic interest in STEM education and careers. If not, the United States will need to recognize the necessity of encouraging and better using the gift of foreign-born talent nurtured by our universities.

As the rules stand, tens of thousands of international students who attend U.S. universities cannot compete for jobs here. Robert Guest, an editor at the *Economist*, wrote a piece for the *Wall Street Journal* in which he compared sending away international students to "Saudi Arabia setting fire to its oil wells." New York mayor Michael Bloomberg (who won election as a Republican) calls the practice "national suicide."

Currently the United States annually awards only eighty-five thousand H-1B visas for highly skilled workers, despite a dearth of U.S.-born workers who can fill these types of jobs.

In addition to paying skilled foreign-born professionals the same wages as comparable American workers, government data show U.S. employers have been required to pay over $3 billion in mandatory government fees since 2000. In other words, despite the higher costs required to hire foreign workers, companies are willing to pay for the talent. The data call into question critics' assertions that H-1B visa holders are hired to save money. Data from U.S. Citizenship and Immigration Services (USCIS) obtained by the National Foundation for American Policy (NFAP) show that, from fiscal year 2000 to fiscal year 2011, employers paid over $2.3 billion to the federal government in H-1B training fees (generally $1,500 per individual). Additionally, a $500 antifraud tax/fee on each H-1B and L-1 visa has cost employers more than $700 million. Including visa adjudication levies, premium processing fees, and costs associated with dependent family members, the total amount employers paid to the federal government to hire H-1B visa holders since 2000 approaches $4 billion. Employers must also typically pay legal fees of $1,800 to $2,500 per H-1B temporary visa, as well as staff time. Sponsoring an individual for a green card (permanent residence) can be as high as $35,000.

Ironically, U.S. policy governing immigration has remained unchanged for nearly half a century despite the fact that immigrants are the ones fueling the U.S. economy. We needn't place artificial limits on the contributions that immigrants are able and willing to provide. While U.S. policy is geared to the economic realities of the past, it is woefully inadequate at encompassing the landscape of the future. The world moves around us, and we remain stuck in place.

In *The Immigrant Exodus: Why America Is Losing the Global Race to Capture Entrepreneurial Talent*, Vivek Wadhwa also recognizes the precarious position the United States is in due to its archaic immigration policy because immigrants can now choose to return home or never come at all.

Wadhwa warns of a decline in immigrant entrepreneurship in the United States, which has traditionally fueled the U.S. economy. His research has shown that the United States can save itself by incentivizing immigrants to stay with policy changes.[1]

Also in agreement, Thomas Friedman wrote in the *New York Times* in 2009 an open letter to America,

> Dear America,
>
> Please remember how you got to be the wealthiest country in history. It wasn't through protectionism or state-owned banks or fearing free trade. No, the formula was very simple: build this really flexible, really open economy, tolerate creative destruction so dead capital is quickly redeployed to better ideas and companies, pour into it the most diverse, smart and energetic immigrants from every corner of the world, and then stir and repeat, stir and repeat, stir and repeat, stir and repeat. We don't want to come out of this crisis with just inflation, a mountain of debt and more shovel-ready jobs. We want to—we have to—come out of it with a new Intel, Google, Microsoft and Apple.

It is important to note that we don't just want another Intel, Google, Microsoft and Apple, but rather we need to be equipped to quickly respond to the next big thing, the development of nanotechnology and biotechnology clusters. Those companies are still important, but the real innovation will come from outside the establishment to create the new jobs and economies of the future.

We need to create an entrepreneurial environment that brings together different groups of people to promote innovation. MIT, Stanford, Yale, and Harvard are among some schools that have been able to create such an environment. They have created a culture that builds and rewards entrepreneurial vision and emphasizes a team approach that brings together people of different backgrounds and skills. Let's take a closer look at MIT. The university steadily creates and enhances entrepreneurial-launching structures, such as the $100K Competition and the Deshpande Center for Technological Innovation. The results of such an entrepreneurial environment have been astounding. Data from a 2009 study suggest that MIT alumni alone have founded 25,800 firms, employing about 3.3 million employees and generating about $2 trillion in annual revenue. Between two hundred and four hundred companies are started each year by MIT staff and alumni. If these companies formed a nation, they would have ranked as the world's eleventh-largest economy. Most strikingly, the institute takes an entrepreneurial approach to entrepreneurship itself. Now, though, there are also excellent foreign universities that train and encourage the development of new industries from Fudan, India's school of Science and Technology, and Iran's Sharif University.

However, as the United States becomes less hospitable, formally and perhaps informally, those bright, motivated individuals are being courted by other immigrant-friendly countries, such as Canada, Singapore, New Zealand, and Israel, not to mention their own native countries. In the global race for the next generation of startups, the United States has a privileged position, but that status as a preferred destination is in danger of being diminished as collateral damage in a debate with other protagonists, motivations, and constituencies. We can only hope that some good sense comes into play alongside the fear, stereotypes, and lack of solid data currently characterizing the problem.

When it comes to the issue of immigration in the United States, there are a myriad of complexities swirling around each point within the debate. But, most often, the underlying, unspoken sentiment seems to be: Do we have enough? Enough resources to accommodate all those around the world who would want to partake of the American Dream? Enough goodwill toward those who are often culturally, and sometimes religiously, quite different than the "typical" American? Enough domestic stability to withstand the inevitable shockwaves caused by the influx of foreign sensibilities? Or, do we instead think that enough is enough?

In another federal program known as EB-5, wealthy foreigners can in effect buy U.S. immigration visas for themselves and their families by investing at least $500,000 in certain development projects. Participants can get a temporary visa by investing $500,000 to $1 million in a federally approved business. If the business creates or preserves at least ten jobs in two years, the investor and his immediate family are eligible for permanent residency in the United States.

In the past two decades, much of the EB-5 investment has gone into commercial real estate projects, like luxury hotels, ski resorts, and even gas stations. Lately, however, enterprising brokers have seen a golden opportunity to match cash-starved charter schools with cash-flush foreigners in investment deals that benefit both. In the first nine months of 2012, the government approved three thousand petitions from foreigners seeking to participate in the program—nearly twice as many as were approved all last year, according to the Department of Homeland Security.

The public debate concerning many of our national issues might be different if our policies were explicitly aimed at boosting talent and competitiveness. Instead of being afraid of competing for finite resources, we should recognize that talent expands the sum of economic rewards. We need not have the view that immigration takes something from the native born, but rather recognize that, with creative thinking and sound policies, we can actually boost employment and make the American Dream big enough to encompass all who want to partake.

A case in point is the global race to any of the previously mentioned clusters. A cluster would create jobs and bring prestige to the area that hosts it. So while there currently exists no overarching economic policy with regard to immigration, we also need to take note that a key driver in the demand for international migrants over the next twenty years will be the slowing growth, and then decline, of the labor force. The United States is expected to have its labor force aging out somewhere around the year 2020. Compare this to developing countries, where about 31 percent of the population is below the age of fourteen, with a forecast to add nearly one billion workers to the world's labor force by 2025.[2]

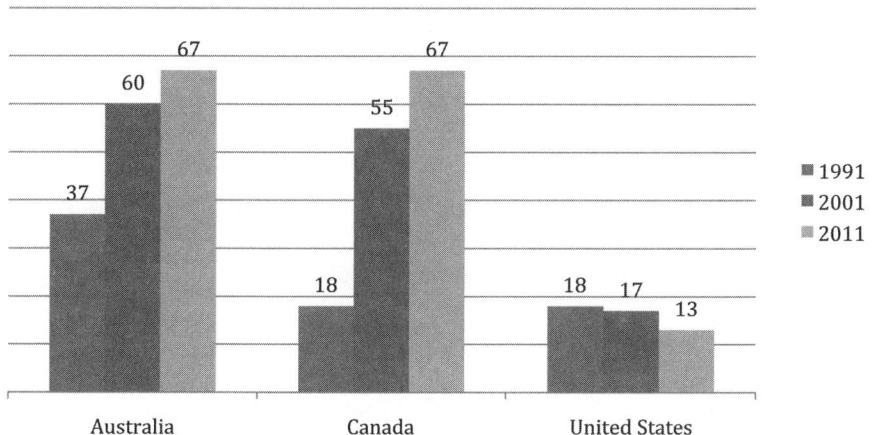

Comparison of Percentage of Permanent Residency Visas Dedicated to Workers and Their Dependents

Austrialian Government, Department of Immigration and Border Protection, www.immi.gov.au/; Citizenship and Immigration Canada, "Fact and Figures," www.cic.gc.ca/english/resources/statistics/menu-fact.asp; U.S. Department of Homeland Security, http://www.dhs.gov/.

In Canada there is no annual limit on the number of work permits issued; Canadian companies in labor-tight industries eagerly use the Temporary Foreign Worker Program to recruit foreign talent. Attracting information technology workers has been deemed a priority in Canada, and special immigration provisions for IT workers have been implemented to facilitate their entry into the Canadian workforce.

There is a fundamental difference between the thinking behind temporary foreign workers in the United States and in Canada. A Canadian temporary work permit is seen as the first step to becoming a permanent resident and then a Canadian citizen, whereas American H1-B holders are aware that their stay in the United States is only temporary.

Canada now has one of the highest intakes of immigrants in the world, with a per capita rate double that of the U.S. rate, even after taking into account the flow of illegal migrants from Mexico and Central America.[3]

Recently, Canadian immigration minister Jason Kenney announced that the federal government is also considering legislating away its massive backlog of immigration applications and allowing provinces to cherry-pick from one big pool of would-be newcomers in a bid to transform Canada's immigration system into one that's driven by the economy. In a speech to business leaders at an Economic Club of Canada luncheon, Kenney promised "transformational change" to immigration that emphasizes the need for skilled newcomers who can fill gaps in the country's labor market. He suggested the pre-2008 backlog of nearly one million applications is bogging down the system and hindering reforms. He outlined several pilot projects and strategies the government is considering to eliminate it. "People with flexible human capital, high levels of language proficiency and a prearranged job are set for success so that will be an important guidepost as we move toward transformational change," he said

Noting New Zealand "legislated an end" to its backlog in 2003 by creating a pool from which all applicants could be selected based on specific criteria as opposed to time spent in the queue, Canada is looking at a similar option. Meanwhile, a new pilot project, Kenney said, is now in place to give provinces the opportunity to "mine the backlog" for newcomers who meet local labor force needs.

The Canadian federal government has already struck deals with British Columbia, Alberta, Saskatchewan, Manitoba, Ontario, Nova Scotia, Newfoundland, Labrador, and the Northwest Territories to sort through the backlogs. Officials predict this will allow Canada to welcome an additional three thousand to four thousand newcomers this year through the provincial nominee program, which gives the provinces and territories a greater say in immigrant selection.

Furthermore, high-level consultations have begun between government officials and employers across the country to discuss ways of creating a more active immigration system in which employers play a greater role in recruiting people from abroad. Kenney said the government is looking at obtaining consent from applicants in the backlog, so they might be considered directly by Canadian employers who are looking for particular skilled workers. This would mean giving employers direct access to the backlog database so, for example, hospitals in Manitoba can find foreign doctors and nurses who have said they would like to settle in the region.

"Employers are best positioned to decide who can best fill the open jobs rather than a passive and bureaucratic system," Kenney said, dismissing the idea that such an initiative could give the private sector too much power at the expense of the federal government. "It's not about privatizing the immigration system, it's about a more active role of recruitment for people so they have jobs when they show up. I'd rather have an engineer working as an engineer than as a cab driver. That's really where we're trying to go with this."

In 2007, Microsoft opened a Development Center in Vancouver, Canada. The most significant reason for doing this, and the one that stimulated much debate, centered on immigration and temporary foreign workers. With a high demand for foreign information technology workers, Microsoft chairman Bill Gates has long lobbied the American government to ease restrictions on H-1B visas. Recognizing that American immigration policy is not likely to change in the near future, Microsoft realized that Canada's more open immigration system for foreign skilled workers is a more attractive option. The Canadian software development center will allow "the company to recruit and retain highly skilled people affected by immigration issues in the U.S."[4]

Those Microsoft employees on H-1B visas, who would have to leave the United States when their visas expire, now have the option to transfer to the Microsoft development center in Canada. This works well for Microsoft. It can maintain these trained and valued employees; it can benefit from Canada's more open temporary foreign worker program to recruit additional IT workers from abroad; and its foreign employees can more easily become permanent residents and Canadian citizens. Employees are therefore more long term. The new Microsoft Canada Development Centre also works well for Canada. The country will benefit from the influx of foreign IT workers and the increased investment in Canada's software development industry.

It should cause U.S. policymakers some concern that the heading on Microsoft's Vancouver Development Center's web page says it is the "Destination for the World's Best."

Immigration Minister Kenney went so far as to go to Ireland this year for an official visit to promote Canada as a destination for international talent. "The Government of Canada is committed to building an immigration system that actively recruits talent rather than passively processing all applications that we receive," said Kenney. He visited Dublin's Working Abroad Expo recruitment fair, where he promoted Canada's strong economy and encouraged talent from Ireland to apply for jobs to work in Canada.

The Construction Sector Council of Canada forecasts that it will need an estimated 319,000 new construction workers between 2012 and 2020, as resource projects peak and retirements continue to rise across the country. The forecast estimates a need for one hundred thousand jobs due to expansion demands in the mining, oil and gas, electricity, and transportation sectors.

The government of Canada is building a fast and flexible economic immigration system with a primary focus on meeting Canada's labor market needs. The government is exploring provinces, territories, and employers' approaches to developing a pool of skilled workers, who could be selected to immigrate to Canada and who are ready to begin employment. "This is the next frontier in Canadian immigration: looking at opportunities to attract the best talent and going out there and getting it," said Kenney.

Meanwhile, across the ocean, Singapore's immigration policy, according to UNESCO, is one that "maximizes the economic benefits of immigration while minimizing its social and economic costs." For instance, its early immigration policy emphasized the immigrant's potential economic benefit, but there was an exclusive criteria for the selection of immigrants whose cultural background matched or was similar to that of the local Singaporean population (e.g., Malaysians). As the country's labor needs changed, so did its sources of foreign talent. Currently, skilled workers and professionals are sought from different parts of the world, while unskilled workers are predominantly sought from the Asian region.

Under the Singapore Employment Act, a foreigner must have a valid work visa to be able to work in Singapore. Today, the foreign workforce in Singapore is categorized into two broad groups: foreign talent and foreign workers. Foreign talent are skilled employees who have a professional business or educational background, whereas foreign workers are the unskilled labor force.

Skilled professionals and entrepreneurs living in Singapore on a work visa are eligible to apply for a permanent residence in due course. A permanent resident status may be granted within six months to two years, while citizenship eligibility may take up to two to ten years of residence. Unskilled workers on a work visa are permitted to work in Singapore for a certain period of time only and thereafter are expected to return to their home country.

The World Bank, in its report "Doing Business," consistently ranks Singapore as the easiest country to conduct business, outranking the United States, Hong Kong, and the United Kingdom.

In the United States, few competitions are more cutthroat than college admissions. Yet it might surprise many to learn that Harvard, with its incredible academic reputation and world-class endowment, works hard to recruit students. Each spring it mails a staggering seventy-thousand-plus letters to high school juniors with the best SAT and ACT scores, whom it has identified after buying their names from the College Board. According to Dean of Admissions Bill Fitzsimmons, every year some 70 percent of the students who ultimately attend Harvard are on this list.

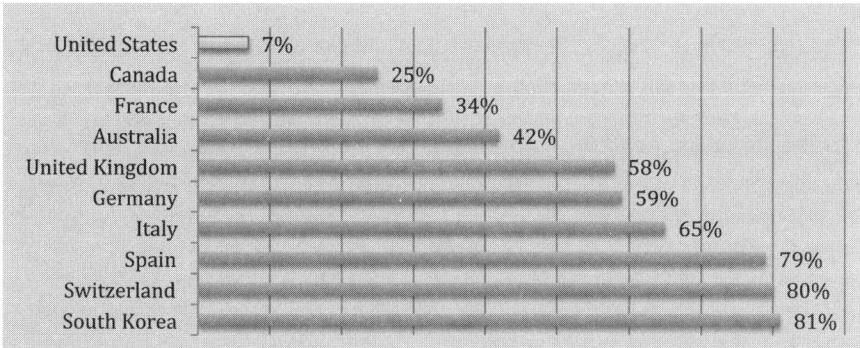

Percentage of Work-Based Immigrants in Various Countries
Pia Orrenius and Madeline Zavodny, "From Brawns to Brains: How Immigration Works for America," Federal Reserve Bank of Dallas 2010 Annual Report, www.dallasfed.org/assets/documents/fed/annual/2010/ar10b.pdf.

If our top educational institutions are being proactive in ensuring they elicit the best of the best, U.S. foreign policy should follow their example and assist corporations in identifying and in recruiting the top global talent to contribute to U.S. innovation.

Yet from many prestigious U.S. higher-education institutions, we are sending a large percentage of the already large foreign student body population out of the United States upon graduation. Once we have educated and trained them, they are now equipped to enter the fields of the future. Unfortunately, these fields are also being nurtured and are developing in other locations around the world.

So in looking at how other countries are handling immigration policy, and even taking a page out of our own Harvard and MIT handbook, it seems in a market-driven economy we need to apply some of the same principles to our greatest asset: our people. When thinking of our human capital, it bears repeating, "Capital goes where it's wanted, and stays where it's well treated." Knowledge and skills are the global currency of the twenty-first-century economies.

The most realistic solution for U.S. policy on immigration is to bring the system out of the 1960s and into the twenty-first century by recognizing that, in a global economy, immigration policies must be as responsive to market forces as economic policies. The global contest for talent is likely to define which countries lead the world economy for decades to come.

America was originally built by immigrants, and it continues to be built by the hard work of immigrants. Immigrants are the secret to our success, let's not forget that.

> Woodrow Wilson, in a July 4, 1914, speech at Independence Hall, Philadelphia:
>
> We set this nation up . . . to vindicate the rights of man. We did not name any differences between one race and another. We opened our gates to all the world and said: "Let all men who want to be free come to us and they will be welcome."

NOTES

1. Vivek Wadhwa, *The Immigrant Exodus: Why America Is Losing the Global Race to Capture Entrepreneurial Talent*, (Philadelphia, PA: Wharton Digital Press, 2012).

2. World Bank, "Global Economic Prospects 2006: Economic Implications of Remittances and Migration."

3. Garnett Picot and Arthur Sweetman, "Making It in Canada: Immigration Outcomes and Policies," *The Institute for Research on Public Policy* 1 (2011).

4. Paul McDougall, "Microsoft Looks to Dodge Visa Limits with Canadian Software Center," *InformationWeek*, July 5, 2007, http://www.informationweek.com/microsoft-looks-to-dodge-visa-limits-wit/200900554 (accessed July 2013).

25

Would I Do It Again?

It's sobering to look back at the choices you have made in your life and their subsequent outcomes and to try to decide what you would do differently if given the chance. I guess everyone by a certain age starts to question the wisdom and validity of their choices. Choices that when made seemed so definitely right, not in the moral sense, but rather in the pragmatic sense. Of course, we are all at the mercy of external forces, regardless of the choices we make or try to make.

Like a feather being carried on the wind, I, too, have been blown around and changed. The life of an immigrant is one of having to survive the tempests that blow in greater force and a more haphazard direction than that of the nonimmigrant. But while I might have a hard time evaluating the wisdom in each decision I have made, I am not able to avoid facing the inevitable consequences that have resulted from those decisions.

We all start out in life as a bona fide member of a tribe, and the unity of a tribe is based on kinship—on kin and kind. It used to be that we rarely encountered someone from another tribe. And, typically, the enemy tribe is the stranger one.

For me, while I have retained close ties with my family, I have lost ties with my kind, for my "kind" no longer exists. This is truly the story of the immigrant. By giving something to his adopted country, he in turn loses a part of himself.

I have regularly met to have lunch with an older group of managers, ministers, ambassadors, government officials, and seniors active during the Shah era of Iran. We discuss U.S. policy toward Iran and comment on its success and failures. After a few meetings, I realized I am no longer an Iranian. I am an American of Iranian decent. During Iran's green revolution in 2010, I was on TV and in the media extensively. Because of this, along with my background, at the age of sixty I was invited to join a group of highly educated, younger Iranians to discuss and to be a part of the plan for a future Iran. After much thought and consideration, I decided I have become too distant from today's Iranian culture and society to be part of something that seemed to be the purvey of the younger generation. I guess I felt too established and maybe not hungry enough to hazard it all to gamble on something so uncertain and potentially risky. I had lost the fire in my belly. I could have gone if I really wanted to. But Iran has changed since I immigrated here; I would have probably felt uncomfortable in that environment, and the other members would not have perceived me as a "true" Iranian. Yet I am not just an American. I am also an Iranian, who is well assimilated into this country's culture and history, its people, and my kin. I am now much older and rooted in the United States. I hope that by mentoring thousands of students I have helped to inspire the next generation, and I can only imagine that my colleagues in education feel similarly. I can only hope that, as immigrants, we have helped to pass the torch onto the next generation of immigrants, who will take up the distinctly American call for those willing to take the risk.

I also can't help but ask myself what would we, as immigrants, have accomplished, contributed to our heritage, and the world at large, if we had not immigrated. The story of older immigrants as they look back at their lives reminds me of Robert Frost's poem "The Road Not Taken."

> Two roads diverged in a yellow wood,
> And sorry I could not travel both
> And be one traveler, long I stood
> And looked down one as far as I could
> To where it bent in the undergrowth;
>
> Then took the other, as just as fair,
> And having perhaps the better claim
> Because it was grassy and wanted wear,
> Though as for that the passing there
> Had worn them really about the same,
>
> And both that morning equally lay
> In leaves no step had trodden black.
> Oh, I kept the first for another day!
> Yet knowing how way leads on to way
> I doubted if I should ever come back.
>
> I shall be telling this with a sigh
> Somewhere ages and ages hence:
> Two roads diverged in a wood, and I,
> I took the one less traveled by,
> And that has made all the difference.[1]

We have become Americans of Iranian, Polish, Korean, African, and French decent. We are proud of our accomplishments. We did it our way, and it has been rewarding for our lives and for the lives of Americans.

NOTE

1. Robert Frost, "The Road Not Taken," *PoemHunter.com*, http://www.poemhunter.com/poem/the-road-not-taken/ (accessed October 31, 2013).

References

Achievement.org. n.d. Pierre Omidyar, Academy of Achievement. http://www.achievement.org/autodoc/page/omi0int-4 (accessed July 17, 2013).

Al Jazeerza English. n.d. One on one: Zbigniew Brzezinski. *YouTube.com.* http://www.youtube.com/watch?v=03ApSE6mgHE (accessed July 8, 2013).

American Civil Liberties Union. 2007. Department of Justice statistics show clear pattern of racial profiling. April 29, 2007. http://www.aclu.org/racial-justice/department-justice-statistics-show-clear-pattern-racial-profiling (accessed July 9, 2013).

American Experience. Transcript: Henry Ford. n.d. WGBH, PBS. http://www.pbs.org/wgbh/americanexperience/features/transcript/henryford-transcript/ (accessed July 8, 2013).

American Psychological Association. *APA.org.* n.d. Crossroads: The psychology of immigration in the new century. http://www.apa.org/topics/immigration/report.aspx (accessed August 16, 2013).

Ansari, Azadeh. 2009. Iranian-Americans cast ballots on Iran's future. *CNN.com.* June 16, 2009. http://www.cnn.com/2009/US/06/12/iran.elections.voting/ (accessed July 24, 2013).

Anthony, Sebastian. 2012. The first flexible, fiber-optic solar cell that can be woven into clothes. *ExtremeTech.com.* December 7, 2012. http://www.extremetech.com/computing/142755-the-first-flexible-fiber-optic-solar-cell-that-can-be-woven-into-clothes (accessed July 9, 2013).

Australian Government. Department of Immigration and Border Protection. n.d. http://www.immi.gov.au/ (accessed October 31, 2013).

Bates, Karen Grigsby. 2012. How Koreatown rose from the ashes of L.A. riots. *NPR: National Public Radio.* April 27, 2012. http://www.npr.org/2012/04/27/151524921/how-koreatown-rose-from-the-ashes-of-l-a-riots (accessed July 24, 2013).

Bier, David. 2013. To grow, the U.S. economy needs more low-skilled immigrant workers. *Forbes.com.* May 6, 2013. http://www.forbes.com/sites/realspin/2013/05/06/

to-grow-the-u-s-economy-needs-more-low-skilled-immigrant-workers/ (accessed August 17, 2013).
Biography.com. n.d. Sergey Brin. http://www.biography.com/people/sergey-brin-12103333 (accessed October 22, 2013).
Blackmon, David. 2013. The Texas shale oil & gas revolution—Leading the way to enhanced energy security. *Forbes.com.* March 19, 2013. http://www.forbes.com/sites/davidblackmon/2013/03/19/the-texas-shale-oil-gas-revolution-leading-the-way-to-enhanced-energy-security/ (accessed July 10, 2013).
BookTV.org. n.d. Conrad Black, "Flight of the eagle." http://www.booktv.org/Watch/14688/Book+TV+Interview+Conrad+Black+Flight+of+the+Eagle.aspx (accessed July 10, 2013).
Booth, William. 2012. Mexico is now a top producer of engineers, but where are jobs? *Washington Post.* October 28, 2012. http://articles.washingtonpost.com/2012-10-28/world/35498580_1_mexico-city-president-enrique-pe-a-nieto-engineers (accessed July 24, 2013).
Borjas, George. 1990. Immigrants—not what they used to be. *Wall Street Journal.* November 8, 1990. http://www.thesocialcontract.com/artman2/publish/tsc0202/article_107.shtml (accessed October 29, 2013).
Brookings Institute. n.d. Brookings: Quality. Independence. Impact. http://www.brookings.edu (accessed July 8, 2013).
Brown, Heather, Emily Guskin, and Amy Mitchell. 2012. Arab-American media. Pew Research Journalism Project. November 28, 2012. http://www.journalism.org/analysis_report/arabamerican_population_growth (accessed July 24, 2013).
Brown, Susan K., and Frank D. Bean. 2006. Assimilation models, old and new: Explaining a long-term process. Migration Information Source. October 2006. http://www.migrationinformation.org/feature/display.cfm?id=442 (accessed July 24, 2013).
Bureau of Labor Statistics, U.S. Department of Labor. n.d. Foreign-born workers: Labor force characteristics. May 22, 2013. www.bls.gov/news.release/pdf/forbrn.pdf (accessed October 25, 2013).
Bush, Jeb, and Thomas McLarty. 2009. Independent task force report on U.S. immigration policy. Council on Foreign Relations. July 2009. www.cfr.org/immigration/us-immigration-policy/p20030 (accessed July 10, 2013).
Carpenter, Steven. 2010. TC teardown: Chegg is a money machine. *TechCrunch.com.* June 5, 2010. http://techcrunch.com/2010/06/05/teardown-chegg/ (accessed July 17, 2013).
Caruso, David, Michael Kunzelman, and Max Seddon. 2013. Zubeidat Tsarnaeva, mother of Boston Marathon bombing suspects, says she's just someone who found deeper spirituality. *Huffington Post.* April 28, 2013. http://www.huffingtonpost.com/2013/04/28/zubeidat-tsarnaeva-mother-boston-marathon-bombing-suspects_n_3176009.html (accessed July 24, 2013).
CBSNews. 2013. Family of accused bombers divided over allegations. April 19, 2013. http://www.cbc.ca/news/world/story/2013/04/19/boston-marathon-bombing-suspect-profile.html (accessed July 24, 2013).

Chabad.org. n.d. Intolerence: Based on letters and talks of the Rebbe, Rabbi M. M. Schneerson. http://www.chabad.org/library/article_cdo/aid/150549/jewish/Intolerance.htm (accessed October 29, 2013).

Chatterjee, Rituparna. 2011. How Silicon Valley's new Indian entrepreneurs are blooming in all hues. *EconomicTimes.com.* July 31, 2011. http://articles.economictimes.indiatimes.com/2011-07-31/news/29835690_1_indian-entrepreneurs-sramana-mitra-serial-entrepreneur (accessed July 17, 2013).

Chegg.com. n.d. Management team. http://www.chegg.com/managementteam (accessed July 17, 2013).

Christian Reformed Church Office of Social Justice. 2013. 10 immigration myths busted. http://www2.crcna.org/pages/osj_immigrationmyths.cfm (accessed August 18, 2013).

Citizenship and Immigration Canada. n.d. Fact and figures. http://www.cic.gc.ca/english/resources/statistics/menu-fact.asp (accessed October 31, 2013).

CNN.com. 2013. Timeline: A look at Tamerlan Tsarnaev's past. April 22, 2013. http://www.cnn.com/2013/04/21/us/tamerlan-tsarnaev-timeline (accessed July 24, 2013).

Coalition for Humane Immigrant Rights (CHIRLA). n.d. Beyond myths and stereotypes: Facts about immigration and crime. chirla.org/files/FactsheetImmigrationanCrime.pdf (accessed July 14, 2013).

Cohen, Tim, and Bill Mears. 2012. Supreme Court mostly rejects Arizona immigration law; gov says "heart" remains. *CNN Politics.* June 26, 2012. http://www.cnn.com/2012/06/25/politics/scotus-arizona-law (accessed July 7, 2013).

Colleluori, Salvatore. 2013. Fox News amplifies fabricated link between immigrants and crime. Media Matters for America.com. June 18, 2013. mediamatters.org/research/2013/06/18/fox-news-amplifies-fabricated-link-between-immi/194504 (accessed July 14, 2013).

Committee on the Judiciary. 2007. U.S. economy, U.S. workers, and immigration reform. U.S. Government Printing Office. May 3, 2007. http://www.gpo.gov/fdsys/pkg/CHRG-110hhrg35117/html/CHRG-110hhrg35117.htm (accessed July 8, 2013).

Cooper, Havovi. 2013. Immigrants should learn English. *Businessweek.com.* http://www.businessweek.com/debateroom/archives/2008/08/immigrants_should_learn_english.html (accessed July 15, 2013).

Cooper, Michael, Michael S. Schmidt, and Eric Schmitt. 2013. Boston suspects are seen as self-taught and fueled by web. *New York Times.* April 23, 2013. http://www.nytimes.com/2013/04/24/us/boston-marathon-bombing-developments.html?pagewanted=all&_r=0 (accessed July 24, 2013).

Council on Foreign Relations. www.cfr.org/ (accessed August 14, 2013).

Davis, Kenneth C. 2007. The founding immigrants. *New York Times.* July 3, 2007. http://www.nytimes.com/2007/07/03/opinion/03davis.html?_r=0 (accessed August 28, 2013).

Deflem, Mathieu. n.d. *Sociology of crime law and deviance* series. *EmeraldInsight.com.* www.emeraldinsight.com/books.htm?chapterid=1791225&show=html (accessed July 14, 2013).

Dodson, Brian. 2013. Metamaterials breakthrough could lead to the first wide-spectrum optical invisibility cloak. *Gizmag*. June 12, 2013. http://www.gizmag.com/metamaterials-wide-spectrum-optical-invisibility-cloak-stanford/27813/ (accessed July 9, 2013).

Douthat, Ross. 2013. When assimilation stalls. *New York Times*. April 27, 2013. http://www.nytimes.com/2013/04/28/opinion/sunday/douthat-when-the-assimilation-of-immigrants-stalls.html?_r=0 (accessed July 24, 2013).

Dudley, Brier. 2013. Ballmer's biggest success was out of the spotlight. *Seattle Times*. August 24, 2013. http://seattletimes.com/html/businesstechnology/2021682849_brierballmerlegacyxml.html (accessed August 27, 2013).

Duran, Jorge, Douglas S. Massey, and René M. Zenteno. 2001. Mexican immigration to the United States: Continuities and changes. *Latin American Research Review* 36, no. 1: 107, 109.

Durkin, Erin. 2013. Mayor Bloomberg blasts immigration policy to Stanford grads. *New York Daily News.com*. June 17, 2013. http://www.nydailynews.com/new-york/mayor-bloomberg-blasts-immigration-policy-stanford-grads-article-1.1374798 (accessed August 14, 2013).

Encyclopedia Britannica. n.d. South Korea: Economic and social developments. http://www.britannica.com/EBchecked/topic/322280/South-Korea/34997/Economic-and-social-developments (accessed July 8, 2013).

Engineering @ San Jose State University. n.d. Alumni profiles: Omid Kordestani, Google Inc., senior vice president of global sales and business development. http://www.engr.sjsu.edu/alumni/profiles/omid-kordestani (accessed October 22, 2013).

Entrepreneurship of All Kinds.org. http://entrepreneurshipofallkinds.org/ (accessed August 14, 2013).

Erdmann, Vera, and Tanja Schumann. 2010. European engineering report. *Institut der deutschen Wirtschaft* Köln. April 2010. www.vdi.de/uploads/media/2010-04_IW_European_Engineering_Report_02.pdf (accessed July 20, 2013).

Fairlie, Robert W. 2012. *Open for business: How immigrants are driving small business creation in the United States*. Princeton, NJ: Partnership for a New American Economy, 2012. 1–40.

Federation for American Immigration Reform.org. http://www.fairus.org/ (accessed August 14, 2013).

Financial Research, Investment Analytics Tools—FactSet Research Systems. 2013. FactSet data—FactSet research systems. http://www.factset.com/data/factset_data (accessed July 10, 2013).

Fiscal Policy Institute Data Release. 2012. What kind of businesses do immigrants own? Detail by country of birth. June 2012. http://fiscalpolicy.org/wp-content/uploads/2012/06/immigrant-business-owners-by-country-of-birth-20120615.pdf (accessed August 27, 2013).

Fischer, David Hackett. *Liberty and freedom: A visual history of America's founding ideas*. New York: Oxford University Press, 2005.

Flow of History.org. n.d. Gathering and interactions of peoples, cultures, and ideas: A brief timeline of U.S. policy on immigration and naturalization. *The Flow of History.* http://www.flowofhistory.org/themes/movement_settlement/uspolicy timeline.php (accessed July 10, 2013).

Fonte, John. 2013. New Hudson study: America's patriotic assimilation system is broken. *Hudson Institute.* April 8, 2013. http://www.hudson.org/index.cfm?fuseaction=publication_details&id=9569 (accessed July 24, 2013).

Forbes.com. n.d. World's most innovative companies: Google. http://www.forbes.com/companies/google/ (accessed October 22, 2013).

Fram, Alan. 2010. Poll finds discrimination against Hispanics is high. *Seattle Times.* May 20, 2010. http://seattletimes.com/html/nationworld/2011916375_biaspoll21.html (accessed July 15, 2013).

Frost, Robert. n.d. The road not taken. *PoemHunter.com.* http://www.poemhunter.com/poem/the-road-not-taken/ (accessed October 31, 2013).

General Books LLC. 2010. *eBay employees: Meg Whitman, Pierre Omidyar, Randy Wigginton, John Donahoe, and Rajiv Dutta.* S.l.: General Books LLC.

Ghadar, Fariborz. 2012. Dispel the immigration myths. *CNN.com.* December 11, 2012. http://www.cnn.com/2012/12/11/opinion/ghadar-immigration-policy (accessed July 14, 2013).

Ghadar, Fariborz, and Erik Peterson. 2008. *Global tectonics: What every business needs to know.* University Park: Penn State Center for Global Business Studies.

Ghadar, Fariborz, John Sviokla, and Dietrich A. Stephan. 2012. Why life science needs its own Silicon Valley. *Harvard Business Review Magazine* (July–August 2012). http://hbr.org/2012/07/why-life-science-needs-its-own-silicon-valley/ar/1 (accessed July 9, 2013).

Gitlin, Marty. 2011. *eBay: The company and its founder.* Edina, MN: ABDO Publishing.

globalEDGE.com. Michigan State University. n.d. South Korea: Economy. http://globaledge.msu.edu/countries/south-korea/economy (accessed July 8, 2013).

"Global Nanotechnology Industry Output Expected to Reach $2.4 Trillion by 2015," Yahoo! Finance, http://finance.yahoo.com/news/Global-Nanotechnology-iw-3399006244.html (accessed December 15, 2013).

Golden, Daniel. 2012. Iranians denied U.S. visas hit by political crossfire. *Bloomberg.com.* September 19, 2012. http://www.bloomberg.com/news/2012-09-20/iranians-denied-u-s-visas-hit-by-political-crossfire.html (accessed August 13, 2013).

Greenhouse, Steven. 2010. Muslims report rising discrimination at work. *New York Times.* September 23, 2010. http://www.nytimes.com/2010/09/24/business/24muslim.html?pagewanted=all (accessed October 29, 2013).

Greenstone, Michael, and Adam Looney. 2010. Ten economic facts about immigration. September 2010. The Hamilton Project. www.brookings.edu/~/media/research/files/reports/2010/9/immigration%20greenstone%20looney/09_immigration (accessed July 10, 2013).

Grieco, Elizabeth M., Edward Trevelyan, Luke Larsen, Yesenia D. Acosta, Christine Gambino, Patricia de la Cruz, Tom Gryn, and Nathan Walters. 2012. U.S. Census Bureau, Population Division. *The size, place of birth, and geographic distribution of the foreign-born population in the United States: 1960 to 2010.* Annual Meetings of the Population Association of America, San Francisco, CA, May 3–5, 2012.

H1base.com. n.b. H1B visa cap and H1B quota 2013 (FY2014) system explained—latest H1B 2013 status for quota, cap, news updates—H1B 2012 cap count and tracker—USCIS H1B quota filing updates and cap numbers count—H1B cap 2011, h1b cap 2012, h1b quota 2012. http://www.h1base.com/visa/work/H1Bvi (accessed August 18, 2013).

Hagel III, John, John Seely Brown, and Duleesha Kulasooriya. 2011. The 2011 shift index: Measuring the forces of long-term change. *Deloitte Center for the Edge* 1 (2011): 17.

Hakimzadeh, Shirin. 2006. Country profiles: Iran: A vast diaspora abroad and millions of refugees at home. Migrations Policy Institute. September 2006. http://www.migrationinformation.org/feature/display.cfm?ID=424 (accessed July 9, 2013).

Hanes, Stephanie. 2013. Immigration: Assimilation and the measure of an American. *Christian Science Monitor*. July 7, 2013. http://www.csmonitor.com/USA/Society/2013/0707/Immigration-Assimilation-and-the-measure-of-an-American (accessed July 24, 2013).

Harper, Tim. 2001. Global funding of nanotechnologies and its impact. *cientifica*. cientifica.com/wp-content/uploads/downloads/2011/07/Global-Nanotechnology-Funding-Report-2011.pdf (accessed July 1, 2013).

Harvard Magazine. 2007. Uneasy neighbors: A brief history of Mexican-U.S. migration. May–June 2007. http://harvardmagazine.com/2007/05/uneasy-neighbors-a-brief-html (accessed August 14, 2013).

Hayden, Erika Check. 2012. Nanopore genome sequencer makes its debut. *Nature*. February 17, 2012. http://www.nature.com/news/nanopore-genome-sequencer-makes-its-debut-1.10051 (accessed July 31, 2013).

Hoefer, Michael, Nancy Rytina, and Bryan Baker. 2012. Estimates of the unauthorized immigrant population residing in the United States: January 2011. Department of Homeland Security. *Population Estimates*. March 2012. http://www.dhs.gov/estimates-unauthorized-immigrant-population-residing-united-states-january-2011 (accessed August 4, 2013).

Humphreys, Jeffrey M. 2008. The multicultural economy 2008. *Georgia Business and Economic Conditions* 68, no. 3 (Third Quarter): 1, 2, 3, 4.

Iglicka, Krystyna, and Magdalena Ziolek-Skrzypczak. 2010. EU membership highlights Poland's migration challenges. *Migration Information Source*. September. http://www.migrationinformation.org/feature/display.cfm?ID=800 (accessed July 8, 2013).

Immigrant Learning Center. n.d. Immigrant entrepreneurs and workers in leisure and hospitality businesses. http://www.ilctr.org/promoting-immigrants/immigration-research/immigrant-entrepreneurs-and-workers-in-leisure-and-hospitality-businesses/ (accessed August 17, 2013).

Immigration Policy Center. n.d. The migrant integration policy index. http://www.immigrationpolicy.org/just-facts/migrant-integration-policy-index-mipex-iii (accessed July 24, 2013).

———. n.d. Rebuilding local economies. http://www.immigrationpolicy.org/just-facts/rebuilding-local-economies (accessed August 9, 2013).

Invernizzi, Noela. 2011. Nanotechnology between the lab and the shop floor: What are the effects on labor? *Journal of Nanoparticle Research* 13 (2011). http://cms.springerprofessional.de/journals/JOU=11051/VOL=2011.13/ISU=6/ART=333/BodyRef/PDF/11051_2011_Article_333.pdf (accessed October 28, 2013).

Jackson, Richard, Neil Howe, with Rebecca Strauss and Keisuke Nakashima. 2008. The graying of the great powers: Demography and geopolitics in the 21st century. Center for Strategic and International Studies, May 2008.

Joshi, Nikhil. 2013. The business case for immigration reform part 1: Low-skilled workers. *Business Forward*. April 2013. http://www.businessfwd.org/blog/body/BF_Immigration_Final.pdf (accessed October 23, 2013).

Justice for Immigrants.org. 2013. Countering the myths. www.justiceforimmigrants.org/myths.shtml#sthash.qJ9mnzUg.dpuf (accessed July 15, 2013).

Kirkpatrick, David D., and Alan Cowell. *New York Times*. http://www.nytimes.com/ (accessed August 14, 2013).

Koba, Mark. 2012. How immigrants are changing US businesses. *CNBC*. September 4, 2012. http://www.cnbc.com/id/48646997 (accessed August 27, 2012).

Korean American Historical Society (KAHS). 2003. 1903–2003: A century of Korean immigration. May 27–June 20, 2003. http://www.kahs.org/news-centennial.html (accessed July 8, 2013).

Korean-AmericanStory.org. n.d. Korean-American Population 1910–2010. http://www.koreanamericanstory.org/index.php?option=com_content&view=article&id=199&Itemid=134 (accessed July 8, 2013).

La Jeunesse, William. 2013. Silicon Valley banks on immigration bill for access to foreign workers. *Fox News*. June 24, 2013. http://www.foxnews.com/politics/2013/06/24/silicon-valley-banks-on-immigration-bill-for-access-to-foreign-workers/ (accessed July 8, 2013).

Lazarus, Emma. n.d. The new colossus. *Poets.org*. http://www.poets.org/viewmedia.php/prmMID/16111 (accessed July 2013).

The Leadership Conference on Civil and Human Rights. n.d. End racial profiling. civilrightsdocs.info. www.civilrightsdocs.info/pdf/discrimination/racial-profiling-and-counterterrorism-w-banner-final-4-15-12.pdf (accessed July 8, 2013).

Lewin, Rhoda G. 1979. Stereotype and reality in the Jewish immigrant experience in Minneapolis. *Minnesota History* 46, no. 7: 258–73. http://collections.mnhs.org/MNHistoryMagazine/articles/46/v46i07p258-273.pdf (August 27, 2013).

Library of Congress. n.d. Polish/Russian immigration: The nation of Polonia. http://www.loc.gov/teachers/classroommaterials/presentationsandactivities/presentations/immigration/polish4.html (accessed July 8, 2013).

Lichtblau, Eric. 2003. Bush issues federal ban on racial profiling. *New York Times*. June 17, 2003. http://www.nytimes.com/2003/06/17/politics/17CND-PROF.html (accessed July 9, 2013).

Linenthal, Edward T. 2003. *The unfinished bombing: Oklahoma City in American memory*. New York: Oxford University Press.

Lo, Barnaby. 2007. Philippines: Have degree, will travel. Where have all the nurses gone? *PBS.org*. December 18, 2007. http://www.pbs.org/frontlineworld/rough/2007/12/philippines_hav.html (accessed October 30, 2013).

López, Ricardo A. n.d. We must stop the negative immigration rage! *Latino Opinion.* http://www.latinoopinion.com/category/prejudice-and-discrimination/ (accessed July 15, 2013).

Ludden, Jennifer. 2006. 1965 immigration law changed face of America. *National Public Radio.* http://www.npr.org/templates/story/story.php?storyId=5391395 (accessed August 27, 2013).

Malone, Michael S. 1985. *The big score: The billion dollar story of Silicon Valley.* New York: Doubleday.

Manpower Group. n.d. ManpowerGroup annual survey reveals U.S. talent shortages persist in skilled trades, engineers and IT staff. Manpower US Pressroom. http://press.manpower.com/press/2012/talent-shortage/ (accessed July 9, 2013).

Massey, Douglas S. 1999. International migration at the dawn of the twenty-first century: The role of the state. *Population and Development Review* 25: 303, 307.

McAllister, Edward, and Timothy Gardner. 2013, UPDATE 3-Rise in shale oil boosts global crude supply estimate—U.S. EIA. *Reuters.com.* June 10, 2013. http://www.reuters.com/article/2013/06/10/global-shale-idUSL2N0EM1KM20130610 (accessed July 31, 2013).

McDougall, Paul. 2077. Microsoft looks to dodge visa limits with Canadian software center. *InformationWeek*, July 5, 2007, http://www.informationweek.com/microsoft-looks-to-dodge-visa-limits-wit/200900554 (accessed July 2013).

MIT Political Science. n.d. Alumni spotlight: AnnaLee Saxenian, PhD, 1989—A view of the valley. http://web.mit.edu/polisci/news/2012/alumni-saxenian-feature.html (accessed August 29, 2013).

Monger, Randall, and James Yankay. 2013. U.S. legal permanent residents: 2012. March 2013. *Department of Homeland Security: Annual flow report.* http://www.dhs.gov/sites/default/files/publications/ois_lpr_fr_2012_2.pdf (accessed July 10, 2013).

Muñoz, Cecilia, Gene Sperling, Alan Krueger, and Sylvia Mathews Burwell. 2013. The economic benefits of fixing our broken immigration system. July 10, 2103. *White House Blog.* http://www.whitehouse.gov/blog/2013/07/10/economic-benefits-fixing-our-broken-immigration-system (accessed July 10, 2013).

Murray, Sara. 2013. Fewer Mexicans head to U.S. as home exerts more pull. *Wall Street Journal.* June 21, 2013. http://online.wsj.com/article/SB10001424127887324069104578529522746064526.html (accessed July 24, 2013).

Myers, Dowell. 2012. The next immigration challenge. *New York Times.* January 11, 2012. http://www.nytimes.com/2012/01/12/opinion/the-next-immigration-challenge.html (accessed July 24, 2013).

National Association of Korean Americans. n.d. In observance of centennial of Korean immigration to the U.S. http://www.naka.org/resources/history.asp (accessed July 9, 2013).

Nevins, Joseph. 2012. Ronald Reagan and comprehensive immigration reform. *North American Congress on Latin America.* November 15, 2012. http://nacla.org/blog/2012/11/15/ronald-reagan-and-comprehensive-immigration-reform (accessed July 10, 2013).

Norouzi, Arash. n.d. Omid Kordestani: Educate people about Iran. *The Mossadegh Project*. http://www.mohammadmossadegh.com/news/omid-kordestani/ (accessed October 22, 2013).

Olds, Kris. 2012. Global citizenship—What are we talking about and why does it matter? *Inside Higher Ed.com*. http://www.insidehighered.com/blogs/globalhighered/global-citizenship-%E2%80%93-what-are-we-talking-about-and-why-does-it-matter (accessed August 14, 2013).

Omidyar Group.com. n.d. Omidyar Group: Pierre and Pam Omidyar. http://omidyargroup.com/ (accessed July 17, 2013).

O'Neill, Joseph. 2008. The new immigrant experience. *NPR.org*. November 26, 2008. http://m.npr.org/story/97468340 (accessed July 2013).

OnTheIssues.org. http://ontheissues.org/default.htm (accessed August 14, 2013).

Organisation for Economic Co-operation and Development (OECD). n.d. International migration outlook. http://www.oecd.org/els/mig/imo2013.htm (accessed October 22, 2013).

Orrenius, Pia, and Madeline Zavodny. 2010. From brawns to brains: How immigration works for America. Federal Reserve Bank of Dallas 2010 Annual Report. http://www.dallasfed.org/assets/documents/fed/annual/2010/ar10b.pdf (accessed October 31, 2013).

Park, Kyeyoung. 1997. *The Korean American dream: Immigrants and small business in New York City*. Ithaca, NY: Cornell University Press.

Parti, Tarini. 2013. "Assimilation" a flash point in immigration debate. *Politico.com*. June 10, 2013. http://www.politico.com/story/2013/06/assimilation-a-flash-point-in-immigration-debate-92469.html (accessed July 24, 2013).

Partnership for a New American Economy. 2011. The "new American" Fortune 500. www.renewoureconomy.org/2011_06_15_1 (accessed July 10, 2013).

———. 2012. Open for business: How immigrants are driving small business creation in the United States. August 2012. www.renewoureconomy.org/sites/all/themes/pnae/openforbusiness.pdf (accessed July 20, 2013).

Passel, Jeffrey S., and D'Vera Cohn. 2008. U.S. population projections: 2005–2050. *Pew Hispanic.org*. February 11, 2008. http://www.pewhispanic.org/2008/02/11/us-population-projections-2005-2050/ (accessed July 9, 2013).

Payvand.com. 2008. Survey of Iranian Americans: 84% support establishing U.S. interest section in Iran. December 11, 2008. http://www.payvand.com/news/08/dec/1117.html (accessed July 24, 2013).

PBS: Public Broadcasting Service. n.d. Caught in the crossfire: Arab Americans. 2013. http://www.pbs.org/itvs/caughtinthecrossfire/arab_americans.html (accessed August 23, 2013).

PBS.org. The City (La Ciudad)—Teachers Guide. n.d. http://www.pbs.org/itvs/thecity/resources1_8_print.html (accessed October 29, 2013).

People with Impact.com. n.d. Pierre Omidyar (founder of eBay): 20 fascinating fun facts. http://www.peoplewithimpact.com/pierre-omidyar/f67e77/ (accessed July 17, 2013).

Pew Research Hispanic Trends Project. 2013. A nation of immigrants. January 29, 2013. http://www.pewhispanic.org/2013/01/29/a-nation-of-immigrants/ (accessed July 14, 2013).

Picot, Garnett, and Arthur Sweetman. 2011. Making it in Canada: Immigration outcomes and policies. *The Institute for Research on Public Policy* 1 (2011).

Putilin, Vladislav, and Anatoly Chubais. 2011. Rusnano annual report. en.rusnano.com/upload/images/normativedocs/RUSNANO_AR2011_ENG.pdf (accessed July 1, 2013).

Roberts, Cokie, and Steven Roberts. 2010. Think like an immigrant. *Evening Sun*. April 16, 2010. http://www.evesun.com/news/stories/2010-04-16/9417/Think-like-an-immigrant-/ (accessed July 2013).

Roco, M. C., C. A. Mirkin, and M. C. Hersam. *Nanotechnology research directions for societal needs in 2020*. September 2010. http://www.wtec.org/nano2/Nanotechnology_Research_Directions_to_2020/ (accessed October 28, 2013).

Rohr Chabad of UNC Chapel Hill and Duke University. n.d. Message from Rabbi Zalman Bluming. http://www.chabaddch.com/templates/articlecco_cdo/aid/345575/jewish/Message-from-the-Rabbi.htm (accessed October 29, 2013).

Rumbaut, Rubén G., and Walter A. Ewing. 2007. The myth of immigrant criminality and the paradox of assimilation: Incarceration rates among native and foreign-born men. Immigration Policy Center. Spring 2007. www.derechoshumanosaz.net/images/pdfs/the%20myth%20of%20immigrant%20criminality%20and%20the%20paradox%20of%20assimilation.pdf (accessed July 13, 2013).

Saxenian, AnnaLee. 1994. *Regional advantage: Culture and competition in Silicon Valley and Route 128*. Cambridge, MA: Harvard University Press.

Schiffauerova, Andrea, and Catherine Beaudry. n.d. Canadian nanotechnology innovation networks: Intra-cluster, inter-cluster and foreign collaboration. *Cairn.info*. http://www.cairn.info/revue-journal-of-innovation-economics-2009-2-page-119.htm (accessed July 9, 2013).

SEIU.org, Service Employees International Union. n.d. "They take our jobs"—Debunking immigration myths. http://www.seiu.org/a/immigration/they-take-our-jobs-debunking-immigration-myths.php (accessed July 14, 2013).

Semple, Kirk. 2012. More U.S. children of immigrants are leaving U.S. *New York Times*. April 15, 2012. http://www.nytimes.com/2012/04/16/us/more-us-children-of-immigrants-are-leaving-us.html?pagewanted=all (accessed July 8, 2013).

Shah, Anup. 2011. World military spending. *Global Issues.org*. May 2, 2011. http://www.globalissues.org/article/75/world-military-spending (accessed July 5, 2013).

Shinal, John. 2013. Tech firms go abroad to hire. *USA Today*. June 5, 2013. http://usatoday30.usatoday.com/MONEY/usaedition/2013-07-05-Silicon-Valley-not-waiting-for-US-immigration-reform_ST_U.htm (accessed August 18, 2013).

Singer, Audrey. 2012. Immigrant workers in the U.S. labor force. *Brookings.com*. March 15, 2012. http://www.brookings.edu/research/papers/2012/03/15-immigrant-workers-singer#4 (accessed July 9, 2013).

Siniavskaia, Natalia. n.d. Immigrant workers in construction. *NAHB HousingEconomics.com*. http://www.nahb.org/generic.aspx?sectionID=734&genericContentID=49216&channelID=311 (accessed October 25, 2013).

Slack, Megan. 2011. By the numbers: 44 million. *White House Blog*. November 3, 2011. http://www.whitehouse.gov/blog/2011/11/03/numbers-44-million (accessed July 8, 2013).

Smeltz, Dina. 2012. Foreign policy in the new millennium. 2012 Chicago Council Survey. http://www.thechicagocouncil.org/files/Studies_Publications/POS/Survey 2012/2012.aspx (accessed October 31, 2013).

Southern Poverty Law Center. April 2009. Under siege: Life for low-income Latinos in the South. http://www.splcenter.org/publications/under-siege-life-low-income -latinos-south/2-racial-profiling (accessed October 25, 2013).

Stockholm International Peace Research Institute. 2013. New SIPRI data on military expenditure—World military spending falls, but China, Russia's spending rises." April 15, 2013. http://www.sipri.org/media/pressreleases/ (accessed July 31, 2013).

Sugrue, Thomas J. 2007. Motor City: The story of Detroit. *Gilder Lehrman American History*. March 2007. www.gilderlehrman.org/history-by-era/politics-reform/ essays/motor-city-story-detroit (accessed July 8, 2013).

Thompson, John. 1995. *The media and modernity: A social theory of the media*. Stanford, CA: Stanford University Press.

Tocqueville, Alexis de. 2007. *Democracy in America* (volume 1, unabridged). Stilwell, KS: Digireads.com Publishing.

Trilateral Commission. n.d. About the Trilateral Commission. http://www.trilateral .org/go.cfm?do=Page.View&pid=5 (accessed August 27, 2013).

Tufts.com. 2013. Pierre Omidyar. *Tufts Now*. October 23, 2013. http://now.tufts.edu/ commencement-2011/pierre-omidyar (accessed July 22, 2013).

UNC Charlotte College of Liberal Arts and Sciences. n.d. Nanoscale science. http:// nanoscalescience.uncc.edu/ (accessed July 1, 2013).

U.S. Department of Homeland Security. n.d. http://www.dhs.gov/ (accessed October 31, 2013).

U.S. Department of State. n.d. *Classes of nonimmigrants issued visas (including crewlist visas and border crossing cards) fiscal years 1992–2010*. travel.state.gov/ visa/statistics/nivstates/nivstats_4582.html.

———. n.d. *Immigrants and nonimmigrant visas issued at foreign service posts fiscal years 1992–2011*. n.d. travel.state.gov/visa/statistics/nivstates/nivstats_4582.html.

———. *Immigrant and nonimmigrant visas issued at foreign service posts fiscal years 1992–2011*. n.d. http://www.travel.state.gov/pdf/MultiYearTableXVI.pdf.

U.S. Department of State: Office of the Historian. n.d. Milestones: 1921–1936—The Immigration Act of 1924 (The Johnson-Reed Act). http://history.state.gov/mile stones/1921-1936/ImmigrationAct (accessed July 8, 2013).

U.S. Energy Information Administration. 2012. How dependent are we on foreign oil? July 13, 2012. http://www.eia.gov/energy_in_brief/article/role_coal_us.cfm (accessed July 31, 2013).

U.S. Government Printing Office. Committee on the Judiciary. 2007. U.S. economy, U.S. workers, and immigration reform. May 3, 2007. http://www.gpo.gov/fdsys/ pkg/CHRG-110hhrg35117/html/CHRG-110hhrg35117.htm (accessed July 8, 2013).

Viegas, Jennifer. 2007. *Pierre Omidyar: The founder of eBay*. New York: Rosen Publishing.

Vobedja, Barbara. 1990. Immigrant tide boosts population: Decides gainers, losers among states, regions. *Washington Post*. December 31, 1990. http://news.google.com/newspapers?nid=1310&dat=19901231&id=u0JWAAAAIBAJ&sjid=i-oDAAAAIBAJ&pg=4916,8134841 (accessed October 29, 2013).

Wadhwa, Vivek. 2012. The immigrant exodus: Why America is losing the global race to capture entrepreneurial talent. Philadelphia, PA: Wharton Digital Press.

Wadhwa, Vivek, AnnaLee Saxenian, Richard Freeman, Gary Gereffi, and Alex Salkever. 2009. America's loss is the world's gain: America's new immigrant entrepreneurs, part IV. Ewing Marion Kauffman Foundation. March 2009. www.kauffman.org/uploadedfiles/americas_loss.pdf (accessed July 1, 2013).

Washington Post. 2010. Nation digest. February 10, 2010. http://articles.washingtonpost.com/2010-02-10/world/36891238_1_illegal-immigrants-gallbladder-immigration-advocates (accessed July 2013).

White House. 2011. Building a 21st century immigration system. May 2011. www.whitehouse.gov/sites/default/files/rss_viewer/immigration_blueprint.pdf (accessed July 1, 2013).

White House Council of Economic Advisers. 2007. Immigration's economic impact. June 20, 2007. http://georgewbush-whitehouse.archives.gov/cea/cea_immigration_062007.html (accessed July 15, 2013).

Whoriskey, Peter. 2012. U.S. manufacturing sees shortage of skilled factory workers. *Washington Post*. February 19, 2012. http://articles.washingtonpost.com/2012-02-19/business/35444240_1_factory-workers-laid-off-workers-jobs (accessed July 9, 2013).

Wines, Michael, and Ian Lovett. 2013. The dark side, carefully masked. *New York Times*. May 4, 2013. http://www.nytimes.com/2013/05/05/us/dzhokhar-tsarnaevs-dark-side-carefully-masked.html?pagewanted=all&_r=0 (accessed July 24, 2013).

World Bank. 2005. Global economic prospects 2006: Economic implications of remittances and migration. November 14, 2005.

Xenakis, John J. 2013. World view: Chechnya, Kyrgyzstan, and analysis of the Boston bombers. *Breitbart*. April 20, 2013. http://www.breitbart.com/Big-Peace/2013/04/19/20-Apr-13-World-View-Generational-analysis-of-Boston-Marathon-bombings (accessed July 24, 2013).

Ziółkowska-Boehm, Aleksandra. n.d. Conversation with Zbigniew Brzezinski, from "The roots are polish" by Aleksandra Ziolkowska-Boehm. *RootsWeb: Freepages*. http://freepages.genealogy.rootsweb.ancestry.com/~atpc/heritage/articles/aleksandra/roots-brzezinski.html (accessed July 8, 2013).

Index

9/11, 7, 126, 141, 143. *See also* September 11
Africa, 13, 24–26, 44, 97, 117, 119, 121, 124, 135, 138, 148, 157, 162, 189
alien, 25, 33, 119, 126, 140
American dream, 1, 21, 44, 47, 77, 85–86, 134–35, 144, 169, 180–81, 199
Amsalem, Michel, 158, 161–64, 172
Arab, 30–32, 35, 45, 97–98, 105–6, 113, 120–21, 124–26, 129–30, 132, 161, 167, 178, 192, 199
Arizona, 73–74, 129, 131, 193
Asia, 7, 25–26, 28–29 45, 55, 82, 84, 117–21, 123, 138–39, 144, 148, 177, 184
assimilation, 1, 10, 17, 23, 25, 103, 135, 137–41, 143–45, 148, 192, 194–96, 199–200
Australia, 6, 64–65, 114–15

bimodal, 60, 73, 87, 89, 91, 93
Boston Marathon, 141, 144, 146, 192
brain drain, 99, 157–58
Britain, 11, 53. *See also* England. *See also* United Kingdom
Brzezinski, Zbigniew, 53–58, 67, 171–72, 191, 202

Canada, 6, 14, 45, 53–54, 65, 101, 105, 138, 162, 172, 180–84, 186, 193, 200
Center for Strategic and International Studies. *See* CSIS
Chegg, 63, 68, 192–93
China, 2, 55–56, 66, 77, 91, 95–96, 103, 105–6, 109, 118, 133, 151, 156, 201
Chinese, 2, 35–36, 28, 49, 59–60, 66, 76, 83, 85, 91, 96, 99, 119, 133, 156, 165
cluster, 95–105, 107–9, 165, 179, 181, 200; automobile, 96–97, 101, 177; biotechnology, 95, 98–99, 165, 174, 179; life science, 91, 100–2, 104, 108, 195; nanotechnology, 95, 99–100, 102–4, 108, 165, 174, 179, 196, 198, 200; shale oil and gas, 95–96, 113, 165; Silicon Valley, 14, 19, 48–51, 68, 95–96, 98–101, 107–8, 151, 167, 169, 193, 195, 197–98, 200
Cold War, 2, 11, 56
The Computer Emporium, 14, 16, 38
conservative, 8, 15, 33–34, 119, 120, 123, 137, 141
crime, 8–10, 22, 97, 129, 130, 193
CSIS, 18, 20

diversity, 44, 126, 164, 172

203

eBay, 60, 62, 67–68, 148, 195, 199, 202
El Salvador, 32–33, 69, 71
emigrate, 44, 157, 167
emigration, 81, 155, 157
England, 76, 92, 96, 147–48. *See also* Britain. *See also* United Kingdom
English language, 8–9, 12, 22, 58, 64, 76, 87, 97, 112–13, 119, 139, 140, 142, 181, 191, 193
entrepreneur, 1–2, 21–22, 34–35, 49, 66, 68, 75–78, 90, 92, 98–99, 134, 140, 157–58, 166, 175, 178–79, 184, 186, 193–94, 196, 202
European, 26, 28, 46, 54–55, 57, 64, 77, 82, 107, 117–18, 121, 123, 133, 138, 148, 166, 194; Eastern, 8, 17, 26, 28, 30–31, 40, 44, 54–55, 57, 97–98, 121, 124, 126, 163; Western, 25, 28–29, 57, 77, 118–19, 154, 168, 171
E-Verify, 30, 33, 74

foreign-born, 5–6, 8, 23, 46, 48, 60, 76–77, 88–92, 99, 121, 123, 139–40, 165, 178, 192, 195, 200
France, 5, 15, 62, 96, 122, 161–63

Garay, Salomon, 67, 69, 71
George Washington University. *See* GWU
Germany, 5, 8, 26, 28, 45, 53, 55, 65, 117–18, 122, 147, 167
Ghadar, Lis, 14–15, 20, 38, 152, 154
Ghadar, Margaret, 11, 34, 37–41
Ghadar, Otessa, 17–19, 151, 153-4, 171–72
globalization, 48, 139, 165
Google, 8, 22, 60–61, 67, 131, 148, 174, 179, 194–95, 202; Project Glass, 174
GWU, 16, 18

Harvard University, 12, 14, 16, 20, 34, 38, 51, 54, 78, 82–84, 100, 108, 113, 127, 131, 162, 165, 172, 179, 184–85, 195–96, 200

illegal immigrants, 29, 33, 47–48, 88, 90, 121–22, 173
immigration laws, 25, 73–74, 81, 95, 104, 106, 128–29, 165; Chinese Exclusion Act, 25–26; immigration act, 26, 86, 20; Immigration Reform and Control Act. *See* IRCA
immigration policy, 1, 6, 10, 21, 26, 28–30, 34, 43, 48, 78–79, 107, 118, 122, 131, 145, 177–78, 183–85, 194, 196, 200
immigration reform, 32–33, 35, 78, 88–92, 122, 131, 137, 140, 194, 197–98, 201
India, 22, 26, 60, 63, 68, 75–76, 91, 95–96, 99, 119, 149, 156–57, 165, 179, 193
industry, 11, 15, 19, 27, 32, 39, 49, 60, 63, 74, 88–91, 95–103, 105–6, 108, 113–14, 121, 126, 128, 152–53, 172, 183, 198; construction, 58–60, 70, 84, 88–89, 92, 184, 200; hospitality, 60, 90, 92, 196; trucking, 88
Intrados, 17–18, 34, 39–40, 127, 151–52
Iran, 11–16, 18, 20, 30, 32, 35, 37–40, 61–62, 67, 75, 91, 112–13, 120, 124, 133, 135, 152, 154, 158–59, 164, 167–68, 171–72, 174, 179, 187–89, 191, 195–96, 199
Iranian, 11–16, 30, 32, 35, 37–40, 62, 75, 113, 120, 124, 135, 154, 158, 168, 171, 174, 187–89, 191, 195, 199
IRCA, 29, 122; Naturalization Act, 25, 28, 119

Japan, 26–27, 30, 44, 81–82, 91, 106, 117–18, 125, 166
Japanese, 26–27, 30, 44, 81, 117, 125

Korea, 49, 59, 75, 81–86, 133–34, 144, 146, 168, 189, 191, 194–95, 197–99
Koreatown, 134, 136, 292

Latin America, 44, 51, 89, 123, 131, 138–39, 163, 194, 198

LAWA, 74
Legal Arizona Workers Act. *See* LAWA
liberal, 33–34, 108, 120–21, 201

Massachusetts Institute of Technology. *See* MIT.
Mexico, 29, 32–33, 46–47, 69, 71, 74–75, 96, 105, 107, 121, 126, 138, 156, 162, 171, 182, 192
Microsoft, 65, 149, 179, 183, 186, 198
Middle East, 26, 30–31, 37, 97–98, 120–21, 124, 126, 138, 153
migration, 7, 43–46, 48, 50, 54, 58, 65, 76–77, 82, 92, 96, 133, 138, 145, 155, 158–59, 186, 192, 196, 198–99, 202
MIT, 12–15, 17, 20, 32, 37, 51, 85, 162, 172, 179, 185, 198

native-born, 22, 40, 75, 87–91, 121, 128–29, 138–40, 154

Oklahoma City, 124–25, 131, 197
opinion, 9, 24, 34, 131, 134, 145, 154, 173–74, 193–95, 198

Pahlavi, Mohammad Reza Shah, 11–12, 15–16, 19, 38, 108, 172, 187, 200
Park, Yoon-shik, 78, 81–86, 171–72
Penn State, 18–19, 25, 102, 107, 112, 151, 195
Pennsylvania State University. *See* Penn State
Poland, 26, 53–54, 56–58, 75, 96, 122, 196
prejudice, 16, 117–19, 121, 123, 125, 127, 129, 131, 198
President Obama, 30, 32, 62, 148–49, 173

racial profiling, 128–29, 131–32, 191, 197
remittance, 92, 156, 186

revolution, 15–16, 38, 44, 54, 99, 104, 109, 119, 120, 152, 154, 158, 187, 192
Russia, 17, 26, 31, 45, 57–58, 61, 95, 103, 105, 109, 141–43, 174, 197, 201. *See also* Soviet Union

September 11, 7, 30, 125–26, 130, 143. *See also* 9/11
Singapore, 45, 65, 180, 184
Soviet Union, 17, 39, 53–57, 122. *See also* Russia
STEM, 34, 66, 76, 78, 91, 96, 100, 104, 177–78

unauthorized immigrants, 5, 29, 46, 74
undocumented immigrants, 7, 24, 32, 74, 122, 127
United Kingdom, 28, 64, 77, 91, 101, 184. *See also* Britain. *See also* England
United States, 1–2, 5–6, 8, 11, 13–14, 16, 18, 21–35, 37–38, 40–41, 44–48, 51, 53–54, 56, 58–66, 69, 71, 73, 75–79, 81–85, 87–88, 90–91, 95–96, 99, 100–1, 103–6, 115, 117–20, 122–23, 125–30, 134, 137–43, 154, 156–58, 162–69, 171, 173–75, 177–85, 194–96, 199; border control, 33; civil rights, 27–28, 55, 119, 134; economy, 1–2, 6, 21, 24–25, 29, 31–32, 40, 44–45, 47–48, 60–61, 66, 73, 75–79, 87–88, 91, 96, 102, 123–24, 126, 158, 167, 178–79, 185; government, 7, 11, 17–18, 26, 29, 33, 39, 47–48, 50, 55, 74, 77, 81, 97, 104, 117–20, 125–29, 137, 143, 157–58, 171, 178, 180, 183; homeland security, 9, 20, 22–23, 25, 46, 149, 189–81, 196, 198, 201; population, 5, 23–24, 28–29, 46, 50, 60, 77, 87–88, 90, 121, 127, 129, 130, 138–40, 148–59, 181; U.S. Citizenship and U.S. Immigration Services, 30, 68, 178, 196

visa, 6–7, 28, 32, 34–35, 45, 48, 54, 63–66, 68, 70–71, 78, 91, 96, 98–99, 106, 114, 149, 157, 162–63, 165, 167, 178, 180–81, 183–84, 186, 195–96, 198, 201; ADE, 65; agricultural visa, 64 (*see also* H-2A visa); F-1, 6 (*see also* student visa); H-1B visa, 6, 65, 91, 96, 98, 104–6, 149, 178, 183; H-2A visa, 64 (*see also* agricultural visa); H-2B visa, 65; student visa, 6, 78 (*see also* F-1); temporary, 63, 178, 180

World Bank, 14–15, 17, 83–84, 92, 121, 162, 184, 186, 202

World Trade Center, 124

World War I, 29, 53

World War II, 29, 44, 66, 81, 117–18, 167, 171

Yahoo!, 60, 148, 167

About the Author

Fariborz Ghadar is the William A. Schreyer Professor of Global Management, Policies and Planning and founding director of the Center for Global Business Studies at the Smeal College of Business at the Pennsylvania State University. He is also a senior advisor and distinguished scholar at The Center for Strategic and International Studies in Washington, D.C. Iranian born, Dr. Ghadar became a citizen of the United States in 1979. As a consultant, academic, and author, he has established himself as a leading authority on future global business trends, global economic assessment, the petroleum industry, immigration, international finance and banking, and global corporate strategy and implementation. He is the recipient of numerous educational awards and was named *BusinessWeek*'s top 10 Stars of Finance. Dr. Ghadar has also written over a dozen books and multiple articles, and he is frequently quoted in internationally circulated publications.

JV 6465 .G53 2014
Ghadar, Fariborz.
Becoming American